Accounting for Genocide

Canada's Bureaucratic Assault on Aboriginal People

Dean Neu and Richard Therrien

Fernwood Publishing • Zed Books

Editing: Brenda Conroy
Cover photo: Prince Edward Island Public Archives and Records Office
Design and production: Beverley Rach
Printed and bound in Canada by: Hignell Printing Limited

Published in Canada by: Fernwood Publishing
Site 2A, Box 5 8422 St. Margaret's Bay Road
Black Point, Nova Scotia, B0J 1B0
and 324 Clare Avenue
Winnipeg, Manitoba, R3L 1S3
www.fernwoodbooks.ca

Published in the rest of the world by Zed Books Ltd.
7 Cynthia Street, London N1 9JF, UK
and Room 400, 175 Fifth Avenue, New York, NY 10010, USA.

Distributed in the USA exclusively by: Palgrave, a division of St Martin's Press LLC
175 Fifth Avenue, New York, NY, 10010, USA.

Zed Books
ISBN:1 84277 188 4 hb
ISBN:1 84277 189 2 pb

Fernwood Publishing Company Limited gratefully acknowledges the financial support of the Department of Canadian Heritage, the Nova Scotia Department of Tourism and Culture and the Canada Council for the Arts for our publishing program.

A catalogue record for this book is available from the British Library.

National Library of Canada Cataloguing in Publication

Neu, Dean E., 1960-
Accounting for genocide: Canada's bureaucratic assault on aboriginal people / Dean Neu, Richard Therrien.

Includes bibliographical references.
ISBN 1-55266-103-2

1. Native peoples—Canada—Government relations. 2. Indians, Treatment of—Canada. 3. Native peoples—Canada—Economic conditions. 4. Native peoples—Canada—Social conditions. I. Therrien, Richard II. Title.

E92.N48 2003 323.1'197071 C2003-900134-2

Reprinted: March 2005

Contents

Acknowledgments

The mountains of information on which this book is based have come to us through much intellectual and academic hard work, but none of it would be relevant without the commitment of those individuals most affected in their daily lives by government bureaucracy and racist policies who have chosen to speak truth to power—relentlessly, in some cases putting their very lives at risk. They remain nameless and countless; to them we owe a special debt of gratitude.

Personally, I came to this project as a non-academic and I owe a debt of gratitude to Dean, who conceived, created and sustained this project, while demonstrating the difficult craft of balancing human compassion with hard-edged analysis. And, of course, to Karen, my spouse, for picking up the household slack and listening with undue patience to my ranting, raving, bewilderment and all too vocal complaining. —*Richard*

Unlike Richard, I came to this project as an academic with all the baggage that being an academic brings; thanks to Richard for showing me the importance of passion and particularly the importance of moving beyond the pedestrian prose of academic writing.

I also owe a debt of gratitude to the various organizations and individuals who have supported and nourished this work. The financial support of the Haskayne School of Business, the Canadian Academic Accounting Association and the Social Sciences and Humanities Research Council was invaluable, as were the research assistance of Monica Heincke and the administrative help of Sylvia Fuchek. The constructive comments and encouragement of Wayne Antony, Robert Molteno, David Newhouse and Daniel Paul encouraged us to sharpen our arguments and to consider issues that we had previously missed. The editorial, design and administrative help of Brenda Conroy, Beverley Rach, Debbie Mathers and the rest of the Fernwood staff removed most of the manuscript's rough edges. Finally, I need to acknowledge my partner Alison, who provided me with advice and encouragement when it was most needed. —*Dean*

Introduction

> It seems to me that a really strong show of force is the only way to keep the casualties down to a minimum.... Perhaps at long last, we will bite the bullet and understand that the gun barrel created this country and that once more it will have to be used if Canada is to remain our home and native land.—Canadian journalist, Barbara Amiel, referring to the Oka stand-off between the military and Mohawk peoples, quoted in Barlow and Winter 1997: 184

Two warriors on the television screen square off, nose-to-nose, unblinking, one camouflaged and masked, the other uniformed and helmeted, one Indigenous, the other Caucasian. Neither flinches. The image, burned into the minds of the witnessing Canadian public, is from July 1990, Oka, traditional Mohawk territory in the Province of Quebec. The Quebec Provincial Police have executed a raid on Mohawk warriors who have erected a barricade to prevent the expansion of a golf course over their ancestral burial grounds. The area in dispute, known as "the Pines," is part of a larger territorial land claim of 266 square miles. After seventy-eight days during which shots will be fired, one life lost and Canadian Armed Forces brought in—vastly outweighing the Mohawks in arms, including heavy artillery—three Mohawk warriors will be apprehended to face over fifty charges.

On another continent a similar drama unfolds. Gold and diamond extraction companies are encroaching on the ancestral territories of the Indigenous Wai Wai, Wapisiana and Macusi peoples of Guyana, which gained independence from the United Kingdom in 1966 (World Rain Forest Movement November 1998). In 1969 the commissioners of the Amerindian Lands Commission deemed the Wai Wai "too unsophisticated" to have title to their traditional homeland. In 1997, immediately after the Wai Wai, Wapisiana and Macusi formed the Tachau's Amerindian Council, the Minister of Amerindian Affairs accused them of treason and threatened legal action if they refused government surveyors access to their land.

Guyana may be a world away from Quebec, but the global economy's appetite for resources knows no boundaries. The government surveyors in question are obliged to trespass because their masters, the Guyanese government, have signed an agreement with Vancouver-based Vannessa Ventures Ltd., granting them 5.1 million acres of land for the purpose of conducting geophysical and geological surveys for gold and diamond sources (Programme 2001).

At about the same time that the Tachau's Amerindian Council is being formed in Guyana, in Mexico's poor southern province of Chiapas forty-five people—mostly women and children—are killed by pro-government paramilitaries (Russell 1998). On the eve of the spring 2000 election that will topple the Partido Revolucionario Institucional (PRI), the reigning power in Mexico for over seven decades, paramilitaries ambush a group of Tzotzile Indians, leaving three dead and three wounded, including a six-year-old. Eighty Percent of Chiapas' population is Indigenous Mayan. Three hundred police officers and two hundred army troops search the area of Chenalho, a stronghold of the Zapatista Liberation Army (EZLN). Military presence in the area has reached up to seventy thousand troops. The first uprising of the EZLN, in January 1994, was chosen to coincide with the implementation of the North American Free Trade Agreement (NAFTA). The Acteal massacre, in 1997, followed the revelation by human rights activists that the Mexican defence department had drafted plans to use paramilitaries for counter-insurgency purposes and that the most prominent group had received a half-million-dollar contribution from the Governor of Chiapas.

In the same spring of Mexico's democratic turfing of its legendary oppressive regime, former U.S. Vice President Al Gore's campaign for the presidency is marred by demonstrators taking part in an international protest against Occidental Petroleum of Santa Monica, California, on behalf of the five thousand-member U'wa tribe of Colombia. The oil fields near Samore, on U'wa ancestral territory, contain 1.4 billion barrels of crude—worth about $35 million on the international market. Oil field exploration and development will take away the U'wa livelihood. Since 1940 they have lost over 85 percent of their land to development. In early 2000, several thousand soldiers are needed to guard workers at the multibillion-dollar project. (Occidental paid the Colombian Army to keep a base near one of its refineries.) In February tear-gas is used in a clash with demonstrators. U'wa leaders threaten tribal suicide if Occidental is allowed to continue drilling. Bending to global activist pressure, President Andres Pastrana agrees in 1999 to increase the size of the U'wa reservation, and in March of 2,000 the Colombian Court ordered Occidental to stop drilling on tribal land.

But exploration continues. Occidental is a high profile supporter of President Clinton's $1.6 million package in military aid to Colombia, and Energy Secretary Bill Richardson is representing Occidental's interests in meetings in Cartagena. The company has "donated nearly half a million dollars to Democratic committees and causes since Gore has joined the ticket" (Silverstein 2000). The Gore family owns about $1/4 million in shares of Occidental stock, and in 1970, when Al Gore Senior left the Senate, he accepted a $1/2 million position at Occidental from his long-time friend and Occidental founder Armand Hammer. Hammer has been a political ally of the Gores for generations, and Vice-President Gore and Occidental CEO Ray Irani are friends, often appearing at social functions together.

According to David Maybury-Lewis (2001), co-founder of the human rights organization Cultural Survival, there are approximately 200–300 million Indigenous people in the world today, and on every continent they are struggling for survival. Indigenous peoples claim their territories on the grounds of prior occupancy and, having been conquered by or incorporated into alien states, are considered outsiders within the countries they call home.

The annihilation of Indigenous peoples is often considered an inevitable by-product of civilization, a process by which backward cultures are naturally eliminated through progress—which can't be stopped. Cultural elimination is often, by default, accepted government policy. The welfare of the country as a whole is held aloft as a higher moral good, for which traditional tribal customs must be sacrificed. Under this guise, Indigenous peoples' land is exploited, usually for extractable resources to be used in First-World manufacturing. If Indigenous peoples call for protection against this hegemony, they are accused of wanting special treatment and their political identity is debased by the term "special-interest group." There is a pervasive misunderstanding, Maybury-Lewis (2001) tells us, that Indigenous peoples are fighting to preserve the traditional ways of their past—but in fact they are fighting for their right to have a say in their own future. They see clearly that they are being dispossessed of their traditional territories, not for the sake of the country as a whole, but for the sake of private profit.

The struggles of the Sami in Scandinavia, the Mohawks, Nisga'a and Inuit in Canada, the Mayans in Chiapas and the U'wa in Colombia are essentially a single struggle. Their enemies use similar forces of government, backed up by similar administrative technologies, and in all cases, from centuries past to the present, Indigenous peoples are fighting to survive the genocide perpetrated against them for the sake of economic exploitation.

Between 1800 and 1914, the amount of the world's land surface controlled by Europeans increased from 35 to 84 percent (Headrick 1981). And in the majority of places to which the Europeans' control reached, the problem of Indigenous peoples was, and continues to be, a pervasive theme in internal politics (Barta 1987). The "Indian Question" continues to be of national and international importance. In Canada, the issues of self-government, land claims, taxation and ownership of natural resources are visible outcroppings of an unstable set of social relations between First Nations and other Canadian peoples (Mercredi and Turpel 1993). In this book we focus on the colonization of Canada's Indigenous peoples, placing it in the context of similar processes occurring globally throughout the last century and before.

In the earlier years of colonization, the settling of Europeans on Indigenous lands was backed by force of arms. But violence can take many forms. The deliberate introduction of diseases, such as smallpox and tuberculosis, the removal of children from their homes, forced acculturation, physical punishment for using one's native tongue, slave labour; these forms of coercion have been accomplished through and even enforced by bureaucratic mechanisms—and by individual bureaucrats. It is in individual actions and face-to-face confrontations that bureaucratic management of entire peoples becomes real and palpable. Throughout this book, the violence of human action, of one group of people imposing its will upon another, is intertwined with the violence of bureaucracy and the economic-political rationalizations that always accompany and empower the more overt uses of force. The recollections of George Manuel, a founder of the Fourth-world movement, active in the seventies, serve as a poignant example of the layering and intertwining of these various levels and types of violence. His statement, for example, referring to residential schools as a "laboratory and the production line of the colonial system" (Manuel and Posluns 1974: 63) may sound polemical and abstract, but when put into the context of a personal story, the details reveal the depth of the crime. A cattle truck pulls up to the reserve; an Indian agent calls out the names of the children who will be trucked to a distant urban centre; children are crying, mothers weeping. The child, as children everywhere always do, blames him- or herself: What have I done wrong, why am I being taken away? The utter foreignness and power of the abductors only adds to the horror. But indoctrination works on many levels; the victims are helpless against this thorough and relentless social engineering, applied twenty-four hours a day. They adapt, in order to survive; the new language, the new food, the new clothes, the new images, symbols and authority figures begin to take hold, a certain bonding between individuals in the captive community somehow strengthens the boundaries that contain them. "Learning to see and hear only what the priests and brothers wanted you to see and hear," the Native leader George Manuel recalls of his own abduction, "even the people we loved came to look ugly" (Manuel and Posluns 1974: 67). In this simple statement, we witness the brutal sophistication and irresistible force of racism, applied bureaucratically and rationalized economically at arm's length, working insidiously as psychological terrorism. The violence, having been turned inward, becomes a toxic and effective self-loathing, culturally and individually. Can there be a more elegant violence than this?

However, the dreamed-of success of that particular brand of violence is far from having been realized. The Fourth World that George Manuel and his international brothers and sisters in arms have given shape to in the last three decades, as we shall see in the final chapter, is a force to be reckoned with, a force that is meeting head-on the new colonialism of global trade. Landmark court decisions such as *Delgamuukw* (see also chapter eight) and the organizing power of electronic information sharing by resistance groups, for example, the virtual web campaign so effectively utilized by the rebels in Chiapas (see chapter nine), are examples of that challenge and indeed may prove to be the central driving force in thwarting the corporatization of the planet. Here the boardrooms and Indigenous councils meet face to face—because the last reserves of our natural resources remain, ironically, in the far reaches of the planet to which so many traditional cultures have been pushed. Hope springs from seeing and naming the violence of bureaucracies and economic rationalization for what it is: a continuance, no less painful, of the more overt forms of violence that have always driven colonization.

Cultural survival for Indigenous peoples is an economic battle fought on the ground in their own communities and in the bureaucracies of government and the boardrooms of transnational resource-extraction corporations. Accounting is the backbone of the rationalization used in defending this exploitation. Relationships between Indigenous peoples and governments are filtered and managed through a complex field of bureaucratized manipulations, controlled by soft technologies such as strategic planning, law and accounting. By the time individuals sit down to negotiate face to face, the choices available have been severely diminished. Those government processes are firmly entrenched within the broader phenomena of modernity, colonialism and genocide. We will show that accounting techniques and calculations have been, and continue to be, essential tools in translating imperialist/colonialist objectives into practice and that genocide is often the result.

Native protests, including Oka, erupted right across the country in Canada's summer of 1990; it was the beginning of a decade that would see many such confrontations, a decade that would also witness the groundbreaking Supreme Court *Delgamuukw* decision and the first modern treaty, with the Nisga'a Nation of British Columbia (both in 1997). But after Oka, the federal government's response was, predictably, to strike a Royal Commission, with the result—a 3500-page document (Royal Commission on Aboriginal Peoples [RCAP] 1996)—not arriving till five years later. The delay prompted Assembly of First Nations leader Ovide Mercredi to march to the parliament buildings. The Prime Minister refused to see him.

For many Canadians the drama played out in the summer of 1990 seemed either a throw-back to the days of "cowboys and Indians" or an elaborate publicity stunt meant to bolster Native demands for special status. There was something surreal about watching the real-life stand-off unwind over the hot summer months, a weird mix of Third-World gunboat diplomacy and Hollywood western, right here in the backyard of a nation often heard congratulating itself on its own civility and international peace-keeping reputation. The reality, however, is that if the media were paying closer attention to the issue of Indigenous cultural survival worldwide and if we, as citizens, had had a better understanding of both the contested histories of settler society and our continuing complicity in genocidal practices directed at Indigenous peoples, the Oka stand-off would not have been seen as extraordinary at all. Oka was and continues to be one of many battles in an historically extended war—the struggle for cultural survival on the part of Indigenous peoples shared not only by other First Nations within the borders of Canada but worldwide.

In Canada, as in most other places, these disputes are a consequence and continuance of colonial history. The *Royal Proclamation of 1763* recognized the rights of Indigenous peoples to unceded land and stated that the government would purchase any land that it desired for settlement (Anon. 1983). But what, especially from the Native perspective, is a purchase? Can land be purchased? How symmetrical must the two bargaining positions be in order for the transaction to be equitable? What values are attached, in either case, to the symbols of exchange? Land transactions, and in particular these exchanges, clearly involve accounting. What role did accounting play in the overall process of colonization itself?

This book looks at accounting's mediative role in defining power relationships and how this role was used in the colonization of Canada's First Nations. We argue that since the early 1800s and continuing into the present, accounting—defined as a system of numerical techniques, funding mechanisms and accountability relations—has been used by the state as a method of indirect governance in its containment, control and attempted assimilation of First Nations peoples.

Since 1857, in federal government legislation, accounting has played an important role in manipulating First Nations peoples. Federal government funding has specifically been used to encourage institutional assimilation (Dyck and Institute of Social and Economic Research 1991: 3). The introduction of municipal forms of government, money bylaws and taxation policies have all been referred to as a type of "coercive tutelage" (Frideres and Krosenbrink-Gelissen 1993) aimed at colonizing First Nations' peoples (Boldt 1993: 140–45).

The November 1996 release of the royal commission report dealing with Aboriginal issues (RCAP 1996) is only the most recent in a series of government attempts to redefine relations between themselves and First Nations peoples. Repeated revisions to the *Indian Act*, the release of the 1969 "White Paper on Indian Policy" and the Penner Report on Indian self-government have all attempted to specify the rights and obligations of the federal government *vis-à-vis* Canada's First Nations peoples (Boldt et al. 1985)

Accounting as a means of indirect governance doesn't exist in a vacuum; rather, it is a central organism in the culture of bureaucracy. Bureaucracy and accounting, we demonstrate, are integral components of modernity in which colonization continues to play a key role. That colonization predicates the mass movement of peoples and the subjugation, displacement or absorption of one culture by another brings to light questions of nationhood, statehood and, by inference, statelessness. Statelessness is a problem of governance, particularly modern governance. We examine how, in seeking solutions, bureaucracies and their accounting techniques have been applied to entire populations, especially "stateless" populations.

Cost-cutting and other numerical "solutions"—at first sight deceptively free of moral entanglements—come to light, upon close scrutiny, as genocidal government policies. We show that solutions sought by colonial governments to the problems they faced in dealing with Indigenous populations is an integral part of the historical arc of modernity, which may have reached its apogee in twentieth-century Europe's Holocaust and which may very well be continuing, under the auspices of global trade, into the new century.

This book makes clear that accounting/funding relations between colonizers and Indigenous peoples have been used by the state since the early 1800s to encourage action-at-a-distance and that, though the techniques of governance vary according to time and circumstance, accounting techniques have been and continue to be used to encourage "governmentality"—a practice that today may have dire ecological and social consequences for those caught in the web of one-world, twenty-first-century global economics.

Note

The name and location of the government department responsible for Aboriginal peoples in Canada has changed many times. We use the term "Indian Department" to refer to this department unless it is important to refer to the specific name at specific junctures in time.

Chapter One

This Land is Our Land

Cultural Survival in the Global Marketplace

Our contemporary *zeitgeist* may be enmeshed with notions of the new economy, information technology and the global marketplace, but the apparently benign appearance of the wired marketplace may veil a far more disturbing reality: essentially, the basis of our economies is still resource extraction, and those resources, as they become more scarce, are increasingly found in the ancestral territories of Indigenous peoples (Amin 2001). In other words, the Information age is in reality a continuation of the industrial age under a new moniker, an even deeper advance of economic imperialism into Indigenous territories—an advance whose end can only be the complete elimination of the cultures still living in those "resource rich" territories.

Except to those individuals and organizations politically engaged in cultural survival, human rights and ecological sustainability, the issue of protecting Indigenous cultures seems secondary, only brought to public attention when the media are focused on Native uprisings and Indian blockades, such as Chiapas and Oka. But this issue is a critical component of the new economy, run right through its centre like a hot wire, and Indigenous leaders and respected activists such as David Suzuki have been warning us for decades that the loss of Indigenous cultures signals the collapse of our eco-systems (Knudston and Suzuki 1992).

"Loss of Indigenous cultures" is not quite an accurate way to put it; rather it is a deliberate obliteration. This "loss" is not the inevitable falling away of outworn customs in the face of unstoppable modern progress. The fact is that bureaucratic mechanisms are employed in the destruction of Indigenous cultures, and bureaucrats, with their biases, confusions and intentions, have historically made choices and planned ways to undermine, control and in some cases destroy targeted populations. Before we examine those bureaucratic mechanisms, to which accounting is central, we examine the central cultural bias that supported those who found themselves in the New World.

Demons, Slaves and Aristotle

Separating an Indigenous population from its traditional territory is a primary need of land acquisition and resource extraction. This is because the fundamental relationship between Indigenous people and their land base is irrevocable: Tradition is Place, and sovereignty over Place is the basis for a sustainable future. The tight interweaving of existence, self-definition and territory is the essence of Indigenous identity—a reality that is a complete anathema to the principles that allow non-Indigenous cultures to objectify land into real estate, divorce it from tradition and exploit its natural bounty without regard for the long-term future. The fusion of Indigenous cultures with their land is so complete that the only way to take that land is to destroy the Indigenous culture.

We discover, while examining the tools and mechanisms utilized in the destruction of cultures, that the moral and philosophical rationalizations needed by those so engaged—since they considered themselves above all to be civilized and God-fearing—may be found, somewhat surprisingly, in Aristotle. The Aristotelian doctrine of natural slavery professed that one part of mankind is set aside by nature to be slaves in the service of masters born for a life of virtue, free of labour.

Perhaps nowhere is the status of what has come to be called "heterophobia" more evident than in the use of Aristotle's theory of natural slavery as it was applied to the treatment of the Aboriginal inhabitants of the New World. To shed light on this most basic prejudicial attitude of Europe's interlopers we go back to Valladolid, Spain, 1550. Here, a celebrated and much observed public debate took place between two reigning intellectuals, Bartolomé de las Casas and Juan Ginés de Supulveda. The question: Is the race of the American Indian naturally inferior to the European and a born slave according to the theory of Aristotle?

Lewis Hanke (1970: 3–4) describes European notions of Amerindian beings as a product of minds saturated with medieval visions of devils and monsters:

> Spanish captains went forth to their conquest expecting to encounter many kinds of mythical beings and monsters depicted in medieval literature: giants, pygmies, dragons, griffins, white-haired boys, bearded ladies, human beings with adorned tails, headless creatures with eyes in their stomachs or breasts, and other fabulous folk. For a thousand years a great reservoir of curious ideas on man and semi-men had been forming in Europe, and was now freely drawn upon in America ... and by the end of the fifteenth century a rich body of fantastic ideas was ready for use in America.

The expansion of Spain and the increased use of the printing press in the early sixteenth century brought forth a considerable volume of travel literature to Europe (Hanke 1970: 2). The "terrestrial paradise" that Columbus claimed to have discovered, the "Fountain of Youth" that so many adventurers were seeking, the "Seven Enchanted Cities which were believed to have been established by the Portuguese who had fled when the Arabs moved into the Iberian Peninsula"—all reflect the degree to which the New World was seen through medieval spectacles (Hanke 1970: 3). Trumpet-blowing apes, singing feathered monkeys, giants and wild men "rending lions barehanded or smashing their skulls with trees or mighty clubs" were depicted in literature as well as pictorially. The inhabitants of the New World, according to one writer, were "blue in color with square heads" (Hanke 1970: 4). The caption of one wood engraving, circa 1505, depicting American Natives reads:

> They go naked, both men and women; they have well-shaped bodies, and in color nearly red; they bore holes in their cheeks, lips, noses and ears, and stuff these holes with blue stones, crystals, marble and alabaster, very fine and beautiful. This custom is followed alone by the men. They have no personal property, but all things are in common. They live together without a king and without a government, and every one is his own master. They take for wives whom they first meet, and in all this they have no rule. They also war with each other, and without art or rule. And they eat one another, and those they slay are eaten, for flesh is common food. In the houses salted human flesh is hung up to dry. They live to be a hundred and fifty years old, and are seldom sick. (Wilberforce Eames, *Bulletin of the New York Public Library*, September 1922, quoted in Hanke 1970: 4–5)

Vestiges of these fantastic heterophobic imaginings were still present during the settlement of North America. Such images, attaching themselves to the archetypes of a particular culture, become rooted in the collective psyche and do not dissolve easily. As we shall see later, the poetry of Ottawa writer and Indian Department official Duncan Campbell Scott is tinged with the shadowy remains of these hallucinatory perceptions. The question of how to treat these "creatures" was basic to the conquering nations. Was a war against them justified? Could they be compelled to serve the King? Could they be made to change?

In August 1492, Columbus set sail—six months after the fall of the Moorish Kingdom, quickly followed by the expulsion of the Jews from Spain. Christian hegemony was freshly established in Spain and ready to spread far and wide. That same year, when the scholar Antonio de Nebrija presented Queen Isabella with the first Spanish Grammatica, his response to her enquiry as to what it was for, was: "Your majesty, language is the perfect instrument of empire" (Trend 1967: 88).

Europe in the age of empire, Ronald Wright tells us in *Stolen Continents*, was technologically but not socially advanced:

> It had the best ships, the best steel, the best guns; it also had conditions desperate enough to make its people want to leave and use these things to plunder others. [In] Spain 700 years of war against the Moors had produced a warrior culture filled with loathing and contempt for other ways of life, not a new spirit of enquiry. The reconquista of Iberia, which ended in 1492, would be the model for the conquista of America. (1992: 12)

The Spaniards took the Aristotelian doctrine of natural slavery one step further: "inferior beings were also being benefited through [their] labour ... the proposition became invincibly attractive to the governing class" (Hanke 1970: 12). A Spanish declaration known as "The Requirement" described the steps to be taken when the Indians refused to acknowledge their overlordship and to allow the faith to be preached to them:

> We shall take you and your wives and your children, and shall make slaves of them, and as such shall sell and dispose of them, as their Highnesses may command; and we shall take away your goods, and shall do all the harm and damage that we can, as to vassals that do not obey. (Hanke 1970: 17)

The debate over the humanness of Indigenous peoples continued into the nineteenth century and gradually shifted towards whether or not it was possible to Christianize or civilize them. "In every century since the great debate," says Hanke, "the dispute has been re-studied and re-ventilated with no loss of conviction or passion on either side.... The problem discussed at Valladolid over four centuries ago still represent[s] two basic and contradictory responses to the question posed by the existence of people in the world who are different from ourselves" (Hanke 1970: 95).

The Indigenous peoples of the early days of occupation were, to the occupiers, conceptual Indians—demons and beasts—not real people at all. But this demonization was and is not limited to aborigines. Throughout history both Jews and Indians have been presented as frightening: the wild and savage Indian, the wandering stateless Jew. The conceptual Jew was seen as demonic, according to Zygmunt Bauman, a "potent force; a force simultaneously intensely fascinating and repulsive, and above all, frightening.... Construed in such a way, the conceptual Jew performed a function of prime importance—that of providing a visual representation for the consequences of being a transgressor of boundaries ... of not remaining fully in the fold, of any conduct short of unconditional loyalty and unambiguous choice; he was the prototype and arch-pattern of all non-conformity, heterodoxy, anomaly and aberration" (Bauman 1989: 39).

The Problem of Statelessness

The historical impermanence of national boundaries and the need to control the populations within them, as well as maintaining a vigilance against "the outsider," increases the vulnerability of any group labelled "stateless." Statelessness, as defined by those outside the identified group in both Jewish and Indian cases, was "the problem." Statelessness and heterophobia are so closely linked with bureaucratic modernity that it may be impossible to tell which came first, the modern bureaucracy or the Western mono-cultural obsession (Bauman 1989). Fear of the "other" is normally managed by the military—its duty is to defend the border, that imaginary line which most fundamentally defines the outsider. But when the outsider is found within the borders and is perceived neither as a patriot nor as a citizen of another country, fear of the other can easily be encouraged by the politically ambitious to reach a frightful pitch.

"Statelessness" is a bureaucratic definition; the problem of what to do with a stateless people is a problem of modern governance, and consequently, the "solution" is primarily a bureaucratic one, whether it lies in the direct extermination of individuals or in the slow procedural elimination of their life-support systems or with their total cultural assimilation (Hilberg 1985). Thus, the problem of the stateless (read "wandering") Jew is linked thematically and historically to the problem of how to adapt the Indigenous person (read "backward savage") to "civilization."

The conquest of the New World—the Americas in general and Canada in particular—could not be perceived by the conquerors as successful without the cultural genocide of the conquered peoples. Aboriginal culture represented to the European everything "progress" and "civilization" were trying to leave behind. The hubris of European hegemony and the notion of Christian superiority over "pagan" or "heathen" societies rendered the subjugation of those peoples not only a perceived natural right but in some cases a moral obligation—albeit sometimes indistinguishable from a capitalist obligation.

Statelessness and heterophobia go hand in hand. Before the stateless can be absorbed or expunged they must first be demonized. Zygmunt Bauman, in his exploration of the Holocaust as a normal outcome of modernity, uses the metaphor of a gardener's vision as the perfectly planned society, a metaphor which can be aptly applied to the case of imperialism's problem of dealing with the "uncivilized savage."

> The end [of genocide] itself is a grand vision of a better, and radically different, society. Modern genocide is an element of social engineering, meant to bring out a social order conforming to the design of the perfect society. (Bauman 1989: 91)

Weeds in the Garden

The society Bauman is referring to is of course modern society. But the same hunger for social perfection drove the Victorians and accompanied imperialism into the New World. "The ideal world about to be built," says Bauman,

> conforms to the standards of superior beauty.... This is a gardener's vision.... Some gardeners hate the weeds that spoil their design—that ugliness in the midst of beauty, litter in the midst of serene order. Some others are quite unemotional about them: just a problem to be solved, an extra job to be done. (1989: 92)

To the weeds, however, it makes little difference—they are going to be exterminated one way or another. Weeds must die "not so much because of what they are, as because of what the beautiful, orderly garden aught to be" (92).

"Hitler's victims" according to Zygmunt Bauman "were ... killed because they did not fit, for one reason or another, the scheme of a perfect society.... People tainted with ineradicable blight of their past origin could not be fitted into such an unblemished, healthy and shining world. Like weeds, their nature could not be changed" (Bauman 1989: 93).

The perception of Bauman's Europe as an ideal garden does not differ significantly from the perception of the New World as a wild land to be tamed, domesticated, turned into a Victorian garden. When the conquerors went looking for paradise they were not looking with fresh eyes. They were bringing with them preconceptions of wild lands and ideals of a newly planned garden. Indigenous peoples were seen as demons to be weeded out of the Victorian conqueror's ideal new world.

A threat to social organization is always preceded by an acknowledged perception of differentness—an order set apart from the main social order—and there is a political need for this apartness to be defined. An over-enthusiastic attention paid to differences or a heightened sense of defensiveness when faced with the other results in a kind of heterophobia. Adventures into the New World were adventures precisely because of the unknown nature of the order into which the empires were thrusting themselves, and in the ethos of this "adventure into the unknown," race and culture took on a heightened perceptual importance. In Canada, the early trappers and *coureurs de bois* and their Native counterparts were able to find common ground, and out of this a rich Metis culture developed. But for the ruling classes the differences seemed only to call forth a rigid and oppressive bureaucratization of the settlement process (and soon after, if not concurrently, the industrialization of the wilderness) driven by heightened perceptions of racial and cultural differences: civilized versus savage.

Bureaucracy and Accounting

The questions of where images of demons and the other ultimately come from or what manner of soil feeds the roots of heterophobia are inexhaustible ones. While we were tempted to simply refer to these phenomena as natural prejudices or the spirit of the times, it may be more useful to address how day-to-day practices contribute to and reinforce such stereotypes. After all, Edward Said (1993: 8) reminds us,

> Neither imperialism nor colonialism is a simple act of accumulation and acquisition. Both are supported and perhaps even impelled by impressive ideological formations that include notions that certain territories and people require and beseech domination, as well as forms of knowledge affiliated with domination; the vocabulary of classic nineteenth-century imperial culture is plentiful with such words and concepts as "inferior," or "subject races," "subordinate peoples," "dependency," "expansion" and "authority."

In thinking about this question in relation to the Nazi Holocaust, Zygmunt Bauman points to the role of bureaucracy and its techniques: "The 'Final Solution' did not clash with the rational pursuit of efficient, optimal goal-implementation. On the contrary, it arose out of genuinely rational concern, and it was generated by bureaucracy true to its form and purpose" (1989: 17). The procedures were routinely bureaucratic: "means-ends calculus, budget balancing, universal rule application" (17). The main outcome of these bureaucratic technologies is to buffer the actions of individuals from their consequences (Funnel 1998). A rational thinking human being operating within a bureaucracy is logically answerable to the administrative dictates of that organization. The functionary's gaze is inevitably back up the chain of command from which the directive has come; it is not outward to the end result, which is in someone else's official jurisdiction. If a person or persons happen to be the recipients of the logically directed action, they are not within the sphere of the functionary's observations. Thus, the actions are not clearly immoral or unethical; morals or ethics simply do not logically or structurally enter the equation. Observes Bauman (1989: 25): "The increase in the physical and/

or psychic distance between the act and its consequences achieves more than a suspension of moral inhibition ... [it renders] the victims themselves psychologically invisible."

Bureaucracy, however, depends on administrative techniques such as accounting to translate policy objectives into practice. Accounting, along with other administrative sciences, provides the tools for planning, motivating and controlling actions. As we observe in subsequent chapters, through mundane techniques such as cost/benefit analysis, budgeting and the development of incentive and disincentive schemes, accounting helps to turn into reality governmental ideas such as the removal/containment of Jewish populations and the assimilation of Indigenous peoples.

Genocide

In this study we are, in the context of the struggle for cultural survival, making reference to genocide. This genocide may be different in some aspects than the one that brings to mind gas ovens. Though definition is important when using such inflammatory terminology, our wish is not to get caught up in the semantics of the word or the measurability of the crime; we mean rather to draw attention to the concrete economic, political and especially bureaucratic manipulations behind the mechanisms that have been employed in the destruction of targeted populations (Churchill 1994). Within bureaucracy, accounting may be its most salient operation, and as we shall demonstrate, accounting is by no means free of politics or ideological construction (Tinker 1985). It is our submission that not only is it impossible for accounting to be value-neutral—since there are values inherent in the act of numerical evaluation itself—accounting can be, and has proven to be, most effective in the hands of those who have taken it upon themselves to manage (i.e., quantify, define and manipulate) populations. The role of imperialist bureaucracies in the genocide of Indigenous cultures remains a prime example of the destructive concrete outcomes of theoretical calculation. But first: what do we mean by genocide?

According to Raphael Lemkin, who coined the term, genocide is "the criminal intent to destroy or cripple permanently a human group" (Lemkin 1947: 147). This statement is important because it forms "the backbone of the U.N. Convention on the Prevention and Punishment of the Crime of Genocide" (Andreopoulos 1994: 1). The Convention, adopted in December 1948, defines genocide as:

> any of the following acts committed with intent to destroy, in whole or in part, a national, ethnic, racial or religious group, as such:

a) Killing members of the group;
b) Causing serious bodily or mental harm to members of the group;
c) Deliberately inflicting on the group conditions of life calculated to bring about its physical destruction in whole or in part;
d) Imposing measures intended to prevent births within the group;
e) Forcibly transferring children of the group to another group. (Andreopoulos 1994: 1)

As we will see in subsequent chapters, this definition provides an excellent starting point for thinking about the consequences of government initiatives directed at Indigenous peoples. With some reorganization, the U.N. definition provides us with a vocabulary for distinguishing between immediate genocides and longer term practices that ultimately have the same effects (Chalk 1994). Drawing upon the insights of Charny (1994), our analysis shows how accounting techniques helped to translate government policies into practice: the end result often being (1) genocide in the course of colonization, (2) ecocide and/or (3) cultural genocide:

Genocide in the Course of Colonization

Genocide that is undertaken or even allowed in the course of or incidental to the purposes of achieving a goal of colonization or development of territory belonging to an Indigenous people, or any other consolidation of political or economic power through mass killing of those perceived to be standing in the way. (72)

Genocide as a Result of Ecological Destruction

Genocide that takes place as a result of criminal destruction or abuse of the environment, or negligent failure to protect against known ecological and environmental hazards, such as accidents involving radiation and waste from nuclear installations, uncontrolled smog, or poisonous air from industrial pollution, pollution of water supplies, etc. (76)

Cultural Genocide

Intentional destruction of the culture of another people, not necessarily including the destruction of actual lives. (77)

These categories are consistent with the original U.N. Convention in that genocide in the course of colonization seems to envision provision (a) of the convention whereas ecocide and cultural genocide appear to envision provisions (b) through (e).

A New Threat: Genetic Imperialism

The image of the boring accountant poring over figures and ledgers in the back room of some obscure government department has been upgraded. In the global marketplace, the laws of commerce supercede the law of the land; moral and ethical standards are measured by profit margins. The quantification of information has given monetary value to speed and volume. The sexy image of the day-trader playing with numbers at lightning speed to determine the shape of the stock market has gained ascendancy. But numbers still account for actions, and those actions have profound effects on human populations—often half a globe away from the computer keyboard. Action-at-a-distance, once the domain of governments, is now boldly partnered with global corporate culture. And the information technology which has been harnessed by the new economy brings with it even more sinister forms of imperialism. Nowhere is this more evident than in the struggle of Indigenous peoples against a new threat to their survival: genetic imperialism.

Gene sequencing and American patent laws have come together to "discover" yet another "new world"; what is ancient knowledge and traditional medicine to Indigenous peoples has now been turned from backward superstition to advanced science. Pharmaceutical companies, seed companies, agri-chemists and geneticists are invading the ancient traditions of ethno-botany and traditional healing practices. U.S. companies are now "discovering" plants and animal life that have for centuries been used by specific cultures for specific reasons, and routinely patenting them because they are novel to their own narrow experiences. Going so far as to patent gene sequences and even human cell lines, this genetic imperialism is far more invasive than land theft and grave robbing. It is predatory in the extreme, demanding that the host culture accept the system of patents and trademarks of the parasitic culture.

In traditional cultures, the proper use of curative substances is integral to and intertwined with the mytho-historical spiritual knowledge of the keepers and practitioners of the healing arts. The genetic breakdown and artificial reproduction of the isolated components, however, is an exact reflection of the compartmentalized stratification and numerical breakdown techniques used by the dominant culture to colonize the Indigenous culture. Digital genetic breakdown and the reconstitution of botanical values into specialized uses, stripped of context, is intellectual theft for private gain and undermines the most fundamental strengths of traditional cultures; it is another tool, similar to accounting, used for genocidal designs on Indigenous peoples.

Chapter Two

Unspoken Terror

The dominating nation must do something about a territory's original occupants if it is to settle its lands and maintain an empire from afar. Using settlers to crowd out the Indigenous peoples and gaining control by importing an elite to oversee the territorial operations are commonly used strategies. The Indigenous inhabitants are the targeted subjects of a social control so concentrated its outcomes can be indistinguishable from genocide.

This chapter links the cultural genocide of Indigenous peoples with the twentieth-century Holocaust in Europe. It is helpful first to examine studies linking the Holocaust with modernity itself; it is western civilization that cradles the two continents, the rise of civilization through the past four centuries and extermination by Holocaust and by cultural genocide. If the roots of genocide find fertile sustenance in modern civilization and the "discovery" of the New World stands as a milestone along the path of modern history, then perhaps such an examination can shed light on the unspoken terror of cultural genocide. However it is also important to specify more clearly what we mean by the term accounting and its role in these processes.

Ubiquitous Accounting

Accounting is ubiquitous in modern-day society. Universities, colleges and a variety of other institutions offer courses on accounting, financial planning and finance for people who wish to pursue related career paths. The popular press and even public broadcasters regularly report accounting-based information on corporations. As a result, terms such as annual reports, earnings per share calculations, profit and loss numbers, price-earnings ratios and earnings forecasts have entered the public lexicon. Likewise, on a personal level, the notions of accounting and accountability are central to family budgeting, retirement planning and the annual ritual of submitting an income tax return.

Because financial information is so ubiquitous, it is often taken for granted, thus helping to construct an image of accounting as a neutral and objective practice, concerned with the "identification, measurement, and communication of financial information about economic entities to interested persons" (Kieso et al. 1991: 2). Indeed, the metaphor of the "map" has been used to describe the apparent neutrality and objectivity of accounting information (Solomons 1991). It is assumed to be a defined field, with a concrete scope.

However, like other social constructs, the notion of accounting is itself contested. Conventional definitions stress the identification, measurement and communication of financial information to interested parties. This information is usually assumed to relate to the activities of corporations, and the interested parties are usually assumed to be investors and creditors. This definition, while highlighting certain aspects of the social practice we call accounting, obscures other aspects (Burchell et al. 1980). In particular, this definition downplays both the broader functioning of such techniques and the ways in which they both operationalize and reproduce relations of power and domination (Cooper and Sherer 1984). Thus, our preferred definition explicitly acknowledges these aspects. Accounting here refers to the system of numerical techniques, funding mechanisms and accountability relations that mediate relations between individuals, groups and institutions.

Implicit within this definition is the acknowledgment that power relationships are also measured and rationalized by accounting techniques (Tinker 1980); that the use of numerical and representational techniques rationalize unequal social relationships by "inciting" action through the construction of incentive schemes and funding relations (Preston, Chua and Neu 1997); and that numerical techniques encourage action-at-a-distance and bring home distant knowledges to the centres of calculation (Miller and Rose 1990).

Note that this definition does not contradict the more conventional notion of accounting. Instead, it emphasizes not only the broader nature and functioning of accounting techniques and calculations (Tinker 1985) but also that what counts as accounting is historically contingent, in that how we "account" for certain activities will depend on both our objectives and our values (Miller and Napier 1993). As later chapters illustrate, the government objectives pertaining to the control and containment of Indigenous peoples, along with certain values regarding the "worth" of Indigenous peoples, motivated the development and introduction of specific accounting techniques.

This view of accounting emphasizes both the informational and incentive aspects. Incentive mechanisms and funding relations encourage certain types of behaviours on the part of individuals, agents and institutions in distant locales. As we point out in later chapters, the Canadian government regularly manipulated the nature of annuity payments in the attempt to encourage certain sorts of behaviours. These manipulations were intended to change behaviours by influencing the minutiae of daily life.

Incentive relations do not have to be direct, however. Governments can provide indirect incentives to third parties or they can change accountability mechanisms which impact upon third parties as a way of encouraging certain actions directed at colonized territories and peoples. The examples of bounties for the scalps of Indigenous peoples would be an example of an indirect, third party incentive. Such incentives were used in Nova Scotia during the 1700s (Paul 2000: 102–103) and remained on the books until the late 1800s in the United States (Churchill 1994). More recently, changed accountability mechanisms along with financial incentives have been used throughout the Americas to encourage transnationals to develop resource extraction industries on or near Aboriginal territories (Galeano 1997).

This view emphasizes that accounting is an entirely utilitarian mechanism of representation, and therefore its *raison d'être* cannot be divorced from its masters—the technicians who operate the tools—nor from their historical and political context. To avoid the context of accounting's operations would be to submit to its erroneous claims of objectivity (Tinker 1991).

In the chapters that follow, we examine the roles played by accounting in envisioning, encouraging and facilitating the practices of cultural decimation. Accounting as a technology of control and a technique of government was central to meeting the objectives of colonialism. It is clear that we are using the term accounting in a broader and more comprehensive way than is normal; we mean by "accounting" the entire technology of numerical ciphers and its holistic attachments to the bureaucracy that employs that technology.

Modernity, Problem Populations and Normal Holocausts

The appropriateness of the term genocide used in conjunction with the European treatment of North American Natives has usually been discussed in the context of providing comparisons between Hitler's extermination machinery and the forces of imperialism in the colonies—an argument which may too easily degenerate into a comparison of numbers or degrees of horror and the semantics of direct or indirect genocide. For our purposes, we view the question from the perspective that both Jews and Natives were perceived as problems of governance: the "Jewish problem"; the "Indian problem."

If perfection was a goal of modernity, the Victorians and later the Third Reich, we can also say that our present global market-driven society might be in the clutches of similar obsessions. Ours is a perfection of absolute rationality, of strict ends-means calculus, of monocultural purity and single-economy focus; if the drive towards monocultural purity continues, Indigenous people will have even less of a place in the twenty-first century. "Western, modern society is defined as civilized society," Bauman reminds us, "and a civilized society in turn is understood as a state from which most of the natural ugliness and morbidity, as well as most of immanent human propensity to cruelty and violence, have been eliminated or at least suppressed" (Bauman 1989: 96).

Zygmunt Bauman sets out the terms by which the Holocaust can be viewed as "a unique encounter between factors by themselves quite ordinary and common" (8). The Holocaust, he claims, was not the antitheses of modern civilization but rather an event

> born and executed in our modern rational society, at the high stage of our civilization and at the peak of human cultural achievement, and for this reason it is a problem of that society, civilization, and culture. (8)

Everything that rendered the Holocaust possible, he claims, was

> normal—in the sense of being fully in keeping with everything we know about our civilization, its guiding spirit, its priorities, its immanent vision of the world—all of the proper ways to pursue human happiness together with a perfect society. (8)

The factors which, according to Bauman, typify the modern social reality out of which the Holocaust erupted and which we are using to examine the earlier cultural genocide of the first peoples include:

1) dismantling of non-political power resources and institutions of self-management
2) monopoly of means of violence
3) social engineering goals
4) decoupling of political state from social control
5) reliance on management designs
6) scientific organization for technological success
7) practical, efficient use of rationality
8) means-ends calculus, budget balancing
9) universal application of rules.

Physical violence during the conquest was commonplace, but the imperialists also had other means to ensure cultural genocide. Through the force of literate culture over oral culture and economic symbolism over bartering and gift-giving traditions, they overpowered the Natives economically. Imposing the written word as contract and monetary equivalence as bargaining tools in the treaty process was a "monopoly of means of violence" as described by Bauman (point 2, above). In other words violating peoples' sole source of sustenance is a violent act. Treaties were used to dismantle Native cultures' land-base—their most fundamental and necessary "non-political power resource" (point 1)—without which they could not survive and which rendered them prime fodder for the social engineering experiments (point 3) of the colonial administrators. The Nazi death-camps, social engineering experiments in the extreme, may have found their infancy in the social engineering projects of Canada: assimilation and absorption, compulsory enfranchisement, isolated model Victorian villages for entire tribes, residential schools for children and Indian reserves.

Jews and Indians—weeds threatening the perfection of the gardens of Europe and Victorian North America—whether through bureaucracy or the military, or more likely hand in hand, eradication was the objective. Bauman reminds us that the purpose of planned violence in genocide is to destroy the marked category (nation, tribe, religious sect) as a viable community capable of self-perpetuation and defence of its own identity. If this is the case, the objective of the genocide is met when

> 1) the volume of violence has been large enough to undermine the will and resilience of the sufferers, and to terrorize them into surrender to the superior power and into acceptance of the order it imposed; and
> 2) the marked group has been deprived of resources necessary for the continuation of the struggle. With these two conditions fulfilled, the victims are at the mercy of their tormentors. (116)

The promise of emancipation through the civilized work of settlement and agriculture was extremely problematic to a people whose lives were sustained by the very ground they walked on, its rivers and streams and vegetation supplying them with all their nutritive requirements—a people whose entire spiritual-cultural-economic subsistence was based on the appropriate usage of land, with "ownership" in the European sense having no status in their world view. The imposition of real estate values—an intractable need of imperialism—was in direct contrast to the first peoples' nature-based means of self-sufficiency. But political cunning, the spreading of European disease, rum and hardware, and the ruthless application of numbers were the instruments which forced the abdication of a way of life—and the first peoples were faced with a slow and painful demise.

Removed from their means of livelihood, Natives were forced into social engineering projects under the auspices of their government keepers. Treated as stateless pariahs, with a complete disjunction between their traditional social structures and the political mechanisms that controlled them, they lost all apparent sovereignty. Their lives as government charges—

including the minutia of daily life—were the subject of administrative designs far removed from their actual day-to-day existence. The stated goal of these designs was to completely assimilate the first peoples through education, evangelization and inter-racial marriage, to transform them into upstanding Victorian citizens—in short, to make them disappear.

Cultural Genocide

The term "assimilation" can almost sound like a peaceful process, implying a certain lassitude in the inductee, if not actual collaboration; the term "cultural genocide," though much harsher, is a more accurate one. One of the fundamental differences between cultural genocide and the genocide of the Nazi type is the amount of time each takes. Which is worse—the murdering of millions of human beings over a short period of time, or slowly dissolving their existence through dehumanization and disease and coercion over several generations? How can we account for suffering? How do we measure human misery? Regardless of rationalizations, however, the end result of the two methods of extermination are similar.

In much the same way that the Third Reich found a solution to the "Jewish problem," Ottawa applied its bureaucratic muscle to the "Indian problem." Though each case differed in many ways from the other, both means of dealing with a "stateless " people involved "co-operation between various departments of state bureaucracy; of careful planning … budgeting, calculation and mobilizing necessary resources: indeed, the matter of dull bureaucratic routine" (Bauman 1989: 116–17).

The Nazi solution of extermination (of persons) was different in degree and type of violence from the Canadian solution of assimilation (extermination of culture), but there was not much difference in attitude and intent. After attempting several jurisdictional methods of moving the "stateless" Jewish population around, through forced migration, the Reich came to the conclusion that Jews could neither be "rehabilitated" nor assimilated and thus chose outright extermination. Canada, on the other hand, chose to practise their social engineering and assimilation skills—skills that were largely dependent on accounting mechanisms. Consider, for example, the following manipulations: the determination of reserve size; the membership-registration of tribes and bands; the movement of individuals from territory to territory; the "giving" of annuities and tight budgetary controls over land transactions; the buying of tools, the selling of goods, the acquiring and exchange of provisions; and legislated interference in inheritances and family wills.

Canadian Indian policy may not have been as overt or concentrated as the Holocaust would prove to be—but it was nonetheless violent and achieved much the same ends. Indeed, it might even be said that Canadian policy has been more effective than Nazi policy, since none of Canada's First Nations have yet to regain full statehood, whereas the Jews have Israel. And we are not concerned here with numbers killed or degree of horror, but with endemic racism and the intentional facilitation by government bureaucracies in rendering cultures extinct.

"Choice" and Managerial Design

"Particular care was taken" Bauman says in describing the Jewish extermination, "that at every stage of the road the victims should be put in a situation of choice, to which criteria or rational action apply, and in which the rational decision invariably agrees with the managerial design" (Bauman 1989: 23). This is a principle at work with the first peoples while they were "choosing" to "sign" treaties and is borne out by Duncan Campbell Scott's version of the Treaty 9 signing, for which he was a commissioner, in an article he wrote for *Scribner's Magazine*, December 1906, entitled (erroneously, as it turned out), "The Last of the Indian Treaties" (Scott 1947: 109). Scott, who was a reputable poet, a member of the Royal Society of Canada and the highest placed bureaucrat in the Department of Indian Affairs at the time, first authoritatively informs the reader that "the Indians were a real menace to the colonization of Canada" (111), then whets the Victorian appetite with descriptions of the "Indian nature ... full of force and heat ... ready to break out at any moment in savage dances, in wild and desperate orgies in which ancient superstitions were involved with European ideas but dimly understood and intensified by cunning imaginations inflamed with rum" (111). He then goes on to describe the negotiating process at Fort Hope. In the end, after deliberating through the night amongst themselves, the chiefs emerged from their tent with a decision favourable to the commissioners. Here is Scott's rendition of Chief Missabay's response:

> "Yes," said Missabay, "we know now that you are good men sent by our great father the King to bring us help and strength in our weakness. All that we have comes from the white man and we are willing to join with you and make promises which will last as long as the air is above the water, as long as our children remain who come after us." (Scott 1947: 116)

Finding themselves in the same untenable situation that the European Jews would later find themselves in, Native chiefs were "signing" treaties in desperate attempts to survive. Clearly, Chief Missabay made a rational decision—to save the lives of his people—that fit neatly into the government's managerial design, a design in perfect accord with the mother country's imperialistic strategies.

Bureaucratic Solutions

When faced with the evidence of the Holocaust, we are almost always overwhelmed by its naked brutality; the degree of inhumanity expressed through such an undertaking seems incomprehensible. And yet the same undertaking applied to Indigenous peoples—stretched over a century or two, dressed in a rationale of progress, economics and civilization—seems somehow to lose this quality of brutality and becomes not only comprehensible but even defensible. There seems to be a difficulty in equating Indigenous eradication, often perceived as a natural force arising out of civilization's march through time, with the more shocking horror of the Holocaust. The temptation to devalue the crime perpetrated against Indigenous peoples is great; the march of civilization was inevitable, where civilization is seen as the most natural outcome of modernity's ingenuity. In succumbing to this temptation, however, we end by defining genocide according to the length of its duration rather than by its brutalities.

In *The Cunning of History*, Richard Rubenstein says that the Holocaust "was the first attempt by a modern, legally constituted government to pursue a policy of bureaucratically organized genocide both within and beyond its frontiers" (Rubenstein 1978: 6–7). But we argue that cultural annihilation, practised for several centuries leading up to the Holocaust, was a form of extermination, organized bureaucratically to harmonize with notions of civility.

The tools of the earlier, civilized extermination were more subtly coercive than those of the Third Reich. Demonization of the subject race, forced acculturation, removal from the means of livelihood, outlawing the use of native tongues, concentration into land reserves—all of these operations were rationalized through bureaucratic reasoning and rational accounting methods. If genocide is gruesome in its lack of subtlety, then forced assimilation as a means of cultural annihilation is sly in its false generosity—the Indians were treated as children "for their own good," the King "watchful over their interests and ever compassionate."

Both gross and subtle forms of annihilation are highly dependent on efficient bureaucracy for their success; both are extreme forms of social engineering; and both require dehumanization and demonization of the target population to render the task more socially acceptable. The general population, which seeks security of livelihood and personal safety, comes to view these as threatened by the demonized race. In both cases, the violence unfolds at such a sure and reasonable pace (with the same precision, in the case of the Jews, as cattle being delivered to slaughter) that it gives the illusion of being inexorable. And in both cases, the victims appear to be the authors of their own demise, and the forces of oppression appear to originate from somewhere beyond the individual functionary's sphere of influence.

In its simplest terms, the political rationale for annihilating a people turns essentially upon a definition of statelessness—the political way of saying, “You don’t belong.” The stateless person targeted by government purists, says Rubenstein, “although not a criminal, was for all practical purpose an outlaw. He was subject to the kind of police surveillance and control that was not in turn subject to judicial review” (Rubenstein 1978: 32).

Dehumanization, according to Hannah Arendt (1951), is an important link between bureaucracy and genocide. It renders the target population “politically and legally superfluous” and results in “political status by a process of bureaucratic definition” (quoted in Rubenstein 1978: 32).

Though Indigenous peoples were not in strictest terms rendered stateless by the colonialists, they were perceived to be stateless by their “managers” and treated as pariahs by the settlers. They were subject to extra-judicial surveillance and control, and the method by which they could “join” the state was patently bureaucratic—and economic: enfranchisement, by which they would give up their Indianness, their special status, and “hand-outs.” Failing that, they could have their Indianness (brain)washed out of them through education or absorbed by racial intermarriage.

This absorption of the Indigenous peoples was logically planned and bureaucratically executed with much the same hubris and arrogance that the Third Reich would later prepare the annihilation of the Jewish people. When we follow the arc of the Indigenous peoples’ demise from conquest to modernity into the twentieth century, it ends unequivocally with forced migration, slavery and internment. By World War I, Canada’s Indigenous peoples were working at forced labour on land which had been expropriated from them. Through the bureaucratic application of means-ends calculus and budget-balancing, over a generations-long process, they had been socially engineered into this position of slavery.

Taming the Wilderness

The history of the territory that we now call Canada is inextricably bound up with the history of the British Empire. And empire is really a shorthand for talking about processes of colonialism and imperialism. Edward Said in his book, *Culture and Imperialism*, defines imperialism as “the practice, the theory, and the attitudes of a dominating metropolitan centre ruling a distant territory” and “colonialism, which is almost always a consequence of imperialism, as the implanting of settlements on a distant territory” (Said 1993: 8). Furthermore, Said tells us that imperialism/colonialism should be viewed as a set of processes and practices that make it possible for the colonizers to continue to dominate both the colonized territory and its inhabitants. As Said reminds us, those processes and practices are integrated into day-to-day consciousness through the classic nineteenth-century language of imperialist culture: Subject races were naturally inferior; expansion, authority and domination went unquestioned (96). As we also saw in chapter one, the equation of "savages" with a wilderness waiting to be tamed fit nicely with imperialist appetite for more lands to be conquered.

If the building of the British Empire depended on the accumulation of territories in far-off places of the world, what were the techniques that allowed the wilderness to be tamed? Historian James Headrick suggests that the adoption of new technologies for military purposes provided the means—or hardware—for imperialism. The development of steam gunboats along with breech-loading and repeat-firing guns; the identification of quinine as a protection against malaria; and the development of steamships, railways and communication cables all contributed to the colonization of distant territories and peoples (Headrick 1981: 42).

Talking about his experiences in Algeria, Franz Fanon comments that force was always present in early encounters between the imperial power and Indigenous inhabitants of distant territories (Fanon 1963: 38). Further, he suggests that the possibility of force never disappears—rather it continues to form the backdrop to current-day interactions between empires and colonized peoples.

Although the building of empire clearly depended on military hardware, the software of empire was equally important (Bell, Butlin and Heffernan 1995). Academic disciplinary knowledge, including anthropology, geography, medicine and accounting, allowed bureaucrats in London to plan, motivate and control the colonies. Headrick comments:

> Stronger than death-dealing war-ships, stronger than the might of devoted legions, stronger than wealth and genius of administration, stronger even than the unswerving justice of Queen Victoria's rule, are the scraps of paper that are borne over the seas, and the two or three slender wires that connect the scattered parts of her realm. (Heaton 1887–88, quoted in Headrick 1988: 98)

To describe the way that societal governance in modern-day societies has shifted from the use of force to the use of dispersed and heterogeneous administrative techniques, Michel Foucault coined the term "governmentality" (Foucault 1991). Government, according to Foucault, is not really a single mode of control exercised by and through the state but is rather an "ensemble of institutions, calculations and tactics … a diversity of forces and groups" that in a number of ways "regulate the lives of individuals" (102). These institutions and individuals use a variety of techniques and expertises to influence the activities of specific populations (Gordon 1991). Accounting is one of these techniques.

Mundane and indirect bureaucratic mechanisms such as accounting play a critical role, according to Miller and Rose, in the art of governing and can be referred to as "technologies of government." They are "actual mechanisms through which authorities of various sorts have sought to shape, normalize, and instrumentalize the conduct, thought, decisions and aspirations of others in order to achieve the objectives they consider desirable" (Miller and Rose 1990: 8).

At first glance, the dichotomy between hardware and software allows us to distinguish between colonization achieved by force and colonization achieved by other means. Hardware, however, is not limited to weapons; it also includes such items as submarine telegraph cables and on-land telegraph lines. Today it would undoubtedly include the computer. The software of the past bound the empire together without the use of direct force against colonized peoples; in the same way, on-line day-traders today are not applying direct force on Indigenous peoples to give up their mineral- or timber-rich traditional territories.

Substituting bytes of information for "scraps of paper" and computers for "slender wires," we can see that, as far as technologies of governance go, not much has changed in the last century. For those who choose to commodify information—a process dependent on accounting—information is power. And so it was long before the so-called wiring of the planet.

Beyond Force

Taming the wilderness must, of course, depend on information—intelligence in the military sense, forms of knowledge in the bureaucratic sense. Edward Said, in *Orientalism*, talks about how Napoleon not only relied on "expert knowledges" to plan his Egyptian expedition but also enlisted several dozen "savants" to build a living archive of the territory and its peoples (1979: 80–81). According to Said, the bureaucratically acquired, strategically planned accumulation of information regarding the target population is primary to the success of its subjugation: "Knowledge of subject races ... is what makes their management easy and profitable" (1993: 36). Furthermore, constructing Indigenous inhabitants of a distant territory as "inferior" or "savages" condones the use of techniques in ways that would be impossible in the homeland. The belief in the inferiority of Indigenous peoples encourages politicians, government bureaucrats and "experts" to make decisions about what is good for Indigenous peoples based singularly on the perspectives of the dominating nation, ably supported by accounting techniques.

Software, such as accounting techniques, helps imperial powers come to "know" distant territories and their inhabitants. In both the colonial context and in the more familiar first-world context, accounting can be envisioned as a method of indirect societal governance, a micro-process enabling action-at-a-distance, thereby facilitating indirect rule. Although the application of techniques of governance will differ across time and space, accounting can and does function as a mode of governmentality in different sites much in the way eighteenth-century navigators, for example, were able to colonize distant places "because, in various technical ways, these distant places were 'mobilized' and brought home to centres of calculation" (Miller and Rose 1990: 9). Accounting, in this view, is not a passive recording of numerical information but rather a dynamic force in controlling events—and therefore populations—from a distance. As Said reminds us, "knowledge gives power, more power requires more knowledge, and so on in an increasingly profitable dialectic of information and control" (1993: 36).

As well as mobilizing knowledges of distant locales and bringing them home to centres of calculation, accounting helps to target specific populations. In his discussion of governmentality, Foucault notes that modern government is concerned with population and ensuring that "the greatest possible quantity of wealth is produced, that the people are provided with sufficient means of subsistence, that the population is enabled to multiply" (Foucault 1991: 95). However, in the colonies, it is a hierarchy of populations that influences the exercise of government (Neu 2000a). Thus, numerical techniques such as the census are used first to come to know Indigenous inhabitants, and then other numerical techniques such as funding relations are used to manage the customs, habits and behaviours of these same inhabitants.

Distantiation—the Human Integer

The separation of moral questions from questions of administrative efficiency by organizational routines and bureaucracy, it is argued, made the Holocaust possible (Bauman 1989). Genocide may be embedded in apparently neutral administrative practices with the result being that these "processes of destruction, although massive, are so systematic and systemic, and ... therefore appear so 'normal' that most individuals involved at some level of the process of destruction may never see the need to make an ethical decision" (Bauman 1989: 102).

Within these administrative processes, accounting and other calculations figure prominently, since numbers serve to reduce people to statistics, an important step in accomplishing genocide:

> Dehumanization starts at the point when, thanks to the distantiation, the objects at which the bureaucratic operation is aimed at can, and are, reduced to a set of quantitative measures. (Bauman 1989: 102)

Likewise, Warrack Funnel, commenting on the role of accounting within the Nazi bureaucracy, writes:

> The conversion of Jews to a one-dimensional metric, an integer as a component of tabulations that could be arithmetically manipulated, stripped of identity and all other qualities.... They could then be discussed in the public domain through their surrogates found in the calculations on accounting. (1998: 452)

These comments draw our attention to the ways in which numbers not only substitute for people but also depersonalize them. Stat(e)istics are dry abstractions from real living people. It is much easier to make dispassionate decisions about numbers than it is to confront the impacts that such decisions have on the lives of real people.

Exercising Governance

In military operations, the act of governing is quite visible. We see soldiers on the streets, we see military machinery such as tanks and airplanes. The contrast between uniforms of the military and civilian clothing signals who is doing the governing and who is being governed. We recognize that the military is responsible for ensuring compliance. However, when the software of empire is used, the sites and agents of governance become much less clear-cut.

One of the features of modern-day governance, upon which Foucault comments, is the way in which government is exercised through a variety of different sites and agents. While governments may use direct financial incentives to encourage Indigenous peoples to act in a certain way, they may also provide these financial incentives to third parties who, in turn, undertake actions which impact upon Native peoples. For example, in 1749, the Governor of Nova Scotia, Cornwallis, issued a proclamation stating:

> His Majesty's Council, do promise a reward of ten Guineas for every Indian Micmac taken or killed, to be paid upon producing such Savage taken or his scalp (as in the custom of America) if killed to the Officer Commanding at Halifax, Annapolis Royal or Minas. (Paul 2000: 109)

This indirect action had very real consequences for Mi'kmaw (Micmac) people; by the end of a three-year period, the Mi'kmaw population had been reduced by 80 percent. While modern-day governments might not use this specific incentive, other indirect financial incentives continue to be used. Residential schooling and relaxed environmental standards for transnationals are two more modern forms of indirect financial incentives that governments have used to encourage actions that impact upon Native peoples.

Beyond Bookkeeping

Accounting is more than it seems. It has the power of language, with its ability to represent in terms that mediate relations and accountability between individuals, groups and institutions what may appear to be simply an objective reality. (What, after all, could be more objective than numbers?) However, it also has the power to motivate via incentive relations and to control through accountability relations. The bureaucratic mechanisms that helped colonial powers translate their objectives into practice relied heavily on accounting's ability, through the symbolism of numbers, to represent power relationships. The construction of incentive schemes, the definition (and often redefinition) of funding relations and the manipulation of the distribution of those funds—all based on the seeming objectivity of measurement and monetary rationalization—precipitates action-at-a-distance. As the following chapters highlight, accounting was central in maintaining the imbalance of power between settler society and Indigenous peoples, while allowing bureaucrats to govern from afar. This is a power that in the end may rival even tanks and heavy artillery.

Chapter Three

Waste Lands

> Whereas it is just and reasonable, and essential to our Interest, and the Security of our Colonies, that the several Nations or Tribes of Indians with whom we are connected, and who live under our Protection, should not be molested or disturbed in the Possession of such Parts of Our Dominions and Territories as, not having been ceded to or purchased by Us, are reserved to them, or any of them, as their Hunting Grounds.—*Royal Proclamation*, 7 October 1763, quoted in Anon. 1983

Historical Struggles over "Purchased" Territories

At least three decades before Confederation, the colonial government was looking forward to the extinction of the Indigenous occupants of the new land. While the suppression of cultural practices, containment of populations, mandatory education of the young and transfer of territories would all play their parts in securing this, a key bureaucratic operation—withdrawal of funding—would offer the *coup de grâce*.

In this chapter, we look at the political background to the increasing use of accounting technology in controlling the costs of empire, and in the following chapters we examine in more detail the two key sites for cost-cutting: military expenditures and "presents." We also examine the bureaucratic process by which the Indian problem became absorbed into a land problem. We look at how ownership of land evolved, the perceived need to fill the "waste lands" with immigrant populations, and the resulting costs to the empire and pressures brought to bear on the colonial government to achieve self-sustenance. These pressures, which gave rise to the rebellions of 1837–38 and resulted in the Durham Report, conclude a narrative arc which begins with the *Constitution Act* of 1791 and points us towards the Confederation of the provinces in 1867. Throughout, we witness the gradual erosion of Indigenous peoples as legitimate participants in the design of their own future.

The Evolution of Land Ownership

Land ownership and "purchase" in the context of colonial-Indigenous relations meant different things to each side. From Britain's perspective, successful colonization of the Canadian provinces required two separate and distinct exchanges with Canada's Aboriginal people: the straightforward exchange of land for money; and the exchange of goods—cast as "presents"—for military support from the Indians.

> The terms were sometimes for a certain quantity of Presents, such as have been before described, once delivered, or for an annual payment in perpetuity, either in money, or more generally in similar Presents. (Great Britain 1847: 5.1)

Successful colonization not only depended on subjugating Indigenous peoples but also on securing and maintaining the territory against other nations with imperialist intentions, first France and then the United States. Military support was obtained through the yearly distribution of goods, consisting chiefly of clothing and ammunition (Great Britain 1847: 5.2). Lands ceded by Aboriginal peoples were used primarily for European settlement and occasionally to re-settle other tribes which had been loyal to Britain in its war with the United States, operations which were a significant proportion of the costs of maintaining the colonies (Great Britain 1857–1858: Appendix 21). How each side of the land transactions perceived the terms was, as we shall see, an on-going point of contention—and a pivotal one in the imperial government's implementation of accounting technologies in order to rationalize the costs of maintaining the empire. The distinction between the two perceptual exchanges, for example, allowed for the subsequent reconsideration of the annual distribution of presents, an issue we will explore in chapter four.

Aboriginal peoples, on the other hand, did not see these two transactions (land for money; military support for presents) as separate. They believed that their initial surrender of land to France and the military support given to both France and Britain were part and parcel of a single agreement. The yearly distributions were assumed to be an annuity payment for the land, not a separate payment for military support. This sentiment is nicely captured by one of the notes in the 1847 Government Report recording an Aboriginal witness:

> Father, these presents are not in fact presents. They are a sacred debt contracted by the Government, under the promise made by the Kings of France to our forefathers, to indemnify them for the lands they had given up, confirmed by the Kings of England since cession of the country, and up to this time, punctually paid and acquitted. (Great Britain 1847: 5.1)

The question of how certain territories had come to be "owned" in the first place goes back to the *Royal Proclamation* of 1763, which ostensibly set out how land was to be acquired from its Indigenous occupants. Although the *Royal Proclamation* recognized Aboriginal title to unceded lands and stated that negotiations between Britain and Aboriginal peoples would be on a nation-to-nation basis, the *Constitution Act* of 1791 legitimized the presumption of ownership by force and royal decree, resulting in large tracts of land being given to a privileged few, who amassed as much of it as possible for speculation and profit (Milloy 1983: 56).

Land Grants and the Indian Problem

The *Constitutional Act* of 1791 directed that one-seventh of all land granted should be reserved for the clergy. Consequently, noted Lord Durham in his report of 1839, of a township containing 80,000 acres:

> one-seventh reserved for the clergy and one-seventh for the Crown ... five-sevenths remain for the disposal of government, a large portion of which is taken up for grants to U.E. Loyalists, militiamen, officers and others: the far greater part of these grants remain in an unimproved state. (Durham and Coupland 1946: 119)

Durham also pointed out that the Church of England "had a far larger share of the public money than the clergy of any other denomination" (Durham and Coupland 1946: 94–95). By 1825, though the population was only 150,000, seventeen million acres of Upper Canada had been surveyed, and of that, fifteen million had been granted. The disposal of land was inextricable from the powerful position held by the Family Compact. According to Durham:

> by grant or purchase, they [The Family Compact] have acquired nearly the whole of the waste lands of the Province; they are all-powerful in the chartered banks, and till lately, shared among themselves almost exclusively all offices of trust and profit.... (Durham and Coupland 1946: 79)

The Family Compact, he wrote, by means of influence on the executive council "wielded all the powers of government.... The bench, the magistracy, the high offices of the Episcopal Church, and a great part of the legal profession, are filled with the adherents of this party" (79).

Through pressure from the Reformers some regulation was eventually imposed restricting the size of land grants dispersed by the government to its own officers and friends, but those regulations were easily circumvented by the "ingenious invention" (Myers 1914: 82) of the System of Leaders and Associates. Simply, a group of associates would apply for individual parcels of land, then after receiving deeds for the land would hand them over to their leader. "In Lower Canada ... 1,425,000 acres were made over to about sixty individuals, during the government of Sir A. Milne" (Myers 1914: 82).

> In Nova Scotia, out of about six million acres of useful land, 5,750,000 have been lavished in free grants. Lastly, [quoting Durham's Report] "the whole of Prince Edward Island was given away in one day, in 1767, to about sixty grantees...." United Empire Loyalists were also the beneficiaries of this government largesse. In Upper Canada, the United Empire Loyalists received 3,200,000 acres. (Myers 1914: 83)

Returning soldiers and Loyalists rarely had farming experience, nor were they especially inclined to the pioneering life. As a consequence their granted lands were often sold for a pittance to speculating government officials and members of the executive and legislative councils—for example, Solicitor-General Grey, who purchased parcels of between 20,000 to 50,000 acres. "The price for 200 acres was variously from a gallon of rum to six pounds—seldom the latter" (Durham and Coupland 1946: 118).

By the 1830s, the Indian problem had become, ironically, a land problem for the colonial government: too much land and too few (white) people able to work it. For the ruling classes, split between chronic conservatism and so-called "radical" reformism, with unemployment and depression seriously affecting the mother country, the vast "empty spaces" of the New World were an ideal dumping ground for their "surplus population," as well as an exotic land of promise in which to invest their idle capital.

Although Britain had technically purchased the land from Indigenous peoples, violence against Indigenous peoples formed the backdrop for these negotiations. In chapter two we noted that the colonial government in Nova Scotia paid for the scalps of Natives. This policy was discontinued in 1752, but within the United States similar legislation existed until the late 1800s. "In Texas, for example, an official bounty on native scalp—any native scalps—was maintained until well into the 1870s. The result was that the Indigenous population of this state, once the densest in all of North America, had been reduced to near zero by 1880" (Churchill 1994: 37). While official incentives may have been withdrawn, violence against Native peoples continued to be condoned as the scramble for resource-rich land encouraged settlers to view them as nothing but an impediment to the accumulation of land (Churchill 1994: 38). Gold fever encouraged both the massacre of entire villages in Oregon and the arming of miners by the Hudson's Bay Company in British Columbia to attack the interior Salish Nation (Weyler 1992: 281). This tacitly approved violence against Native peoples was the context against which the treaties were negotiated. The decision of Indigenous people to surrender vast tracts of land in return for reserve lands and a small annuity payment was less an exchange than a tactical surrender in an attempt to avoid annihilation.

The political landscape in which the Indigenous struggle for cultural and physical survival took place was rife with immigrant resentment towards the ruling classes of the Canadas, a resentment that finally erupted in the Rebellions of 1837–38. It is one thing to appropriate vast tracts of wilderness from a conquered people; as the British soon learned, it is quite another to know what to do with it.

Immigration

If, under the auspices of the 1791 *Constitution Act*, those who were blessed by virtue of class and title received more land than they knew what to do with, the same could not be said for new immigrants. The titled and absentee proprietors of large tracts of land needed labourers; immigration to the New World needed to be stimulated. British emigrants, mostly from the poor classes, were "herded in foul ships and packed off to Canada under the most inhuman and horrible conditions" (Myers 1914: 87). Of the nearly half million immigrants arriving at Quebec between 1815 and 1839, most of them arrived "in a state of great poverty" (Myers 1914: 88).

Ships, "ill-provisioned, over-crowded, and ill-ventilated" (Durham and Coupland 1946: 123), veritable incubators of disease, easily evaded the *Passengers Act* of 1825. The dying piled up over the seventy- to eighty-day voyage, "the sick abandoned along a stretch of desolate shore" (Schull 1967: 20). The disgusting odour of the arriving ships could be smelled from miles away (Durham and Coupland 1946: 122). And for the hundreds of patients arriving at a time there was simply no accommodation at the Emigrant Hospital of Quebec. Generally the ill and destitute were "forcibly landed by the masters of the vessels, without a shilling in their pockets.... For six weeks at a time from the commencement of the emigrant-ship season, I have known the shores of the river along Quebec, for about a mile and a half, crowded with these unfortunate people, the places of those who might have moved off being constantly supplied by fresh arrivals, and there being daily drafts of from 10 to 30 taken to the hospital with infectious disease" (Schull 1967: 20).

Immigrants who had worked building the canals and railroads of Great Britain and knew little about agriculture or breaking virgin soil drifted towards the cities where they were used as cheap labour. In a time of clearing and road-building, fortunes were being made by contractors and owners.

For the desperate, living hand to mouth, the laws were cruel. Boys were hung—as well as adults—for burglary, robbery and sacrilege. Lashes were common for both genders. Servants were arrested for leaving their masters. "Poor children were torn from their parents, and bound out as apprentices by the overseers of the poor" (Francis, Jones and Smith 1988: 223).

By the early 1800s Upper Canadian settlers outnumbered Indigenous peoples by ten to one. Pressures on Indigenous lands were sharply increased; impoverished refugees, landed gentry and, at the end of the American Revolution, the United Empire Loyalists, all poured into the Maritimes. Settlement activity encouraged incursions on the Aboriginal land base and resulted in a shift in economic activity away from fur trading to wheat farming and timber (RCAP 1996: Chapter 5). The resulting changes were predictable:

> As Aboriginal economies declined because of the loss of the land, the scarcity of game and the continuing ravages of disease, relief payments to alleviate the threat of starvation became a regular feature of colonial financial administration. In short order, formerly autonomous Aboriginal nations came to be viewed, by prosperous and expanding Crown colonies, as little more than an unproductive drain on the public purse. (Cook and McNaught 1963: 316)

Cost Cutting

In Britain at this time there was much discussion about the costs of empire, particularly the costs of maintaining a military presence in the colonies, and the mother country was increasingly unwilling to fund colonial expansion activities (Spiers 1980). Reducing the national debt took on great importance, with the military as a primary target. Although Indigenous peoples had been valued allies, their military support in the Canadian provinces seemed less necessary. France had vacated the continent some sixty years earlier. The declining Indigenous population—less than ten thousand in Upper Canada by 1830—had reduced the threat of armed resistance to government policies (Surtees 1983).

With the pressures on land settlement and use, the Indigenous population, across the ocean from Downing Street, was "discovered" as a site for parliamentary cost-cutting. The framework for this cost-cutting legislation—with a direct effect on the livelihood of First Nations persons—was provided by a series of reports rationalized by the driving force of accounting techniques. In Britain, a military expenditure committee appointed by Parliament examined the military costs of maintaining Britain's far-flung empire (Great Britain 1835). One of its resolutions was that the Indian department in the Canadas—the department that administered the provision of "presents" to Aboriginal peoples—be either greatly reduced or eliminated entirely. In 1845, the *Report on the Affairs of the Indians in Canada* (RAIC) presented the history and background of colonial relations in Canada (Great Britain 1845), and, in 1847, presented its recommendations to the Legislative Assembly (Great Britain 1847). Another report in 1857–1858 revisited many of the same issues (Great Britain 1857–1858).

By using accounting techniques to meld together the separate events of land grants, immigration, Indigenous assimilation and the costs of maintaining the empire, the reports reframed the Indian problem as a land problem. The solution to the latter was to reconcile, via the software of accounting, the competing goods of colonial self-sufficiency, cost containment and the civilizing of Indigenous peoples. The subsequent legislation—*Civilization of Indian Tribes Act* (1857), *Civilization and Enfranchisement Act* (1859) and the *Act for the Gradual Enfranchisement of Indians* (1869)—we contend was genocidal.

The Rebellions

The rebellions of 1837–38 were a direct result of the 1791 *Constitutional Act,* which legitimized the possession of large tracts of land by the colonial elite and left the general population with no representative voice in government. The rebellions brought the Durham Report, which in turn gave birth to the Confederation of 1867. In the Report we can see the progressive partitioning of colonial expenditures. Indigenous peoples were caught in the squeeze—pressure on available resources with a focus on colonial expenditures from above, their own traditional resources slowly being eroded from below. The rebellions can be viewed as a turning point in their history though Native people themselves were largely uninvolved in the central struggles. The clarion call of the times was "self-sustenance." Costs to the empire were divided by the accountants into military costs (read British) and land costs (read economic dependence of Natives on the Crown). This left no place for the Indigenous peoples except as integers on the "expense" side of the ledger.

By the time the rebellions erupted, Indigenous peoples in Upper and Lower Canada had, in their attempt to avoid annihilation, surrendered most of their territories—which were considered purchased by the imperialists at the cost of nominal presents, negligible annual payments and vague promises (Surtees 1983). Few, if any, of the land grantees were farmers; most were titled gentry, politicians and industrialists, often all three rolled into one. Many of them increased their fortunes substantially by selling their land grants in smaller portions to those immigrants who could afford them.

Destitute immigrants imported as cheap labour for the ruling classes, their dreams of self-sufficiency held firmly in check by a colonial government answerable to the Crown, found themselves in a wilderness of unbroken land in a colony that was, by extension and the natural right of kings, dominated and exploited by the same forces they had been fleeing in the first place. While the immigrant poor and the colonial aristocracy vied for survival on the one hand and legitimization of the great land-grab on the other, the Indigenous peoples, almost completely disenfranchised from their source of livelihood and power, observed from the sidelines the colonial squabble over how to share the spoils of conquest—virtually ignored, except as a targeted site for government austerity measures.

The *Constitutional Act* of 1791 provided for an assembly which was elected by the people; however, this assembly—the only popular branch of the legislature—had no power to remove members of either the executive or legislative councils, most of whom had direct ties to, or were themselves members of, the Family Compact oligarchy. The popular assembly was thus left with a single ineffectual form of dissent: personal attack upon the individual members of the upper house, with no recourse to legislative power.

It was the Family Compact that William Lyon Mackenzie, leader of the Upper Canada rebellion, so tirelessly attacked. Through his newspaper *The Colonial Advocate*, Mackenzie made several populist proposals. "My creed" said Mackenzie, " has been social democracy—or equality of each man before society—and political democracy, or equality of each man before the law" (quoted in Creighton 1958: 241).

The poorer classes were further disillusioned by the legislated give-away of huge tracts of land to the aristocracy and the clergy in 1791. To the dissatisfied colonists, mostly farmers and labourers, with some shop-keepers and a few professionals, corporations such as The Bank of Upper Canada, the Welland Canal Company and the Canada Company were responsible for corrupting the government and oppressing the people. In the colonies, according to the reformers, representative government created oligarchic control by governors and councils, and in Britain "centralized bureaucratic control [was] exercised by the Colonial Office," whose officers were "not answerable to public opinion or parliament" and "were inadequately supervised by a colonial secretary who might be in office for only a short period and was sometimes incompetent. Political patronage, exorbitant expense, and other major evils flourished under this system" (Burroughs 1969: xxiii).

Thus, the storm had been brewing for forty years. In Britain, Whig Reformers were on the rise, with rebel leaders fanning the flames in the colonies; fear was mounting that a second American revolution might be brewing. The prospect of losing more colonies to independence, with mounting political pressure at home to reduce the costs of colonialism, forced the government to deal with the rebels on the one hand and to cut the costs of maintaining the empire on the other.

With pressure mounting and a market crash in 1837 throwing immigrant labourers out of work, the explosion was finally ignited when Lord John Russell, MP, introduced his Ten Resolutions to the British House. Among the resolutions was the inflammatory edict that revenues of the Crown would be surrendered to the Assembly only in return for the installation of a permanent Civil List (of bureaucratic appointees, i.e., legislated patronage) and that the governor would be empowered to appropriate funds without legislative sanction. (Since 1832, the assembly of Lower Canada had refused to vote supplies until their grievances had been redressed, resulting in inadequate revenues for local expenses and arrears of bureaucratic salaries [Burroughs 1969: 109–10].) There would be no elected legislative council and no responsible executive. According to *The Spectator* (March 11, 1837), "those resolutions not only negated all the demands of the Colonial suitors for justice, but authorized robbery" (quoted in Burroughs 1969: 110).

Systematic Colonization: Durham, Wakefield and Buller

After the 1837 rebellion, Lord Durham was sent, as Governor General, to clean up the mess. He brought with him, as part of a large entourage, two advisors: Charles Buller and Edward Gibbon Wakefield, fellow reformers and theoreticians in colonial matters. Before we look further into Lord Durham's report, an examination of Wakefield's theory of colonization—a theory that held sway in intellectual and government circles at the time—will illuminate how subtle and perhaps negligible the differences between the Tory status quo and the Whig Reform movement actually were. The theory is also a good illustration of how bureaucracies can be easily infected with theoretical systematization, reframing persons as conceptual integers. It is also important to note that Wakefield was a primary influence on the thinking of Herman Merivale, who in 1848 would become Permanent Undersecretary of State to the Colonial Office and whose policies would have a devastating effect on Indigenous populations. We will acquaint ourselves with Merivale in the following chapter.

All reformist roads during this period of colonization, it seems, led inevitably to government control of land. Whether through land price control, manipulation of peasant ownership and participation or schemes to relieve the burden of the British taxpayer, the end result for the Aboriginals was to have the land pulled out from under their feet. The economic-government machinations around which the rebellions and the resulting Durham Report swirled had at their centre the control of distant populations, differentiated and segmented into hierarchies, with the Indigenous populations occupying the lowest rung. As we shall see, the economic pressure to this lowest echelon was applied with such bureaucratic finesse that the Indigenous people themselves were forced to pay the government for the cost of having their land taken from them.

Edward Gibbon Wakefield was a colourful character to say the least. While serving as a European diplomat in 1816 he took young heiress and ward in chancery Eliza Pattle as a bride in a runaway marriage and ten years later increased his infamy by abducting and marrying Ellen Turner, another school-girl and heiress, a crime for which he served three years in Newgate Prison. It was there, meeting prisoners waiting to be deported to Australia, that he became interested in colonial policy. He later developed his ideas for Systematic Colonization while writing anonymous letters to the *Morning Chronicle*, during the autumn of 1829, masquerading as a settler in Sydney. "The letters themselves were written in a colourful, racy style, with a wealth of illustrative detail concerning the fortunes of an Australian settler with more land than he had the labour or capital to develop" (Burroughs 1969: xvii).

Wakefield had a marked influence on Durham and though neither were considered part of the Family Compact—indeed, in theory, were critical of them—their personal relationship lays bare the internecine manipulations of Downing Street and the landed colonials. After the rebellions, Wakefield was to become the agent of the North American Colonial Association of Ireland, which eventually owned the Seigneury at Beauharnois—the richest of the Lower Canada seigneuries and the very epicentre of the Lower Canada rebellion, at the time owned by Edward "Bear" Ellice, a kingpin of the Family Compact. Ellice was married to the daughter of Charles, making him Durham's uncle. Ellice's son was Durham's private secretary. Ellice had been a Whig MP under Lord Grey in 1818 and served his government until 1834. "He [Ellice] probably knew more about Canada than any other person in politics in England and his influence upon Lord Durham cannot be overestimated" (Burroughs 1969: x). Ellice held large interests in the Hudson's Bay Company and several hundred thousand acres in the northern U.S. and Canada.

Wakefield's theory of Systematic Colonization was designed to alleviate unemployment by supplying homes and jobs for immigrant labourers and new fields of investment for surplus British capital, which "was accumulating in the hands of British Capitalists faster than it could be profitably invested at home" (Burroughs 1969: 43). Systematic Colonization was thus an attempt to transplant a cross-section of English society to the colonies.

Systematic Colonization—eventually to be abandoned by the government—is a brilliant example of social engineering through the mechanics of accounting. Its genius lay in the number of birds it could kill with one stone: the control of settlement, the use of land, the structure of land ownership, economic growth and the exploitation of surplus population (Burroughs 1969: ix). The key integers in the accountant's balance sheet represented the immigrants. "Land grants would be replaced by selling land at a price which would be restrictive enough to prevent labourers from immediately becoming land owners, thus creating and preserving a supply of labour for settlers with capital" (43). These restrictive prices would concentrate settlement in agricultural communities and prevent labourers from becoming landowners too easily. "The proceeds from land sales would be used to finance selected emigration from the British Isles" (43). As labour became scarce, the price of land would be raised; when labour was cheap and plentiful, the price would be reduced. The revenue produced by sale of Crown land would be used "to pay the passages of selected emigrants from the English labouring class, with a preference being given to young married couples" (43).

Charles Buller, another key advisor to Lord Durham, did not think British workers were fit for "the severe and painful labours to which they would thus be exposed." Buller feared that, in spite of any regulations that might be set down, the emigrants would be "tempted, by the desire of becoming independent landholders, to settle themselves upon farms of their own at too soon a period for their comfort and prosperity," then abandon the land to hire themselves out as labourers (Burroughs 1969: 57–59).

The Durham Report, the Family Compact and Self-Sustenance

Durham faced three issues: the split between the two Canadas—French and English; the distribution of waste lands; and representative government. Politically, his report would have to be seen to ease the tax burden on the British electorate while theoretically reconciling local autonomy with imperial unity—a unity which had no place for Canada's first peoples except as entities absorbed into British culture. "Easing the burden of the British taxpayer" really meant controlling the Canadian territories from a distance.

Whatever the ostensible goals of the Durham Report, at bottom the stability of the landed gentry had to be ensured. And in Canada the landed gentry meant the Family Compact. The term did not refer exclusively to blood ties, though these were notable, but to a broader class and social grouping in which the boundaries between the landed gentry, the titled representatives of the Crown and government officials themselves were completely obliterated. Railway ownership, for example, was based on legislation granting definite rights and privileges, as charters of incorporation. In many cases, the politicians granting the charters and the investors themselves were the same individuals. "Other members of parliament were traders, merchants, or shippers, as well as land speculators, and had a personal and immediate interest in bringing about modern methods of transportation" (Myers 1914: 153).

Railroad companies—at the heart of the Family Compact—were privately owned but publicly supported with enormous land grants by the Dominion government. Canadian Pacific, for example, had amassed as much as twenty-five million acres by 1913, and the British American Land Company was chartered on March 17, 1845, to A.T. Galt, who happened to be Commissioner in Canada from 1844–1854 (Myers 1914: 153). Galt, first elected to Parliament in 1849, was also with the St. Lawrence & Atlantic Railroad Company. Allan McNab, promoter of London and Gore R.R. Co., which became Great Northern Railway with McNab as president, was a member of Parliament who received a knighthood and a baronetcy in 1856. He was also Chairman of the Legislative Assembly Standing Committee on Railroads.

The members of the Family Compact, in spite of the Durham Report, were so firm in their alliances with legislators and so strongly associated with government itself, that locations for self-sustenance were obviously to be set elsewhere. Somehow the aristocrat-industrialist's dependence on the Crown's largesse was perceived differently than the dependence of Indigenous peoples and immigrant settlers on those same coffers. Bureaucratically, locating sites for cost-cutting and promoting self-sustenance was to be accomplished through the progressive refinement of partitioning total costs. This partitioning, accomplished with its reliance on a hierarchy of populations and the power of written tabulations, contributed to the Crown's self-fulfilling prophecies that Indigenous peoples would eventually disappear entirely—and therefore government ought to weigh carefully how much was invested in their welfare.

"Self-sustenance" is a noble designation most often used by those who have decided that the cost of supporting the less fortunate has reached its limit. As a semantic tool especially suited to accounting technologies, it can be easily applied to a target population—without judiciously applying its criteria to one's own population. The expert application of accounting measures to a population whose resources have been usurped renders that population economically dependent—i.e., not self-sustaining. Those benefitting from that population's demise are thus defined—by themselves—as self-sustaining. Those who are not able to sustain themselves are seen, by virtue of their dependence, as sites for cost-cutting. In the 1830s climate of economic retrenchment, the Natives would be taking a greater step towards being civilized if they could only sustain themselves without relying on hand-outs from the government. If the colonies would simply do the right thing, said the prevailing wisdom, then the British taxpayers would not have to pay so much for the maintenance of the empire.

Census: Differentiating Populations, Partitioning Costs and Extinction

In chapter two we noted that governance involves the planning, motivating and controlling of populations, but on what basis is this accomplished? One suggestion is that in order to govern, it is necessary "to know," to have detailed knowledge of the various populations. Furthermore, this knowing is accomplished through statistics:

> The events and phenomena to which government is to be applied must be rendered into information—written reports, drawings, pictures, numbers, charts, graphs, statistics.... This form enables pertinent features of the domain ... to literally be re-presented in the place where decisions are to be made about them. (Miller and Rose 1990: 7)

In order for a hierarchy of populations to be achieved, individuals must first be conceptualized as integers and counted.

The explicit government partitioning of citizens into a hierarchy of populations—the Family Compact, the immigrant settlers and Native peoples—encouraged increasing attention to be paid to the lower classes. Immigrant settlers would be governed, in keeping with Wakefield's theory of Systematic Colonization, through the management of land sale procedures. However the real force of governance would be directed to the bottom-most population, since clearly this was the area that offered both the greatest opportunity for cost savings and the least political cost to government officials. But first, it was necessary to gather information on Native peoples.

In the spring of 1837, His Majesty's government undertook a detailed census "for the purpose of encouraging the Indians to adopt agricultural pursuits, and acquire habits of settled industry" (Great Britain 1845: 11). This census sought to represent, under cover of "pertinent data," the population of Indigenous peoples, with an emphasis on how large the population was, where they resided, how they lived, the locations of their hunting grounds, a summary and accounting of those employed in the superintendence of the settled Indians or of the other tribes and the number and description of the clergy or teachers attached to each tribe or party. Thus was the first partition erected between moneys spent on Indigenous peoples and moneys spent on British personnel.

The second partition was erected between military expenditures and land expenditures, creating a completely artificial—but tabulated—division between incomes and expenses from settlement activities on the one hand and the military costs of maintaining those activities on the other hand—as though the two were not inextricably linked. When Lord

Goderich proposed that payments for Native land should come out of "the Casual and Territorial Revenue of that Province" and that the remaining charge, which had originally been "incurred with the view of securing the services of Indians in wars" ought to be borne by British Parliament, he was reframing the expenditures as an issue of land, which was uppermost in the minds of the legislators of the time.

Other such artificial categories were constructed, legitimized by the drawing up of convincing tables, allocating costs of presents, pay and allowances, pensions and contingencies—all of them finding their way into the reports on Indian affairs. For example, Table 1 shows how F.B. Head, in a letter to Lord Glenelg, used such partitions to argue that selected expenses (the presents portion of the expenditures) of the Indian Department could be further reduced (Head 1836: 358).

Lord Glenelg used these categorizations to concur with F.B. Head that the pension portion of the expenses should not be abrogated because of the service the officers had given to Britain. An officer, for example, "in the Evening of his long and well-spent life " should not be neglected "by His Majesty's Government to whose Service he has been for more than Half a Century unremittingly and devotedly attached" (Glenelg 1836: 358). This argument is supported by another table containing the names of Indian Department personnel and their pensions (only one of the pensions was payable to a "Warrior wounded in Action"). This letter makes similar arguments regarding then current Indian Department personnel, again supported by the inclusion of a table listing personnel, their remuneration and their period of service.

The decision to partition Indian Department costs into a land component and a military component—which may as well have been termed "other"—may have convinced British government officials that colonial land sales were self-sustaining, but it also appears to have encouraged increased calls for the reduction/elimination of the military expenditures (presents) component.

One response of colonial administrators was to propose a different accounting allocation, one that both encouraged and signaled self-sufficiency on the part of the Indian Department, while leading to the perverse notion that Indigenous people could, by selling their remaining land to settlers, cover the costs of distributing presents to themselves. Picking up on F.B. Head's suggestion some twenty years earlier, the 1857/58 report on Indian affairs would (unsuccessfully) propose that the Indian Department itself become self-sustaining by:

> paying the Officers connected therewith out of the funds which they administer. To effect this, [it was] proposed to devote the sum annually granted for charitable purposes among the Tribes in Lower Canada by the Provincial Government to meet the

Table 1
Enclosure in No. 32, Summary of the Annual Expenditure of the Indian Department in Upper Canada

	Sterling
Cost of the Presents, say at least	£ 8,500
Pay and Allowances	1,610
Pensions	462
Contingencies, consisting prinicpally of Pay of Persons employed not on the regular Establishment, such as a Clerk, Schoolmasters, Farmers at the several Posts to instruct the Indians in Cultivation, and a weekly Express for Letters, Transport of Persons from Depots to Places of Issue, Buildings for Indians, Rations to Visiting Indians at the annual Issue of Presents, Postage and travelling Expenses	2,000
Gross Expenditure	£12,572

The Proportion for this Province of the British Parliamentary Grant annually voted for the Indian Department in the Canadas is 13,380£ Sterling.

J. Givins,
Chief Superintendent of Indian Affairs,
Upper Canada

Indian Office, Toronto
22d November 1836

RETURN OF THE NUMBER OF RESIDENT INDIANS IN UPPER CANADA who have or will receive PRESENTS during the Year 1836; and also of the Number of VISITING INDIANS who have received PRESENTS during the same Year, showing what Proportion of such Visiting Indians came from the UNITED STATES, and what Proportion from Canada.

The Number of Indians resident at established Indian Stations who have or will receive Presents as above	5,209	
Do. Do. who from not being attached to any Indian Station received their Presents with the Visiting Indians	1,298	
		6,507
The Number of Visiting Indians from the United States who have received Presents as above		2,793
Total		9,300

Source: Head 1836: 130

annual expenditure of the Department in that part of the Colony, and to raise means for the support of the Indians themselves by the sale of their Reserves. (Great Britain 1857–1858:2)

Under this plan the costs of administering the distribution of presents in return for military support would be borne by both settlers and Aboriginal peoples. A portion of Indian Department costs would be deemed to be an expenditure on "charity" and paid for out of provincial revenues. Since provincial revenues and expenditures were ultimately expected to balance, this proposal implied that a portion of Indian Department costs would be covered by the costs of land sales to settlers. The remainder would be borne by Aboriginal peoples who would be "compelled" to use a portion of the proceeds from the sale of their land to, in essence, cover the costs of distributing presents to themselves. Like Goderich's proposal in the 1830s, this re-allocation of costs would demonstrate the self-sufficiency of colonial operations. However, it also represented an attempt to both redefine responsibility for Indian Department costs as being, in part, the responsibility of Indigenous peoples and to label the settler's portion of these costs as charity.

Accounting techniques continued to penetrate into more sites of colonial governance—as if accounting could function as a ready-made technology to instill economy. The 1847 *RAIC Report*, for example, went so far as to recommend that "the management of the Indians be placed under the Civil Secretary, with the view of its being brought more immediately under the notice of the Governor General" (Great Britain 1847: 10.1). The report went even further: why not install the superior technician himself into the administrative machinery? The report recommended that:

> An Accountant be employed under him (the Civil Secretary), who will be specially charged with the management of the various accounts of the Department connected with the estimates, requisitions, annuities, sales of land, etc., and devote any spare time which he may have to the general business of the office. (Great Britain 1847: 10.1)

The institution of such a functionary would undoubtedly be for the Indigenous peoples' own good, as they were slowly being tabulated into non-existence. Their future well-being, Head opined, was beyond Britain's control, and for "humanitarian" reasons, the distribution of presents should not be abrogated because:

> this Expense will shortly be defrayed altogether by the Sale of Lands they have this Year Liberally surrendered to me; and even if that were not the Case, I do think, that, enjoying as we do Possession of this noble Province, it is our bounden Duty to consider as Heirlooms the Wreck of that simple-minded, ill-fated Race, which, as I have already stated, is daily and yearly fading before the Progress of Civilization. We have only to bear patiently with them for a short Time, and with a few Exceptions, principally Half-castes, their unhappy Race, beyond our Power of Redemption, will be extinct. (Head 1836: 357)

Chapter Four

The Only Possible Euthanasia

An examination of the various appointed select committees inquiring into colonial expenses may serve to unveil the bureaucratic methods used in reconfiguring and often decimating Indigenous-government funding relations. Generally, the process begins with the theoretical partitioning of populations and expenses needed to maintain power abroad; then there is an "accounting" of those various segmentations; and finally, bureaucratic rationalizations are employed, based on the gathered numerical information, in applying recommendations that inevitably impact on the targeted segment. The theoretical partitioning of populations and the artificial segmenting of the tasks necessary to maintaining an empire appeal to the logical mind. But without the contextual realities of individuals living their day-to-day lives, these segmentations are illusory. By representing these economic factors, the government of Canada in the early part of the nineteenth century was able to present, through the slight-of-hand of sound committee work, an air-tight economic logic for dissolving their commitments to the Native populations—under the rubric "amalgamation" or, what Herman Merivale, the government's colonization guru of the time, called "the only possible Euthanasia" (Merivale 1967: 511).

Accounting for Military Machinery

As early as 1822, the Colonial Secretary for the Canadian provinces "contemplated a reduction of the Indian Department, with a view to its ultimate abolition" (Great Britain 1845: 7). In 1829, the Lords of Treasury and the Secretary of State issued an order that "the whole expense of the [Indian] Department should not exceed 20,000£." (7). And in 1832, an accounting allocation change recommended that the charges for the Indian Department be separated from other charges relating to colonial operations in Canada, when being presented to Parliament for approval:

> Previously to this period the charges for the presents, including those given on account of the annuities payable for lands surrendered, had been yearly granted by the British Parliament in a separate vote, while the salaries and pensions of the officers of the Indian Department had been paid from the military chest.

> This course being considered irregular, Lord Goderich proposed that for the future, the land-payments or annuities payable for land surrendered, which were confined to Upper Canada, should be charged on the Casual or Territorial Revenue of that Province, while the remaining charge, having been originally incurred with the view of securing the services of Indians in wars, for British, and not exclusively colonial interests, ought, according to His Lordship's view, to be provided by the Imperial Parliament. (Great Britain 1845: 8)

On the February 28, 1834, the British House of Commons ordered "That a select Committee be appointed to inquire into the Military Establishment and Expenditure in the Colonies and Dependencies of The Crown" (Great Britain 1835, Volume 1: 1). The Committee gathered evidence, interviewed witnesses and presented the first volume of its report to the House of Commons in August 1834. The second volume was completed and presented to the House of Commons in 1835. In these reports, the Committee examined military establishments and expenditures in the colonies of Gibraltar, Malta, the Ionian Islands, the West Coast of Africa, the Cape of Good Hope and the Island of Ceylon (in volume one) and New South Wales, Van Diemen's Land and the North American Provinces (in volume two). The published report contains the Select Committee's analysis and recommendations, along with minutes of evidence from the witnesses and supplementary appendices.

The report of the Select Committee illustrates the manner in which the military machinery of empire relied on accounting. In his examination of the administration of the British military during this time period, Sweetman makes a similar point, commenting that the "development of improved techniques of accounting ... created the impetus for efficiency which reflected throughout the [military] administrative system" (Sweetman 1984: 3).

The mandate of the Select Committee and the reports themselves illustrate this intertwining of the hardware and software of empire. The mandate was to inquire into both the adequacy of military establishments and the cost of these establishments. Throughout the minutes of evidence, witnesses were repeatedly asked to juxtapose and balance these two goals. And in the final report, the first two recommendations explicitly deal with these matters:

> Resolved, That it is not the Intention of this Committee ... to relieve the Executive Government from the Duty which constitutionally belongs to it, of providing.... A force sufficient for the Security of His Majesty's Possessions abroad.

And:

> Resolved, That the Committee are of the Opinion, That the strictest Economy should be observed in every branch of Military Expenditure of the Colonies; and that any surplus Revenue that may remain after defraying their Civil Expenses ... be applied to the payment of their Military Charges. (Great Britain 1835, Volume 1: iii)

Thus the mandate of the Select Committee and the final report itself set up the mutual goals of effectiveness and efficiency for the military forces in the colonies (Great Britain 1835, Volume 2: 26). It is worth noting that efficiency here was meant in the strictest economic sense. Such notions of efficiency and economy were prevalent in the reformist discourses of the time and provided the rhetorical space for accounting techniques (Sweetman 1984: 13). In attempting to assess the economy of military operations in distant places, the Committee turned not only to eyewitnesses but to accounting techniques and records. Accounting records provided the Select Committee with a short-form representation of distant events. And by providing this information to decision-makers in the imperial centre, accounting helped to render these distant locales "governable."

Throughout the report is the recognition that accounting is a useful technology with regards to governing military operations. For example, the report contains an extended discussion of the accounting records for individual detachments and whether these records provide appropriate information (Great Britain 1835, Volume 2: 63–84). In the following example, questions posed by the lawyer for the Select Committee to a bureaucrat from the military considers, in keeping with the emphasis on economy, whether the current methods of accounting are economical:

> Q: If those two are able to keep the accounts in the whole of Newfoundland for 276 rank and file, how is it that so large a staff is kept in those parts of Canada where detachments from only 10 to 50 men exist?
> A: The same description of accounts are necessary for a detachment of 50 men as are necessary for a regiment of 800, provided the regiment of 800 is at one post; but if the regiment is scattered over different parts of the country, then that would impose additional labour upon the commissariat, because each detachment would require the same description of accounts to be rendered in duplicate, and the same description of vouchers. (Great Britain 1835, Volume 2: 63)

The notion of economy also motivates discussions regarding the prevention of fraud and regarding how often the accounts of different detachments, regiments and commissariats are audited and by whom (Great Britain 1835, Volume 2: 57–73). From these examples, it appears that accounting techniques were viewed as an integral tool in the government of military operations.

The report not only discussed accounting techniques but used accounting numbers. Accounting data was interspersed throughout the report, usually with the effect of making visible certain aspects of military operations. For example, included in the appendices were tables listing the cost to Britain of military operations in different colonies. Other tables enumerated the number and distribution of effective forces, including a breakdown of officers, non-commissioned officers and soldiers in Canada, whereas yet other tables summarized the "pay, allowances, emoluments, advantages and salaries" accruing to different military personnel in different locations (Great Britain 1835, Volume 2: 96). This cost information was then referred to in the questioning of witnesses regarding the appropriate military force at a particular location.

Thus was the actual state of affairs in the colonies represented as accounting information—to be used by the Select Committee in providing a rational basis for examining economic efficiency of the military. This information also created the illusion that it was possible to compare the military efficiency of disparate locales. For example, a recurrent theme in the questioning of military officials by the Select Committee was the differential cost of military personnel in Nova Scotia *vis-à-vis* the rest of Canada:

> It appears by the Returns that the number of troops in Nova Scotia and in Canada are nearly equal; that there is not a difference of above 200 between the amount of troops in Canada and Nova Scotia: be kind enough to explain to the Committee why there is such a difference between the amount of the expense of the commissariat at Canada and Nova Scotia; and state why it should be three times the amount at the one place as it is at the other, for nearly the same number of troops? (Great Britain 1835, Volume 2: 55)

Here we see the central illusion of representation at work. While common sense tells us how enormously different each locale under consideration would be, and therefore how unique their funding requirements, the committee kept returning to the issue of cost differences, insisting that the two jurisdictions were in the same area—North America!—and insinuating that therefore costs should be the same in both cases (Great Britain 1835, Volume 2: 53, 55, 72). Reducing the

Table 2
Distriution of the Troops in Canada on the 1st January 1835, the Date of the Latest Return Received

Stations	Corps	Field Officers	Captains	Subalterns	Staff	Serjeants	Drummers	Rank and File
Quebec	Royal Artillery	1	4	4	1	3	1	131
	Royal Engineers	1	1	3	-	-	-	1
	15th Foot	-	-	-	-	-	-	5
	24th Foot	-	-	-	-	3	-	9
	32nd Foot	1	2	7	3	27	10	411
	66th Foot	-	-	-	-	-	-	2
	79th Foot	2	3	8	4	29	8	423
Grosse Island	32 Foot	-	-	-	-	1	-	2
Montreal	Royal Engineers	-	1	-	-	-	-	-
	24th Foot	2	4	9	4	20	9	353
	79th Foot	-	-	-	-	1	-	-
St. Helen's	Royal Artillery	-	1	2	1	3	1	69
Isle Aux Noix	24th Foot	-	1	1	1	3		50
Sorel	24th Foot	-	-	-	-	-	-	5
Coteau du Lac	24th Foot	-	-	-	-	1	-	4
Lachine	24th Foot	-	-	-	-	-	-	2
St. Philip's	24th Foot	-	-	-	-	1	-	1
Rideau Canal	Royal Engineers	-	1	2	-	-	-	-
	24th Foot	-	-	-	-	1	-	-
	66th Foot	-	-	1	-	1	-	23
Kingston	Royal Artillery	1	3	4	1	4	2	90
	Royal Engineers	1	1	1	-	-	-	-
	15th Foot	-	-	-	-	-	-	5
	66th Foot	2	5	8	5	30	10	397
Fort Henry	Royal Artillery	-	-	-	-	1	-	9
Toronto	Royal Artillery	-	-	-	-	-	-	8
	Royal Engineers	-	1	-	-	-	-	-
	15th Foot	2	3	6	4	21	7	264
	66th Foot	-	-	-	-	-	-	3
	79th Foot	-	-	-	-	-	-	2
Fort George	Royal Artillery	-	-	-	-	-	-	3
	15th Foot	-	1	1	-	3	1	46
	66th Foot	-	-	-	-	1	-	-
Grenville Canal	Royal Engineers	-	-	1	-	-	-	-
Cataroque	66th Foot	-	-	-	-	-	-	1
Amherstburgh	15th Foot	-	1	2	1	3	1	49
Penetangushene	15th Foot	-	-	1	-	2	-	40
	total	13	33	61	25	159	50	2,408

Adjutant-General's Office
30 March 1835

John Macdonald
Adjutant-General

Source: Great Britain 1835, Volume 2: 98

comparison of locations to accounting data is not surprising since programs of government depend on the illusion of "stable, mobile, combinable and comparable" data—such data rendering the domain under consideration "susceptible to evaluation, calculation and intervention" (Miller and Rose 1990: 7).

Accounting information not only provided a starting point for comparing the military efficiency of different locales as represented in numbers but also for interrogating the military judgments of the expert witnesses. For example, cost data pertaining to the Governor of Newfoundland's ship provided the starting point for the following line of questioning directed at the former Governor of Newfoundland:

> Is there not a vessel or yacht for the governor's use at Newfoundland? Yes, there is.... What is the amount of expense? The contract for the vessel is 2,300£ a year ... do you consider it absolutely necessary that a yacht should be kept up, or so large a vessel as at present? I think that it is quite necessary that the vessel should be kept up: The size at present is not more than adequate for the purpose for which she is wanted. She is not wanted exclusively for the governor's use; she is required when necessary to send detachments of troops to different parts of the islands, and she should be able to carry them ... and she has been sent to cruize [*sic*] when complaints have been made of the conduct of the French with respect to the fishery and to prevent smuggling and other duties. (Great Britain 1835, Volume 2: 32–40)

In this example, accounting data made visible certain aspects of military operations in the Canadian colony. Select Committee members focused their questions on these aspects, asking the military witnesses to justify in military terms the appropriateness of these expenditures.

In another instance, accounting data was used to frame the decision as to whether "regular forces" or the militia should be used to defend Canada [questions directed toward a lieutenant-colonel stationed in Nova Scotia]:

> Q: is the militia force a popular force in Nova Scotia?
> A: I should say it is certainly.
> Q: How are the officers and men paid when embodied?
> A: They are paid by a vote of the House of Assembly....
> Q: Is not the pay very inferior to that which they can obtain by labour or by any work as artisans or labourers?
> A: The pay is very inferior....
> Q: Then taking that into consideration, and taking into consid-

> eration the difficulty of finding employment for emigrants ... do you think there would be any doubt of finding a sufficient number of men for the militia at as low a rate of pay as British soldiers?
> A: Emigrants without money would enlist....
> Q: Supposing the experiment were tried ... do you, in a military point of view see any objection to employing a proportion of that force, and releasing an equivalent proportion of the regular force of the country?
> A: If it were possible to have the militia as perfectly trained as our militia were during the last war, I should see no objection to a certain portion, but I doubt that being practicable. (Great Britain 1835, Volume 2: 28–29)

And:

> Q: Have you yourself attended any of those [present] distributions? ... At what place? ... How many Indians attended? ... At what months in the year? ... what were the articles distributed? ... Did you take all those things up with you, or is there any depot kept there? ... On your arrival there, what measures are taken, and how is the distribution regulated? ... Do any observations occur to you, as to a better and cheaper mode of distribution than that which is now used? (Great Britain 1835, Volume 2: 73–74)

And:

> Q: Can you give us any information as to the distribution of presents, and how far the duties now performed by the commissariat may be performed by the Indian Department, or the duties of the Indian Department performed by the commissariat?
> A: I should think the commissariat would be quite competent to distribute the presents without any Indian Department, which is quite an expensive machine. (Great Britain 1835, Volume 2: 77)

Rendered as a machine, then, and an expensive one at that, the Indian Department, broken down into its parts, each of which are measured and its efficiency weighed, can be dismantled and rebuilt according to the political aims of the commissariat. Thus, the data serves the ideology; "local" knowledges are mobilized by imperial powers and rationalized by accounting numbers. This same data also provided the Select Committee with a starting basis for questioning and interrogating the opinions and judgments of military witnesses. By continually juxtaposing the "truths" as made visible by accounting numbers with the "truths" enunciated by military personnel, the Select Committee sought to rationalize the state of military operations in these distant colonies.

The foregoing analysis illustrates the ways in which the military machinery of empire at this juncture relied on accounting techniques. Accounting techniques appeared to function as not only the guidance system for the empire's military machinery but also as a useful technology for interrogating the military costs of empire during this period of economic retrenchment.

Given the parameters of the Select Committee's mandate and the direction of the questions, the report's final conclusion regarding the Indian Department is not surprising:

> Resolved:
> That the Committee are of the opinion from the Evidence taken, and to which they refer, that the Indian Department may be greatly reduced, if not entirely abolished, and they therefore call attention of the House to the same; and also to the expenses of articles annually distributed to the Indians, and whether any arrangement may not be made to dispense with such distribution in future, or to commute the presents for money. (Great Britain 1835, Volume 2: iii)

The evidence indicated that the military support provided by Indigenous peoples was less needed in the 1830s than in earlier periods. This, coupled with the discourse of economy and the emphasis throughout the committee's process on cost-cutting, made the final recommendation that the Indian Department be abolished quite predictable.

It is important to note that the solutions proposed in the report indirectly addressed the competing dilemmas of government. The specific costs associated with the Indian Department would be reduced over time and, if the solution were successful, Indigenous peoples would both be contained and civilized. Furthermore, over the longer term, this strategy of containment would make it easier for colonial officials to buy and resell the land previously occupied by Indigenous peoples, since this land was no longer central to their subsistence. In these ways, the proposed solution partially reconciled the competing demands of government facing officials at this juncture.

Throughout the chain of events leading to the discovery/identification of Indigenous peoples as a potential site for governance, accounting techniques were salient. As we saw in chapter three, techniques of counting were used to come to know the population of Native peoples. And in this chapter, we see how accounting techniques were used by the Select Committee to interrogate the costs of military operations in the colonies, eventually leading to the recommendation that the Indian Department be abolished. Accounting numbers formed a seamless circle in that they both framed the problem and suggested a potential solution (Smith 1990; Neu and Taylor 1996: 452).

While we believe that accounting was instrumental in the process of "discovering" Indigenous peoples as a potential site of governance, this is not to suggest that discovery occurred at a single moment in time nor that accounting was the only administrative technique which contributed to this shift (cf. Foucault 1984: 80). Rather, accounting, as an integral part of colonial bureaucracy, played a role in helping governmental officials come to both know and construct Native peoples in such a way that they came to be viewed as a particular population to be specially governed.

Presents: Dependence of the Feeble-minded on the Bounty of the Crown

The use of the term "presents" for what now would be called "annuity payments" is a key linguistic trope in the rationalization of government initiatives directed at Indigenous peoples. Normally the word denotes a gift bestowed; a present is voluntarily given and is not predicated upon, or part of, a previous exchange. By using the term the government was able to mask or erase the true rationale for the annuity payments. These payments had been a long-standing feature of government-Indigenous relations:

> From the earliest period of the connexion between the Indians and the British government it has been customary to distribute annually certain presents, consisting chiefly of clothing and ammunition. (Great Britain 1845, Section 1: 5)

The term "presents" had certain ideological effects, primarily the masking and rationalization of colonial interests. Any exchange—gift or otherwise—may serve to delineate the differences between bestower and recipient. The position of gratitude assumed by the recipient of a gift may be interpreted by the bestower as a position of inferiority. The historical distribution of presents to the Indigenous people served to augment and even cement the broader colonialist perception of Indigenous people as inferior and dependent on government support. References to the inferiority of Indigenous people are maintained throughout the correspondence between government bureaucrats and official government reports. The introduction to the 1847 report, for example, outlines the failings of Indigenous peoples:

> The chief obstacles to the advancement of the race are, their want of self-dependence, and their habits of indolence, which have been fostered, if not created, by the past policy of the Govern-

> ment; their ignorance or imperfect knowledge of the language, customs, and mode of traffic of the whites; and that feebleness of the reasoning powers, which is the necessary consequences of the entire absence of mental cultivation. (Great Britain 1847, Section 3: 1.1)

This construction of Indigenous people as lazy, ignorant and feeble-minded made it possible for government bureaucrats to argue that the distribution of presents created a dependency relationship:

> This reliance has doubtless had the effect of encouraging their natural indolence and improvidence; of keeping them a distinct people; of fostering their natural pride and consequent aversion to labour; and of creating an undue feeling of dependence upon the protection and bounty of the Crown. (Great Britain 1847, Section 3: 2)

In linking the notion of voluntary presents with these broader constructions, appropriate modes of government were framed. Emphasizing the voluntary nature of the payments made it possible for Britain to reconsider both the amount and type of presents to be distributed. As Miller and Rose note, "it is out of such linguistic elements that rationalities of government ... are elaborated and seek to specify appropriate bases for the organization and mobilization of social life" (1990: 6). Central to the framing contained in the government reports of this period was the assumption that Indigenous people were inferior. We doubt that government bureaucrats would in the same way argue that interest payments consumers make to debt-holders encourage their indolence and dependency.

Although the term "presents" masked the historical basis of the distributions, at other places in government documents there was some acknowledgement of this history:

> There is no record of any agreement on the part of the British Government, to establish or to maintain these gratuities, nor of any regulation as to the parties who are entitled to share in them. For many years, however, they have been issued annually, and latterly according to a fixed Schedule, to all the Indians resident in Canada, and to those Tribes who took part with the British Government in their wars on this continent, but who continued to reside on their ancient hunting grounds, within the Territory of the United States. (Great Britain 1847, Section 3: 2)

This implies an acknowledgement that the distributions had been occurring since 1759 as part of an exchange for military support. The quote also underlies the importance of written techniques to the act of governing and the manner in which this served to reinforce colonialist relations. Written documents of treaties and land sales historically took precedence over the oral histories of Indigenous peoples, and the verbal agreement often differed from the subsequent written English text. Thus, the accepted histories that subsequently "remembered" past agreements and which framed current policy decisions were those of the colonial powers, not the Indigenous peoples. We explore this further in the next chapter.

Land Treaties: Rent-to-own or Expropriation?

Accounting not only measured and "fixed" the unequal terms of exchange that existed within this particular colonial context but also helped to accomplish and facilitate unequal exchanges. In this way accounting was both active and passive—it helped colonial officials take advantage of the tenuous position of Indigenous peoples and allowed these unequal relations to be represented in monetary terms. It also rationalized and justified these values by reference to the "natural laws of society." So, accounting served not only to construct and rationalize the culture of colonialism, but it also acted as an active agent in expropriation and as a "settling-up" mechanism.

Land cessions in Upper Canada during the early 1800s illustrate some of these varied roles for accounting. In an 1818 attempt to minimize the cost of land purchases, colonial officials changed the method of payment. They decided that, instead of making a lump-sum payment for land purchased, they would instead pay the interest component in perpetuity. The interesting part of such an agreement is that the rewards and risks associated with the land are transferred to the Crown. Yet the payment of interest in perpetuity really boils down to a rental payment for the use of the land—no payment of capital occurred and the amount of the payment was often denominated in nominal dollars—that is, the dollar amount at the time of the transaction. Of course, over time, these dollar amounts became worth less and less. This changed method of structuring the transaction allowed the colonial government to make settlement activities self-sustaining by virtue of the fact no payment had to be made for the actual cost of the land. Such a strategy was clearly desirable given the increasing reluctance of Britain to fund Canadian settlement activities.

Indigenous peoples were suspicious of these changed arrangements but their tenuous bargaining position made it difficult to resist. The following exchange nicely captures both the promises made by colonial officials and the recognition by Indigenous peoples that they had little bargaining power:

> [The colonial official] told the chiefs that the king was buying lands in order to provide for the settlement of "his children." And then he introduced the new method of payment, and stressed its advantage by saying the king "does not mean to do as formerly to pay you at once, but as long as any of you remain on the Earth to give you Cloathing in payment every year, besides the presents he now gives you." (Surtees 1983: 74)

The Chief responded:

> Father; If I was to refuse what our Father has requested, our Women and Children would be more to be pitied. From our lands we receive scarcely anything and if your words are true we will get more by parting with them, than by keeping them—our hunting is destroyed and we must throw ourselves on the compassion of our Great Father the King. (Surtees 1983: 75)

Thus we see how the changed payment method is constructed by the colonial official as being in the best interests of Indigenous peoples and how this same official implicitly promises to continue the current payment of presents. We also get a sense of the desperate circumstances that Indigenous peoples found themselves in—increased settlement and a changing economy had devastated their subsistence lifestyle. These changes, along with activities of colonial officials to keep Indigenous peoples divided—careful use of interpreters, the location of the distribution of gifts, the assignments of Indian agents—weakened the bargaining position of Indigenous peoples to such an extent that they had little choice but to enter into these pseudo purchase agreements. As historian Surtees concludes, "the picture one receives from these arrangements is one of a demoralized, even docile, race of people submitting to the will of government" (Surtees 1983: 80).

In this example, we observe accounting numbers being used to represent not only the amount Indigenous peoples received for their land but perhaps more importantly the value that colonial officials placed on Indigenous peoples themselves. The land that colonial officials desired for settlement activities had to be purchased, but the colonial government was the sole purchaser, since individual settlers were prohibited from purchasing land directly. The absence of any external market or alternative purchasers, coupled with the colonial government's desire to save money and the desperate position of Indigenous peoples, encouraged colonial officials to not only minimize purchase prices wherever possible but also to structure the transactions in such a way that a capital payment for the land was not required.

If accounting techniques were used to help appropriate land and to measure/represent the values implicit within these exchanges, accounting notions were also used after-the-fact to rationalize these unequal outcomes. For example, the 1845 report acknowledges that the consideration given by the government for ceded land was low but states that this amount was better than simply having the land taken away:

> It has been alleged that these agreements were unjust, as dispossessing the natives of their ancient territories, and extortionate, as rendering a very inadequate compensation for the lands surrendered. If, however, the Government had not made arrangements for voluntary surrender of the lands, the white settlers would gradually have taken possession of them, without offering any compensation whatever; it would, at that time, have been impossible to resist the natural laws of society, and to guard the Indian territory against the encroachments of whites. (Great Britain 1845, Section 1: 5)

Accounting notions of present and future values were also used to rationalize previous exchanges:

> Nor can the friend of the Indian claim for him a monetary compensation based on the present value of the land, which has been created solely by the presence and industry of white citizens. Its only value to the denizen of the forest, was as a hunting ground, as the source of his supply of game and furs. Of the cultivation of the soil, he knew nothing. The progress of settlement, and the consequent destruction of the forests, with the operations of the lumber, and fur trader, was shortly to destroy this value; in every case the Indians had either the opportunity of retreating to more distant hunting grounds, or they were left on part of their old possessions, with a reserve supposed at the time to be adequate for all their wants, and greatly exceeding their requirements as cultivators of the soil at the present day, to which were added. (5)

To paraphrase the argument: The "value" paid by the government represented the value of the land to Indigenous peoples at the time; any value added to the land since that time was a consequence of the industry of settlers, implying that the compensation received by Indigenous peoples, while low, was higher than what might have been expected in the absence of the government purchasing the land—hence, a "fair price" was paid.

The government, however, had a monopoly over land purchases, settlers being prevented from purchasing land directly. The circle of ideology, now reflected in land transactions, slowly tightened its grip on the Indigenous peoples—supported by accounting discourses which echoed, enlisted and harmonized with other colonialist discourses as it attempted to minimize the costs of empire.

Accounting Technology: From Hunting to Farming

In chapter two we suggested that governmentality is about the sorting, sifting and classifying of a territory's population. And in terms of specific techniques, such governance involves employing tactics to arrange things in such a way that certain ends are achieved, that one of the targets of such techniques are the habits and customs of the population in question. From the late 1830s onward, we observe accounting techniques being used as a specific technology of government in the attempt to change the relationship of Indigenous peoples to land.

By 1840, colonial administrators had come to the conclusion that containment and/or assimilation of Indigenous peoples were the only viable policy options, since the close watch of the humanitarians and missionaries had effectively ruled out extermination and slavery. These goals, however, were tempered by three broader colonial concerns: the demands of settlers that Indigenous people not interfere with settler economic activities; the demands by Britain for cost minimization; and the demands of humanitarian organizations for the civilization of Indigenous peoples.

Adjustments to the nature and amount of annuity payments and yearly distributions, i.e., presents, provided colonial officials with a method for accomplishing these diverse objectives. Initially, it was thought that the commutation of presents into money would satisfy the goal of cost minimization. However, this suggestion was contrary to other policy objectives since cash payment would decrease colonial influence over the habits and behaviours of Indigenous peoples. The Colonial Secretary, Lord Glenelg, in his correspondence with the governors of Upper and Lower Canada, indicated that such a scheme had been previously proposed but was opposed by both colonial administrators and missionaries. Referring to comments made by Lord Dalhousie, Lord Glenelg responded that the conversion of presents into money "would be received with the utmost alarm" (Glenelg 1836: 2). Although he is not opposed to this in principle, Glenelg claims, the goals of religious and moral improvement must be kept firmly in mind. Instead of commuting presents for money, he encouraged the governors to consider modifying the type of presents being distributed, with a view "to the moral and religious improvement of the Indians, and their instruction in the arts of civilized life..." (2). The commutation should be in the form of "some object of permanent benefit and utility to the parties now receiving them" (2).

Although the text of Glenelg's comments is framed with the apparent goal of civilization in mind, the comments of other colonial officials indicate that the real concern about the commuting of presents for money was the loss of control by both government officials and missionaries. Under the current scheme colonial officials dictated what Indigenous peoples received; they feared losing this control with the distribution of money. So naturally there was greater support for the proposal to simply modify the nature of both annuity payments and presents.

In the continuing attempt to change the habits and customs of Indigenous people, these modifications to annuity payments specifically honed in on the very heart of Indigenous culture: their relationship to the land and the micro-behaviours arising from that relationship. One of the first adjustments made was to change the type of consideration given in payment of the yearly annuity. Instead of providing clothing, blankets and hunting supplies, General Darling proposed that agricultural implements be distributed, as "active steps to civilize and educate the Indians...." (Great Britain 1845, Section 1: 7). This proposal was almost immediately implemented: the Lieutenant Governor of Upper Canada saw this as a way of discouraging the spending of annuity payments on liquor and as a way of encouraging Indigenous peoples to give up their wandering lifestyle. The Lieutenant Governor, "being desirous of checking the evils of this system, and of promoting the civilization of the Indians" applied the annuities towards building supplies, agricultural implements and stock (Great Britain 1847, Section. 3: 7). The implication is clearly that a shift in the type of annuity payment would both constrain the abilities of Indigenous peoples to engage in undesirable activities (i.e., drinking) and would encourage them to take up a more settled (i.e., European) lifestyle.

Interestingly, the shift in the type of annuity payment also necessitated the introduction of additional techniques of accounting that, in turn, tightened the degree of control exercised by the government over Indigenous affairs. Suddenly it was necessary to account for the differences between the amount spent on agricultural implements and the annuities owing. This necessitated additional record-keeping:

> In consequence of this change, it became necessary to credit each Tribe yearly with the amount of its annuity, and to direct the expenditure of the money for the benefit of the Indians. This has further led to the admission of the Indians to a voice in the disbursement of their annuities. The Government has not abandoned its control over these funds, which it still exercises, either to restrain improvident or improper expenditure, or to direct undertakings for their advantage; but the general practice is for the Indians to determine among themselves how the money is to

> be spent; and to apply to the Indian Department, from time to time, for such sums as they require. (Great Britain 1847, Section. 3: 7)

The above quotation is illuminating in that it makes visible the shifting relations between the colonial government and Indigenous peoples: from a nation-to-nation relationship at the time of the *Royal Proclamation* to a paternal relationship in which the colonial government has the majority of the say in how annuity payments will be distributed. Again it is interesting to juxtapose this relationship to other debtee/debt-holder relations and to notice the inversion of influence—usually we think of the debt-holder as having significant influence over the structuring of the interest payment.

Accounting Technology: From Nomadic Wandering to Schooling

In maintaining the reduction of expenditures and forcing change in the Indigenous relationship to land, a second reconfiguration in the payment of annuities was implemented: the encouragement of schooling over nomadic hunting. As early as 1838, a portion of the yearly distribution "now expended in the purchase of stores and presents" was to be directed "to the erection of school houses, the purchase of elementary books, and the payment of resident school-masters, for the benefit of the Indian tribes" (Great Britain 1845, Section 1: 10). It was also suggested that "prizes" be distributed to Indigenous children that did well in school to "stimulate their exertions" (10). In 1845, such a shift was effected with the annual distribution of gunpowder being withheld and the saved amount being directed toward education. The Earl of Elgin found himself "disposed to think it advisable ... the system of withdrawing from such Indians as can dispense with them all presents which tend to perpetuate a hunter's life" (Great Britain 1857–1858: 2).

Other aspects of daily life were also specifically targeted by the manipulations. For example, the 1847 report on Indian affairs recommends shifting from the provision of ready-made clothes to the provision of material with which to make clothes. It was thought that this shift would discourage idleness (Great Britain 1847, Section 3: 4). The type of material to be provided was debated, and whether to provide kettles since they "are useful in the manufacture of sugar and culinary purposes" and whether to provide shoes since they are "part of the European Costume" were all discussed as matters of legislative importance (Great Britain 1847, Section 3: 4).

Amalgamation: The Only Possible Euthanasia

> On the 15th of March, the Secretary of State in reviewing the expenditure of the English Parliamentary Grant, came to the conclusion that the gradual extinction of this vote would not conflict with any just claims on the part of Indians. In announcing the decision of Her Majesty's government that the issue of presents should cease in the year 1858, he expressed his confidence that the Provincial Legislature would never be insensible to the claims which the former occupants of the Canadian Territory have upon the consideration of the great and flourishing European Community by which it is now inhabited. (Great Britain 1857–1858: 2)

While the rebellions of 1837–38 were being fought in Upper and Lower Canada, Herman Merivale, Drummond Professor of Political Economy, Oxford, was lecturing on European overseas expansion. In 1841, he published his influential *Lectures on Colonization and Colonies*, and in 1848 he was appointed permanent Undersecretary of State at the Colonial Office. His tenure would last until 1860, and his mark would be set deeply into the colonial administrative mindset of the period. In examining his writings, his tenure and his influence, it becomes evident that Merivale's is an appropriate voice for the sentiment of the times. He was a keen follower of Edward Gibbon Wakefield and believed that labour was key to sufficient development of land. He also devalued the labour of the Native people, preferring white settlers, and predicted that "the Indian economy would eventually disappear and the Indians would either become extinct or assimilate with the non-Indian population" (McNab 1983: 93).

Of the four alternatives apparent in solving The Native Question—extermination, slavery, insulation, amalgamation—only amalgamation seemed to Merivale sustainable. According to McNab, Merivale saw amalgamation as

> a gradual and ultimately a consciously and ultimately an assimilative policy, entailed in the long term the complete or partial loss of the native culture and economy. (1983: 87)

However, other pressures dictated the government's approach:

> the demands of the settlers for colonial self-government, the desires of British politicians and the Treasury to rationalize the British Empire in economic terms, the failures of missionaries to "civilize" the natives, and, of great significance, the active resistance of the native people against those persons who wanted to change their way of life. (McNab 1983: 87)

Colonial officials under Merivale sought to encourage changed habits and customs, especially pertaining to land, changes consistent with the objectives of settler society, while simultaneously seeming to contain and assimilate Indigenous peoples through the use of micro-techniques. In his lectures, Merivale shared keen insights into the gradual process of disinheriting First Nations from their ancestral territories. He notes the guarantees of perpetuity offered by the *Proclamation* and points out the proviso "unless the Indian shall be inclined to part with them [lands]" (Merivale 1967: 506). Thus, says Merivale, "every art has been introduced to obtain their consent to the usurpations made upon them. Bit by bit," he explains, their hunting grounds become "altogether possessed by the whites" (506). However, following the recommendations of F.B. Head, he exacerbates that same problem by agreeing to "get rid of the responsibility of the home government" (McNab 1983: 92)—in other words, handing over control of Indian affairs to non-Native colonial interests. In 1860, the province of Canada was given responsibility for Indian affairs without consultation with Natives (McNab 1983: 92).

We see in Merivale's lectures a precursor to the sort of contradiction that would later ensnare Duncan Campbell Scott (see chapter six). Merivale saw in the Indigenous people a

> native generosity of spirit, and manliness of disposition; more of a religious element; and yet, on the other hand, if not with less capacity for improvement, certainly less readiness to receive it; a more thorough wildness of temperament; less curiosity; inferior excitability; greater reluctance to associate with civilized men; a more ungovernable impatience of control. And their primitive condition of hunters, and aversion from every other, greatly increased the difficulty of including them in the arrangement of a regular community. (Merivale 1967: 493)

In his lectures Merivale apologetically and contritely puts history behind him, sparing us "the wretched details of the ferocity and treachery which marked the conduct of civilized men" (487) towards the Natives and gives Natives the benefit of acknowledged disadvantage, while leaning slightly towards the noble savage characterization, "a degraded, craving, timid, and artful creature, familiarized with the powers and the vices of the whites, rendered abject or sullen by ill-treatment" (487). But, he waxes optimistically, "true political wisdom, on subjects such as these, consists in making the best of the instruments at our disposal" (490). And which instruments might these be but the "authority of governments" (490). Armed with this authority, he claims, "there is now little fear of their being treated with injustice and oppression by the founders of the colonies" (490) and "we may be satisfied with the improved prospect of our relations with these much abused members of the human family" (490). The implication is that governments—at least governments of his time—rather than being propagators of violence towards the Natives, are actually their protectors.

After the founding of a colony, imperial duties towards the Natives fall, according to Merivale, under two categories: protection and civilization. Protection, of course, from the violent business of the uneducated colonists and from themselves; civilization being, naturally, what he calls amalgamation.

Who will be the arbiters of justice insofar as protecting the Natives goes? The Crown, of course. "That the protection of Natives should in all cases be withdrawn altogether from the colonial legislature, and entrusted to the central executive, is a principle in which, I think, even the most jealous friends of Colonial freedom must acquiesce" (Merivale 1967: 465). One of the advantages of removing judicial power from the popular assembly, he claims, is "to arbitrate dispassionately between classes having so many mutual subjects of irritation" (465). He is referring to the labouring classes of immigrants and to the first peoples as each a class of their own.

Merivale asks the rhetorical question: "How far, and in what mode, are natives ... to be brought within the pale of English law?" (497). In terms of protecting them from crimes committed against them, he recommends the full measure of the law. But regarding "the savages themselves" (497) committing acts against the colonists, he asks "Are they to be punished ... with all the forms of justice, for actions to which they cannot themselves possibly attach the notion of crime?" (497). He answers by comparing Natives to lunatics or idiots, "who are in all societies exempted from their infliction" (497).

The Natives, then, must first be educated in British Law. Meanwhile, it is imperative that they be deterred "from attacks on the persons and property of colonists" (499). How best to ensure this? "By placing them under a species of martial or summary law, to be administered by the chief police functionaries" (499). This would also serve to protect them from a jury and remove "the white settlers themselves from any share in judicial proceedings," thus leaving "an opportunity for the admission of the native to full civil rights at a future period, when converted and instructed, and able to satisfy some efficient test of his fitness for full participation in the rights and duties of civil society" (499).

Turning then to the question of appropriate punishment, he acknowledges the humaneness of the suggestion that punishment exclude death or corporal punishment, but finally doubts its practicability: "It must be remembered that all savages are habitually pilferers," and the biggest problem facing settlers is "securing moveable property and stock against their depredations" (499).

Death, then, according to Merivale, is justifiable towards the savage, and when it is to be applied it must be done immediately following the punishable act—"terror as a retribution" (500). It must not appear to be an act of deliberate justice, because, says Merivale, "no uncivilized mind can possibly entertain" a notion such as justice (500).

And what about justice regarding the Natives' conduct towards each other? Here, Merivale quotes Lord Grey at length, regarding New Zealand's first peoples, demonstrating that the attitude of allowing Natives to practice their customs, though philanthropic, is unworkable—"for," quoting Grey, "savage and traditional customs should not be confounded with a regular code of laws ... it is necessary, from the moment the aborigines of this country are declared British subjects, that they should, as far as possible, be taught that the British laws are to supersede their own." Here again is the intention to protect the Natives from themselves: "Under their own customs" those who suffer "may have the power of an appeal to the laws of Great Britain." But the purpose is clearly assimilation. Otherwise, "the older natives have at their disposal the means of effectually preventing the civilization of any individual of their own tribe" (501).

Regarding "civilization" of the Indians, Merivale considered Native reserves "a temporary remedy" which only tempted them "to relapse into the hunting condition" (508–509). "What," he asks rhetorically, "is the ultimate destiny of the races whose interests we are now discovering?" Three possibilities exist: extermination, segregation or amalgamation with the colonists.

> I firmly believe it [amalgamation] to be the very keystone, the leading principle, of all sound theory on the subject—that native races must in every instance either perish, or be amalgamated with the general population of their country.... I mean the union of natives with settlers in the same community, as master and servant ... at present I am deeply anxious to point out to you that, however improbable the success of any particular project of amalgamation may seem, amalgamation, by some means or other, is the only possible Euthanasia of savage communities." (511)

Chapter Five

Dreaming of Canada

> After this they had the final signing of the treaty. There were no chairs and no tables. Crowfoot and Colonel McLeod stood together. There was no writing at the signing of the treaty. The writing about the treaty is all recent.... That is one reason I do not look at these books written about the treaty, because they are all recent and do not say what actually happened. What was discussed at the treaty and the promises that were made by the Queen's men at the treaty, that is what I believe in, that is what I go by....
>
> At that time, the Indian people did not understand all these things, but this is what they heard the interpreter saying. Each person was paid twelve dollars. It did not matter what age they were. What does a one-year-old child or a two-year-old do with money like that? There were priests, white men from the south, east, and north, and Indian chiefs at the signing of the treaty. And no one explained to the Indian what this paper money was for. They were told it was for trading, but they did not know its value. When they went to buy, even only a package of matches, they just gave all of it. They did not know how to count it, what it was worth.—John Yellowhorn (hereditary chief), Peigan Reserve, March 10, 1975, quoted in Price et al. 1975: 141–43

As Canadian Confederation loomed on the horizon, the thoughts of imperial administrators and Canadian officials turned to settlement, in particular the costs of obtaining land from Indigenous peoples and administering the Indian Department. Throughout this formative period in Canada's history, government bureaucrats attempted to liberate land for settlement, minimize the costs of liberation and control the use of the proceeds to Indigenous peoples. The reliance on accounting and funding created a web of financial relations that penetrated and permeated all aspects of Indigenous affairs.

From 1860 to 1900, Indigenous peoples of the plains and woodlands witnessed the final slaughter and disappearance of the buffalo, the ultimate securing of vast tracts of land for settler access and a flurry of treaty-making activity. The vocabulary of colonialism and domination continued across the great divide of Confederation without missing a beat and affected the language of the treaties themselves. In this chapter, not only is the existence of multiple sites and agents for these vocabularies revealed, but so is the diffusion of government techniques, highlighting how different accounting mechanisms are used to encourage, even force, action directly—for example, the use of food in the face of starvation as a bargaining chip in treaty negotiations. Indirect action is exemplified during the late 1800s when the federal government encouraged, via the introduction of certain funding and accountability mechanisms, third-parties—religious organizations—to operate residential schools (Milloy 1999: 269).

The synchronized march of accounting with government operates on two different levels simultaneously—on one level allowing knowledge of distant locales to be gathered and transported back to Ottawa for decision-making purposes, representing activities in distant locales and making visible the "costs" of operation; on another level mediating the activities of Indigenous peoples in these distant locales, forming a web of financial regulations which govern macro- and micro-aspects of behaviour. While these two aspects of accounting were present during early periods, they reached a new level of maturity and dispersion at this time.

At Confederation, the place we now know as Canada was but a dream of politicians, and this dream could only be realized by claiming the unexploited western lands and finding immigrants willing to settle there. The first step in this process was to liberate land by persuading Indigenous peoples to surrender their traditional territories. In 1871, Secretary of State Joseph Howe appointed Mackenzie Simpson as Indian Commissioner and directed him to negotiate for the cession of land from Thunder Bay westward (Morris 1991: 25). Between 1871 and 1876, the numbered treaties one to six were concluded. As part of these treaties the federal government agreed to make annuity payments and to provide schooling and agricultural implements. Treaty six was noteworthy because it included clauses dealing with both pestilence—

> That in the event hereafter of the Indians comprised within this treaty being overtaken by any pestilence, or by a general famine, the Queen, on being satisfied and certified thereof by her Indian Agent or Agents, will grant to the Indians assistance of such character and to such extent as here Chief Superintendent of Indian Affairs shall deem necessary and sufficient to relieve the Indians from the calamity that shall have befallen them. (Morris 1991: 354)

and a medicine chest:

> That a medicine chest shall be kept at the house of each Indian

> Agent for the use and benefit of the Indians, at the discretion of such Agent. (354)

The arguments over the differences between the written texts of the treaties and the oral agreements between the two parties is central to the dispute over territory and its governance which has continued to this day. Before examining the bureaucratic and numerical rationalizations behind written treaties (i.e., the treaties as viewed by government) we explore the treaty-making process from the Indigenous perspective—as much as such a cross-cultural endeavour is possible—which is above all else a perspective that arises from an oral culture. Treaty-making was already an integral and long-practised convention amongst various Indigenous nations, steeped in traditions that the Canadians seemed incapable of acknowledging.

Accounting Before the Treaties

Prior to the treaty-making process, the Indian Department was largely self-sufficient. In his 1868 report, Secretary of State H. Langevin provides the following overview:

> The branch charged with the affairs of the Indian Lands has the management of the affairs, lands and funds of the Indians. I have instructed the Deputy Superintendent to prepare for me a report of the affairs of his branch, together with tabular statements as complete as possible to give an exact idea of the situation of the Indian Tribes, of the extent of their domain, of the funds belonging to them, and of their income and expenditure.... Your Excellency will perceive that most of the tribes have a sufficient income, but those of Nova Scotia and New Brunswick have no means of acquiring the education necessary to enable them hereafter to share the blessings of civilization.... In a pecuniary point of view the tribes of Ontario are much better off than those in the other Provinces, owing to the fact that the lands reserved for them originally, that is to say, from the first establishment of British Government in this country were situated in localities highly favored in regard to climate and to fertility of soil. (1869: 2)

Langevin's comments are interesting in that they highlight the roles played by "accounts" in facilitating governance. However, the numbers themselves are salient in that they support Langevin's assertion that costs were under control. Total government appropriations for Indian Affairs amounted to $12,797 in 1868 and $14,797 in 1869.

When the signing of the western treaties opened the floodgates for western settlement, the financial obligations of Indian Affairs were changed forever. Government appropriations for Indian Affairs jumped eighteen-fold from $14,797 in 1869 to $276,325 in 1876, with almost all the increase pertaining to Manitoba westward, in particular as a result of treaty obligations. These included annuities, agricultural supplies, schooling costs and provisions for destitute Indians.

Clearly, government officials had not anticipated the magnitude of the costs of meeting their treaty obligations; nor had Indigenous peoples expected that treaty-making would lead to dispossession of their traditional territories. The government, however, was able to redefine its treaty obligations with impunity—an issue that is still alive today in government–Indigenous peoples relations. This redefinition of treaty obligations was reflected in the accounting and administrative procedures of Indian Affairs, particularly during the regime of Deputy Superintendent Lawrence Vankoughnet. Also brought to light was the troublesome question of treaty interpretation and subsequent responsibilities as understood by each party.

Before examining Vankoughnet's day-to-day role in the playing out of government "action-at-a-distance" and its effects on the lives of Indigenous people, we will first put his department's function in the context of the treaties themselves and the negotiating process that gave rise to their signings. Accounting mechanisms and other softwares of governmentality played a major role in maneuvering the Indigenous peoples and the imperialists into a treaty-making position. But what was at work in the treaty negotiations themselves? What did the negotiations and the treaties mean to the tribal chiefs and headmen? Is it possible that the two parties were not even "signing" the same agreement, given the different understandings of such basic concepts as treaty, land, exchange (money, presents) and leadership (queen, chief)? And what of the differences in the more global concepts of time, place and the bounty of the natural world? How did the bureaucratic and governmental mechanisms—of which the written treaties were central—fit into the Indigenous view of how two parties come to an agreement? In other words, from what particular historical perspective did the Indigenous treaty-makers approach the process, and what cultural tools did they bring to the table?

Indigenous History and the Power of Collective Memory

> When I was a young child, I remember my grandmother describing a meeting which she attended as a young woman. The meeting was to discuss the land and whether land should be surrendered from the reserve. She told me the exact location of the meeting, pinpointing the hill where the meeting took place. My grandmother told of all the persons present at the meeting, in-

> cluding the clothing the women were wearing, right down to the colour of their head scarves. Her telling of the story occurred about fifty years after the meeting had taken place. She neither read nor wrote but her mind was strong and sharp....
>
> That kind of detail [what was said by each person and what kind of clothes they were wearing] is also a way of verifying the story. These details can be checked by other people present at the meeting. Recounting the smallest details indicates the memory is accurate.... The detail held by my grandmother's mind about the meeting served to ensure that future generations could listen to the story and feel and hear the context and texture of the discussions. (Venne 1997: 175–76)

Action-at-a-distance, while rationalized through the discriminating use of particular knowledges, is maintained by the dominating power through physical force on the one hand and, in the case of treaties, through the force of the written document on the other. The latter is dependent upon the privileging of literacy over oralcy—writing and reading are seen to be more "civilized" and "advanced." Something that is "written in black and white" is assumed in our literate culture to be synonymous with the "truth," while storytelling is synonymous with "fiction." But the fundamental meaning of the written word is nothing more than a culturally-bound and limited coding and decoding. In effect, however, the written word is only a single means, among many, of passing on information; in oral cultures, storytelling is the primary means of passing on information. The recent *Delgamuukw* decision has done much to deprivilege the written form of recording and interpreting history (see chapter eight). A story, in oral culture, is not something "made up" in the European sense of storytelling, as Venne (1997) so clearly points out.

The use of encoded inscriptions in literate cultures and the use of memory-based storytelling in oral cultures, while variant in mechanism and dynamic, share a fundamental principle: collective memory. Those who read in common a written version of history share a collective memory; those who listen together to an elder's passing on of witnessed events similarly share a collective memory. In oral cultures as in literate ones the information is held among many. But the qualities of reading and listening are significantly different from each other, and the maintenance of the information across time and place differs remarkably in each culture—differences which have serious repercussions when viewed in the context of revisiting or remembering treaty-making. While the written word allows almost interminable reproduction and distribution of a single version of an event, the stories of the oral cultures can only be known "through repeated and continuous contact" with the elders of the community—the keepers of the stories, who have been chosen for their remarkable skills and who have trained for their practice throughout a lifetime. Because the information—the whole story—is held among many, "no one elder knows the complete story.... With stories spread over a number of people, the accuracy of the story is constantly open to review. If one elder is changing their part of the story, then the parts held by the other elders will not fit together" (Venne 1997: 176).

Knowledge of these differences in narrative/historical awareness and practice can have a profound impact on how we perceive the treaty-making process. It also sheds light on how, through the imposition of literacy over oralcy and the forbidding of Indigenous languages, the residential schools ripped apart the very fabric of a highly evolved civilization. Bearing in mind the central role of the elder in that civilization, we can also see how the imposition of "democratic" decision-making processes, which exclude the wisdom tradition of those who carry the historical narratives of their people (to say nothing of the separation of those elders from the children), completely gutted the central organism of Indigenous cultures.

In his book, *Technopoly,* the cultural critic Neil Postman relates the story of Thamus from Plato's *Phaedrus*. The great inventor Theuth, in exhibiting his inventions to the wise king Thamus, received this response for his greatest invention of all, writing, which he believed would increase the wisdom of the people:

> Theuth ... you who are the father of writing, have out of fondness for your off-spring attributed to it quite the opposite of its real function. Those who acquire it will cease to exercise their memory and become forgetful; they will rely on writing to bring things to their remembrance by external signs instead of by their own internal resources. What you have discovered is a receipt for recollection, not for memory. And as for wisdom, your pupils will have the reputation for it without the reality: they will receive a quantity of information without proper instruction, and in consequence be thought very knowledgeable when they are for the most part quite ignorant. And because they are filled with the conceit of wisdom instead of real wisdom they will be a burden to society. (quoted in Postman 1993: 4)

Today we are more than ever conscious of how information has, through technology, been linked to speed, where the speed with which one receives information takes precedence over its meaning. What a stretch, then, to imagine our way back to a time when information had to travel overland, when even reproduction of a document was time-consuming and labour-intensive. But an even larger leap of imagination is needed to identify with the time and patience needed to receive the information kept as a sacred trust and distributed by the elders of an oral culture. According to Venne, "It is through continuous contact with the Elder that one will hear the complete story.... It is not a process of sitting for one hour or an afternoon. The history of Indigenous peoples is learned over many years, as the depth of an Elder's knowledge is immeasurable" (176).

Venne describes the long drawn out protocol and the exchange of gifts involved in retrieving a story and how one may be referred to other storytellers for different parts of it. "Patience is important. An Elder does not always answer on the day the question is asked. Sometimes you are requested to return a few days later. Not only does one learn about listening, but one learns about patience" (177). How absurd then, the impatience displayed by treaty commissioners who were upset about waiting when Poundmaker took longer than four days before giving the commissioners a response, because he first had to make peace with the Blackfoot Confederacy—a winter-long process.

Here, then, we are faced with the ultimate dichotomy in the understanding and remembering of the treaty process. While in a literate culture, glyphs pressed upon the page are intended to fix events in time and place, the function of the elders in an oral culture is to "hold the inherited collective body of knowledge that transcends time and space" (Venne 1997: 177).

Describing the Treaty Six negotiations, the Elder Toussaint Dion, who grew up in Frog Lake Reserve listening to the elders present at the signing in 1876 and specifically identifies his uncle as the holder of this part of the story, continues the narrative, explaining that the negotiations lasted several days:

> The progress of the negotiations was slow because there was a lot of discussion going on, a lot of deliberation took place. And, then, there the Treaty Commissioner made the strong statement. The sun and the water, if these exist, the terms would always be the same. As long as the sun shines and the waters flow. [This the father used to say.] Consequently, the negotiators figured that they had finished their business then. (quoted in Venne 1997: 188)

Sealing the Deal: Peace Pipe or Magic Glyphs?

We have been discussing collective memory as history—bringing the past into the present. But how is the present brought into the future—the essential function of the treaty? How are promises made and negotiations finalized? How do parties guarantee, as much as is humanly possible, that the words exchanged in the treaty-making process will be carried intact into the future? In literate culture, signing one's name is the symbolic gesture that assures that the present, barring an act of God, will be carried into the future. In the oral cultures that concern us here, the smoking of the pipe "would signify to the Creator the intention of the parties to keep the terms of the agreement in a strong binding manner" (Venne 1997: 188).

The pipe ceremony conducted at Forts Pitt and Carlton signified their extreme importance—"evident by the number of Indians in attendance at a time when the people should have been out hunting for their winter supply of food" (Price et al. 1975: 111). Alexander Morris in relating an earlier meeting with Starblanket and Big Child refers to the pipe ceremony without, it seems, an understanding of its importance, its actual sealing of his spoken words in the sanctity of truth. They smoked the pipe, he writes, and "in accordance with their customs ... accepted the friendship of the Cree nation" (Price et al. 1975: 111). Here is a popular European notion that debases the essential function of the pipe in treaty-making.

To the collective memory of the Treaty Six Cree, the commissioners accepted that "the Indigenous people wanted the treaty to last as long as the earth would exist." The pipe was smoked to seal that promise.

> [The chiefs] told the officials that they were using their greatly respected power for a legal transaction [peace pipe].... These promises were made with the smoking of the pipe.... This wasn't done ordinarily for no reason. If one puts a pipe stem to his lips, that was a highly honoured agreement.... He [the commissioner] smoked the pipe stem.... They sang their sacred songs. (Venne 1997: 188)

Here, then, are the sacred technologies of the Indigenous peoples, downgraded to quaint custom by the Canadians, by which the Indigenous treaties were to be brought to fruition. It is important to realize that the written treaties were not in evidence during the discussions and that these discussions in themselves constituted the treaties as far as the chiefs and headmen were concerned. So what, then, according to the elders, were the details contained in these oral treaties?

The Depth of the Plow—Signing Treaties Six and Seven

> My father was at the first signing of the treaties, and so were my two uncles.... He would indicate with his hands approximately one foot in depth: "That is the depth that is requested from you, that is what the deal is, nothing below the surface, that will always belong to you. Only land where agriculture can be viable; other areas where nothing can grow, that will always belong to

> you. You will always be the owner of that land." That is what they were promised....
>
> "And when the negotiation has been concluded, and settlers begin to homestead, it will only be their property that will be fenced off, that you will not be allowed to enter. Other areas which are not homesteaded and remain open will belong to you as long as the sun shines." These are the promises that were made to our forefathers and our fathers. It was most obliging and sounded wonderful when they first dealt with the white man. (Lazarus Roan, Smallboy Camp, interviewed by Louis Rain, 30 March 1974, quoted in Price et al. 1975: 115–16)

From the Canadian perspective, it is the written form which represents the agreement, and any discussions preceding the "signing" of the treaty represent persuasive tools employed to lead the other party to the agreement. The signature seals the deal that is captured in black and white, regardless of the verbal preamble. From the Indigenous perspective the reverse is true: the treaty evolves over continuous discussion through a process of verbal clarification until a common understanding is reached. When both parties arrive at an agreement the treaty has been made. Smoking the peace pipe seals the deal that is ingrained in the memories of the witnesses. The written document is a symbolic acknowledgement of the verbal agreement already sealed. Herein lies the crux of the differing perspectives. A brief examination of Treaty Six may illuminate the differences between the knowledge brought home to the centre of calculation—Ottawa—and the actual unfolding of events in the territories, differences which appear to have worked in favour of the Canadians.

Alexander Morris, Commissioner and signatory of Treaty Six, wrote a thorough report of his experiences as Commissioner, including pre-treaty communications and actual negotiations. In the chapter entitled "The Treaties of Fort Carlton and Fort Pitt," he describes the correspondences and conversations between the two parties in detail, leading up to the actual signing of the treaty (Morris 1991: 168–244). In comparing both these recorded conversations and correspondences and the oral history of Cree elders, with the written treaties themselves as preserved in government archives, it is clear that issues of survival were the prime concerns of the Native chiefs and headmen. In the written treaties, possession of vast tracts of land—120,000 square miles for Treaty Six alone—was the sole motivation of the Canadian Government.

Between 1871 and 1876, as reported by Morris, Indigenous leaders and representatives discussed *ad infinitum*, the following concerns: starvation, disease and poverty, the elimination of the Buffalo, peace between nations, increasing white population, abundance of troops in the district, acts of violence, the setting of fires in forests, the making of roads, construction of telegraph lines, use of strychnine poisoning and lack of provisions for adapting to the new form of agriculture.

Food and Starvation: The Turning Point of Treaty Six

Above all, the plains Cree were seeking assurance that the Queen's representatives wouldn't let them starve to death. Rarely was the surrender of land mentioned. And why should it have been? The Cree negotiated in the belief that they were in the process, with no predetermined outcome, of treating for peace; the possibility of textual changes to the government's written version simply did not exist. Meanwhile the state of well-being of the Cree people was pitiful. One of the earliest correspondences in the process, dated April 1871, was between W.J. Christie, Chief Factor In Charge of Saskatchewan District, Hudson's Bay Company, to Lieutenant Governor Archibald. Christie had been approached by the Cree chiefs, in particular Sweet Grass, to ascertain the government's intentions towards them. In his letter from Edmonton House, Christie writes:

> They referred to the epidemic that had raged throughout the past summer, and the subsequent starvation, the poverty of their country, the visible diminution of the buffalo, their sole support, ending by requesting certain presents at once, and that I should lay their case before Her Majesty's representatives at Fort Garry. (quoted in Morris 1991: 169)

Christie's dispatch included a message, to "His Excellency Governor Archibald, our Great Mother's representative at Fort Garry, Red River Settlement" from Chief Sweet Grass, later a signatory of the Treaty, which describes the plains Cree state of being. It is important to consider that this was translated into English without the Chief having any way of verifying the content:

> Our country is getting ruined of fur-bearing animals, hitherto our sole support, and now we are poor and want help—we want you to pity us. We want cattle, tools, agricultural implements, and assistance in everything when we come to settle—our country is no longer able to support us.... Make provision for us against years of starvation. We have had great starvation the past winter, and the small-pox took away many of our people, the old, the young, and children.... We send these words by our Master, Mr. Christie, in whom we have every confidence. (quoted in Morris 1991: 171)

To the Canadian government the treaties were about land. But which land, what aspect of land, which rights to what sorts of usage? In a colonial mind, land was automatically linked with ownership, usage then being determined according to individual property rights, but such was likely not the case in the Indigenous understanding. Lynn Hickey, in addressing the question of land in the understanding of Treaty Six as surface only or as including subsurface, explains the likelihood of misinterpretation:

> the word "land" may not translate into Cree with the same meaning as it does in English. There is evidence that "land" is usually used with various prefixes which must be added in order to specify more precise meanings. Thus, if the prefix indicating "surface" land were used to explain what settlers needed for farming, Cree-speakers may have understood they were being asked for something entirely different from "land" with some other prefix attached. Since we cannot know which Cree word for "land" was used in translating Treaty 6 negotiations, and since Cree requires great precision in the use of prefixes, there are innumerable possibilities for misunderstandings to have occurred simply over this one issue. (quoted in Price et al. 1975: 42)

Negotiations for Treaty Six were centred, as far as the Cree were concerned, around food. Morris recollects the negotiations with Poundmaker, and in his entry for August 22, 1876, replies to the Chief's concern about assistance once they settled on the reserves:

> I replied that they had their own means of living, and that we could not feed the Indians, but only assist them to settle down.... I explained that we could not assume the charge of their everyday life, but in a time of great national calamity they could trust the generosity of the Queen.... The whole day was occupied with this discussion on the food question, and it was the turning point with regard to the treaty. (Morris 1991: 184–85)

In comprehending the full impact of the discrepancy between the treaty the Indigenous leaders thought they were getting and the later "official" written version, we might thus imagine a scene called "The Signing of the Treaty." Negotiations have lasted, from the Indigenous perspective, for years. The chiefs have been seeking, more than anything else, assurances that the Great White Mother, the Queen, will not let them starve, that a medicine chest will be made available to them, that they will be provided with provisions for farming and that their traditional hunting grounds will be kept intact except for those areas needed by settlers for cultivation, to the depth of a plow blade. The focus of the treating has been peace and survival. The chiefs have time and again acknowledged that they are at the mercy of the Queen. No mention has been made of square acreage (how, we wonder, would that be translated into Cree?), no delineations marking territory have been made, the differences in understanding between concepts of land tenure and use, money and surrender have not been acknowledged, and the entire procedure has been carried on under threat of starvation and extinction. Finally, relatively sure that they have made their needs known, the chiefs, on behalf of their people, believing they have secured assurances of provisions and protection in return for allowing Canadians free movement through their territory, smoke the sacred pipe with their counterparts, and put their X's on a piece of paper drawn with mysterious glyphs proffered by the Queen's representatives. This, in part, is what they have "signed":

> The Plain and Wood Cree Tribes of Indians, and all other Indians inhabiting the district hereinafter described and defined, do hereby cede, release, surrender and yield up to the Government of the Dominion of Canada, for Her Majesty the Queen and Her successors forever, all their rights, titles and privileges, whatsoever, to the lands included within the following limits, that is to say:
>
> Commencing at the mouth of the river emptying into the north-west angle of Cumberland Lake; thence westerly up the said river to its source; thence on a straight line in a westerly direction to the head of Green Lake; thence northerly to the elbow in the Beaver River; thence down the river northerly to a point twenty miles from the said elbow; thence in a westerly direction, keeping on a line generally parallel with the said Beaver River (above the elbow) and about twenty miles distant there from, to the source of the said river; thence northerly to the northeasterly point of the south shore of Red Deer Lake, continuing westerly along the said shore to the western limit thereof; and thence due west to the Athabasca River; thence up the said river, against the stream, to the Jasper House, in the Rocky Mountains; thence on a course southeasterly, following the easterly range of the mountains, to the source of the main branch of the Red Deer River; thence down the said river, with the stream, to the junction therewith of the outlet of the river, being the outlet of the Buffalo Lake; thence due east twenty miles; thence on a straight line south-easterly to the mouth of the Red Deer River on the south branch of the Saskatchewan River; thence easterly and northwardly, following on the boundaries of the tracts conceded by the several treaties numbered four and five to the place of beginning.
>
> And also, all their rights, titles and privileges whatsoever to all

> other lands wherever situated in the North-West Territories, or in any other Province or portion of Her Majesty's Dominions, situated and being within the Dominion of Canada.
>
> The tract comprised within the lines above described embracing an area of 121,000 square miles, be the same more or less.
>
> To have and to hold the same to Her Majesty the Queen and her successors forever. (quoted in Morris 1991: 351–52)

Selling the Land

Increasing pressure for settlement meant the surrender of land had to be stimulated, and government bureaucrats, as early as the 1820s, were devising schemes of "easy credit" to facilitate the sale of land:

> Purchasers would be required to pay 10 percent as a down payment and carry a mortgage for the balance. However, as long as they paid the annual interest, the principal would not be required. The annual income from interest would then be used to make an annual payment, in perpetuity, to the Indian [held in trust by the government] who sold their land. (Surtees 1983: 70)

To facilitate the sale of Indigenous lands, the government maintained a registry of Indigenous land that was available for sale. After Confederation, the terms of the land sales changed slightly, but they continued to be structured in such a way as to provide easy credit terms.

Once the surrender of land was underway, a mechanism was needed for turning the land over to the settlers, while maintaining—or even increasing—the coffers of the Indian Department. The inaugural *Indian Act,* in 1876, while consolidating numerous statutes relating to Indians, contained regulations for financial transactions *vis-à-vis* surrendered territory and provided a mechanism for same. Although the Act contained many detailed regulations, the gist was that, before any land could be sold, the majority of male members of the band must agree to cede the land. Furthermore, since the Act prohibited the sale of Indigenous land to anyone but the federal government, the land had to be surrendered to the government, which then sold it to other parties. And finally, control over the terms of the sale, including the price, rested with the government. The only decision not in the government's hands was whether the land would be surrendered or not.

By the 1890s, settlement pressures had encouraged the government to amend the *Indian Act*. As a way of circumventing band intransigence regarding the leasing of land, the Act was amended in 1884 to give the Superintendent General authority to lease Indigenous lands to non-Indians (Tobias 1983: 47). At the end of the decade, the Act was amended to allow Indigenous peoples to receive up to 50 percent of land-surrender proceeds instead of 10 percent. Historian John Tobias comments that this change in policy had the desired effect of increasing the amount of land available for settlement (49).

These government regulations completely circumscribed Indigenous control over the sale of their land. They essentially dictated to whom the land would be sold, what the selling price and payment terms would be and how much of the proceeds would be under Indigenous control. The willingness of bureaucrats to modify financial regulations (and their incentive effects) to meet changing policy objectives illustrates how governmentality was attempted and operationalized during this period.

Natural Resources

> My grandfather and grandmother were there at the first treaty payment.... This was told to me by my mother-in-law, Mrs. Smallboy. She is over one hundred years old and she is being cared for in Edmonton. I heard this old woman telling the story of the treaty; she was there. Bobtail, the first chief, was her grandfather....
>
> At the time of the first treaty my grandfather, Buffalo Chief, was a councilor, along with old Saddleback and Louie Natchowaysis; their chief was Samson. I used to listen to my grandfather. He, too was issued with a councilor's suit, as they were included with the treaty promises. They were told that, if the land was not suitable for anything, then that portion would not be taken, only the land where the settlers could make their living through agriculture. The commissioners were not to take the game animals, the timber, nor the big lakes—that was the Indians' means of survival. Also anything underground would not be given up, only six inches, enough for the settlers to grow crops. (John Buffalo, Ermineskin Reserve, interviewed by Richard Lightning, 18 April 1975, quoted in Price et al. 1975: 118–22)

If the surrender of the land itself was the primary bureaucratic concern, the extraction of natural resources from remaining reserve land was a close second. The 1876 *Indian Act* gave the Indian Department control over timber extraction rates and terms, and in 1887, an order-in-council pertaining to mining was adopted. This regulation allowed for exploration on both surrendered and unsurrendered Indigenous lands, as long as approval of the Superintendent General of Indian Affairs had been obtained. Should a third party wish to secure a mining location on surrendered land, they could do so by paying the government (in trust for Indigenous peoples) $5 per acre along with a royalty fee of 4 percent of revenues. For mining locations on unsurrendered lands, the Superintendent General would ask the band whether they were willing to surrender the land in question.

While this order-in-council apparently left control of Indigenous lands with Indigenous peoples, the 1894 amendments to the *Indian Act* allowed the Superintendent General to circumvent these regulations if he felt that it was in Indigenous peoples' best interest. Historian John Tobias comments that economic-growth arguments were used to justify the leasing of Indigenous lands "without taking a surrender for purpose of mineral exploration, to expropriate for right-of-ways for highways and provincially chartered railways, and to lease ... farmlands" (Tobias 1983: 49). Like the case of land surrenders, financial regulations pertaining to natural resources provided bureaucrats with a method of structuring Indigenous activities and circumscribing Indigenous agency.

Administering Indigenous Affairs

> No, the majority of Indians did not know money. As an example, our grandmother received payment for three sons, two daughters, and herself at $25.00 per head. She had the money in her hand, but she just gave it to another woman for payment on a horse she bought. They told this story themselves; they did not know money—she paid $150.00 for her horse. (John Buffalo, Ermineskin Reserve, interviewed by Richard Lightning, 18 April 1975, quoted in Price et al. 1975: 118–22)

> At the beginning, fifty dollars were promised to each person; after about six years, that was reduced. They thought of a way to make the Indians believe that the money was being put aside for them.... Then after about six years they reduced the payment again; the chief now was paid twenty-five dollars and the adults and children each received five dollars.... They were told the money was kept at the government.... Long ago they tried investigating it but then it was difficult.... They told the agent but he did not do anything. Some of the councilors wrote letters, but there was never a reply. Maybe the letters were thrown in the garbage. My father also tried to find out about that many times, but he, too, never received a reply. (Fred Horse, Frog Lake, Alberta, interviewed by Richard Lightning, 14 March 1975, quoted in Price et al. 1975: 123–26)

Not only did the *Management of Indian Lands and Property Act* of 1860 give government bureaucrats control over the terms of sale of Indigenous lands, it also let them decide how the proceeds would be spent and what sort of administration fee would be charged for fulfilling these functions. As the following examples suggest, this financial control allowed government bureaucrats to attempt to balance both settlement policy objectives and the containment/control of Indigenous peoples.

In the 1868 *Annual Report from the Secretary of State*, Hector Langevin comments on the ways in which Indigenous lands were being managed to further settlement objectives:

> In the management of Indian lands the object has for several years been steadily kept in view, of inducing actual settlement, thus promoting the great agricultural interests of the country, while also giving an additional value to sufficiently contiguous unsold lands; and furnishing also from Indian funds substantial aid towards opening out leading roads. (Langevin 1869: 3)

As the report indicates, the proper management of Indigenous lands is equated with promoting settlement. In this same report, Langevin also notes that the proceeds from land sales were often used for projects that only loosely benefitted Indigenous peoples.

> It will be understood that the expense of surveys, the construction of roads, special relief to various bands of Indians, assistance in the erection of school buildings, and to other objects, diminished considerably the balance which would otherwise have been added to invested funds. (Langevin 1869: 6)

Settlement costs such as surveys and the construction of roads were often paid for out of land sale proceeds.

Using the trust account data for 1875 as an example, we can see the ways in which the government administered these accounts primarily for its own benefit. First, the *Indian Act* prohibited Indigenous peoples from selling land to anyone other than the government. With this monopoly, the government was able to decide what the terms of sale would be: these terms of sale influenced the amount of cash inflows in any particular year, since cash inflows are a function of both the selling price and payment terms. The government also decided what management fee would be charged for administering land sales (10 percent), what interest rate would be paid on Indigenous funds held in trust and what expenses would be paid out of these accounts. In essence, while these were ostensibly "trust" funds, they were used to sustain the land sale/settlement infrastructure of the federal government. Out of the total $250,000 of cash inflows from land sales and interest in that year, only about 50 percent of these monies were returned to Indigenous peoples in the form of direct annuity payments. While some of the remainder was indirectly spent on activities of benefit to Indigenous peoples, a significant amount was spent on Indian Department infrastructure. Although the numbers changed in later periods, the government logic of using Indigenous funds to support settlement activities did not.

From Indian to Indian Agent to Municipal Government

The 1884 *Indian Advancement Act* was important in that, prior to this time, decisions on how annuity monies were to be spent were made by the Indian agent for individual bands. The 1884 Act sought to confer wider powers upon the band council, including the raising of money, yet appointed the Indian agent chairman of the council (Bartlett 1980: 585). It gave the council the power to levy taxes on the real property of band members and expanded powers over police and public health matters (Tobias 1983: 46). However, it also greatly increased the powers of the Superintendent General in that the provisions spelled out election regulation, the size of the band council and the deposition of elected officials. While this statute gave the appearance of conferring wider powers, it actually reaffirmed the status quo by giving the power to make money bylaws only to those bands declared to have reached an advanced stage of development (Bartlett 1980: 600).

The 1884 Act highlights how governmentality was continually being reworked, the underlying logic of control, however, remaining ever-present. While a surface reading of the Act suggests a loosening of administrative control, a closer reading reveals a shift in the mechanisms of control. Whereas prior to the Act, the Indian Department via the Indian agent determined how monies would be spent, now the band council under the guidance of the Indian agent would make these decisions. Of course, such autonomy could only occur after westernized (i.e., advanced) structures, such as municipal governance (i.e., the band council), were introduced. Further autonomy could only happen after Indigenous peoples had accepted the discipline of westernized administrative structures and internalized the self-disciplining norms inherent in such structures (i.e., reached an advanced stage of development).

Lawrence Vankoughnet: Fiscal Responsibility and the Criminalization of Potlatch

From the period 1874 to 1893, which included the inaugural *Indian Act*, the signings of Treaties Six and Seven and the rebellion of 1885, the office of the Deputy Superintendent was held by a single individual. While politicians and appointees came and went, Lawrence Vankoughnet administered the daily operations of the Indian Department and by the early 1880s was making virtually all the major decisions. In 1861, after graduating from Trinity College, Vankoughnet joined the civil service. With the return of the Conservatives to power in 1878—and following on the heels of Treaty Seven—the young civil servant was, as Deputy Superintendent, working directly under his personal hero and family friend, Prime Minister John A. Macdonald. "In Vankoughnet," Macdonald "knew he had a loyal and conscientious deputy who could manage the Indian Department with a minimum of supervision" (Leighton 1983: 105). Amendments to the *Indian Act* between 1879 and 1884 "complemented the Prime Minister's 'civilization' programmes for the Indians, to enfranchise the more acculturated tribes of the older provinces and to advance the Indians of the North-West through establishment of model farms and industrial schools" (Leslie et al. 1978: 71).

Vankoughnet was known for his obsessive attention to detail and his inability to delegate decision-making. His reputed parsimony was well-suited to the department's centralized authority, "a logical outcome of the changes occasioned by the transfer of the Indian department [from the British Crown] to Canadian authority in 1860" (Leighton 1983: 107). Typically for the times, political loyalty, economy and efficiency were highly regarded within the department, often to the detriment of the people who were affected by the strict way in which policies were interpreted and exercised.

As the costs of fulfilling treaty obligations became more apparent, the minimization of expenditures became the department's internal mantra. Even as the devastation of the buffalo signalled the loss of the plains tribes' nutritional and cultural sustenance, to Vankoughnet it meant only a strain on his department's purse-strings.

> Vankoughnet was fearful that the department was being propelled into excessive expenditure, and he imposed strict quotas for supplementary rations. Per diem allowances for individuals of thirteen and-a-half ounces of flour, three-and-a-half ounces of bacon, and six ounces of beef were ordered reduced. This niggardliness regarding food quotas did more to alienate western tribesmen before the North-West Rebellion than anything else. (Leighton 1983: 107)

Vankoughnet's paternalism and racial biases were typical of the time. When Natives were able to prove themselves capable of white behaviour, he felt they should be rewarded or encouraged to improve, on an individual basis.

Like most nineteenth-century Europeans, he simply could not understand why some Indians preferred the old ways, when white society offered them a more comfortable and rewarding lifestyle. The only explanation of such behaviour that he could accept was that of Indian indifference or laziness. And then he wiped his hands of them—if such Indians would not help themselves, there was nothing the department could do for them.

Vankoughnet's hand was also visible in designing the "Trespass, Timber, and Illicit Sale or Exchange" laws in the *Indian Act Amendment Bill*, May 13, 1879, demonstrating how a bureaucrat exercising a technology of governmentality in applying action-at-a-distance is able to control the most micro-economic transactions of commerce—with a direct effect on an individual's ability to put food on the table. Down to the minutest detail, including collecting a debt, passing on an inheritance to a family member or the division of a family estate, tribal decisions were under Vankoughnet's discretion. It was under his supervision that the "Incitement of Indians to Riot" amendment to the *Indian Act* included two to six months imprisonment for the celebration of the Potlatch—the central political-economic-spiritual mechanism of west-coast Native traditions.

The long arm controlling action-at-a-distance went beyond daily activities of commerce to include an assault on the most basic human right, freedom of movement. Under Vankoughnet and at his behest in correspondence to his friend John A. Macdonald, September 25 and September 29, 1885, a permit system was instituted for Indians absent from the reserve (Indian Affairs 1887).

Despite attempts by Indian Department bureaucrats to curb expenditures, government appropriations pertaining to Manitoba and the Northwest continued to increase, peaking at around $1 million in 1885 and remaining at the $850,000 level in 1900 (Indian Affairs 1885, 1900). While these numbers may not seem like much in today's terms, these same documents indicate that the salary of a teacher was about $100 per year. These unintended consequences spurred government officials to explore other options for minimizing the costs of fulfilling treaty obligations and encouraging settlement.

From the subsequent responses, it is clear that these accounting numbers captured the attention of government. In this case, the magnitude of unexpected treaty obligations encouraged government bureaucrats to focus on the accounting numbers themselves and to govern "by the numbers." Emphasis was placed on lowering the numbers through the centralization of administrative activities in Ottawa and by focusing on the cost savings of particular actions rather than their broader consequences. As Leighton comments, " one is forced to the conclusion that for Vankoughnet, fiscal considerations came ahead of human ones" (Leighton 1983: 108).

The emphasis on minimizing the numbers became an end in itself, not only with Vankoughnet but with the government. The treaty-making period of the latter half of the nineteenth century serves as a prime example of how working "by the numbers" effaced the consequences of policy initiatives on Indigenous peoples and allowed bureaucrats to avoid questions of morality and ethics. As we see in the next chapter, this governing by the numbers was refined even further when Duncan Campbell Scott became Deputy Superintendent of Indian Affairs.

Looking from the vantage point of the present, it is clear that the saving or spending of money has always been in the forefront of the federal government's dealings with First Nations peoples. While the 1996 *Report of the Royal Commission on Aboriginal Peoples* is the most recent in a long series of attempts to redefine relations between the federal government and First Nations, accounting and funding relations have been front and centre since the "birth" of Canada. During this birthing process, laws and government incentives were used to break down traditional forms of Indigenous governance, to centralize authority at the level of the Indian agent and the Department of Indian Affairs and to intensify government control over Indigenous finances. For example, starting with the introduction of regulations appointing the Superintendent of Indian Affairs as financial steward for Indigenous peoples, successive regulations refined, tightened and extended the scope of government financial control. Land sale regulations, natural resource regulations, trust fund administration regulations and reserve governance regulations were subsequently introduced. While many of these regulations appear to be piecemeal solutions to a particular issue confronting government bureaucrats at the time, by the end of the period the result was a series of regulations that governed a multitude of on-reserve activities.

While accounting and other techniques of governance may have cast their gaze further afield in the attempt to deal with the problems of nation-building, "success" was necessarily elusive. Governmentality is an eternally optimistic but perpetually failing endeavour (Miller and Rose 1990). As we see in the next chapter, the dynamic between optimism and failure encouraged both the rethinking and re-invention of accounting techniques of governance.

Chapter Six

Duncan Campbell Scott and the Canadian Indian Department

> Vengeance was once her nation's lore and law:
> When the tired sentry stooped above the rill,
> Her long knife flashed, and hissed, and drank its fill;
> Dimly below her dripping wrist she saw,
> One wild hand, pale as death and weak as straw,
> Clutch at the ripple in the pool; while shrill
> Sprang through the dreaming hamlet on the hill,
> The war-cry of the triumphant Iroquois.
> Now clothed with many an ancient flap and fold,
> And wrinkled like an apple kept till May,
> She weighs the interest-money in her palm,
> And, when the Agent calls her valiant name,
> Hears, like the war-whoops of her perished day,
> The lads playing snow-snake in the stinging cold.
> —D.C. Scott, "Watkwenies" (Scott 1926: 230)

In Canada, the transition from the nineteenth to the twentieth century was a transition from British colony to independent dominion—a nascent country trying on its Confederation persona, still somewhat tied to its Victorian apron-strings but reaching for modernity. A concerted focus on settlement, troubled by the remains of Indigenous populations which had refused to disappear, made the Indian Department of the federal government a key player in civilizing the hinterlands. But Ottawa at the time was far closer in sensibility to London, England, than it was to the Red River, the heartland of the country, or even to its own Canadian Shield backyard. Ensconced in the heart of the Ottawa bureaucracy was a civil servant, an accountant whose tenure bridged the century change. Duncan Campbell Scott, eventually to become Deputy Superintendent of Indian Affairs, was instrumental in designing legislation that, in retrospect, can be seen as driven by a bureaucratic need to cleanse the emerging colonial nation of its troubled—and troubling—Native cultures, if not, at least overtly, its individual members.

Under D.C. Scott's regime, federal government initiatives such as residential schooling and the centralization and rationalization of the

Indian Department, along with more micro-bureaucratic routines, set the context for subsequent government-Indigenous relations. However, in addition to these structures of government, D.C. Scott, the person, epitomizes both the sensibilities and tensions of this era. Under Scott, accounting techniques became a favoured method of translating Indian policy into practice. Scott was not only a well-placed bureaucrat with a deep understanding, as an accountant, of the economic basis of his department's actions, he was also a poet, essayist, prolific letter-writer and esteemed member of the Royal Society of Canada—a man at the centre of the cultural milieu of Ottawa. A literary light of his times, he recorded history both through his subjective, aesthetic perspective and through his official government record-keeping.

Duncan Campbell Scott seemed to live a double life—or at least an enigmatic one. In his official capacity, he was intent on seeing the complete assimilation of Native populations into Canadian society and was not above using legislation and the long arm of the law to force them into "civilization"—and yet in the literary world he was known as a writer who was exceptionally sympathetic to Natives and their culture. Politically, Scott was deeply conservative, yet his poetry on first glance pushed the Victorian boundaries of his fellow cultural travellers. Deeply influenced by the Confederation Poets, he was more drawn to free verse, for example, than his contemporaries. His gift appears to have been his ability to mask his conservatism behind romantic verse that extolled the freedoms of the savages while lamenting their inability to become civilized—though it was through the auspices of his own office, ironically, that serious attempts to force them into civilization were being made. The two sides of D.C. Scott provide us with a way of locating the bureaucratic mechanisms of accounting within the societal sensibilities of the times. The juxtaposition of D.C. Scott's bureaucratic initiatives with his literary output highlights both the parallels and the tensions between Indian Department policies and societal discourses pertaining to Indigenous peoples. For us, D.C. Scott is a representative of the times. His government policies resonate with the nascent emphasis on accounting as an important mode of governance and foreshadow the use of these techniques in future settings. His poetry, with its emphasis on reason over passion, captures the zeitgeist of his era.

Duncan Campbell Scott, as accountant-bureaucrat-poet, gives us a unique entry into Ottawa's handling of the "Indian problem," precisely because he was instrumental in the inauguration and implementation of a powerfully destructive bureaucratic machine and because he was, as his correspondence and poetry show, so blindly Eurocentric and unquestioning about the wisdom of his own cultural values. By exploring the paradox of what seems to be a double life, by insisting that the same individual consciousness both inaugurated racist policy and wrote "sympathetically" about members of the target race, we can deepen our understanding of government-First Nations relations.

In chapter two we examined the ways in which bureaucracy made holocausts possible. We saw how accounting provided a mode of distantiation allowing bureaucrats to believe that they were dealing with objects rather than individuals. Accounting, we said, provided information on Jewish populations in distant locales, for example, allowing policymakers to know how many pieces of human cargo needed to be transported (Funnel 1998: 454). And it provided information on the costs of the resettlement programs and the associated proceeds (Funnel 1998: 457). In these ways, accounting was the lifeblood of the Nazi bureaucracy. It provided the techniques that were necessary to plan, operationalize and manage the Final Solution.

While the roles played by administrative structures and techniques such as accounting, within the holocausts of modernity, are easily identifiable, defining the role of individual agency within such structures becomes problematic. As Raoul Hilberg (1985) reminded us, the bureaucratic machine is too complex to be the work of a few mad minds. Yet key individuals do exercise power and control within such administrative structures. It is these individuals who design the administrative programs and technologies that other civil servants implement. It is these individuals who create a system that allows for the subsequent enlistment of "desk-killers"—those individuals "in a vast bureaucratic organization, who kill from behind a desk without wielding weapons more lethal than a typewriter" (Milchman and Rosenberg 1992: 216).

Though it is clear that bureaucratically D.C. Scott was an essential individual in the destructive operations aimed at first peoples, not only does the cloak of civilization and the pretence of saving the Indians from themselves render him and his fellow bureaucrats difficult to recognize, in Scott's case, his literary career disguises him even more as being on the side of the victims of his own government's legislation—legislation he had a direct hand in designing (Milchman and Rosenberg 1992: 221). This is not to imply that the poet was consciously cynical or two-faced, faking compassion in his Indian poems on the one hand while plotting against their demise on the other. It means rather that in spite of his heart-felt lament for a drowning culture, he was unable to see beyond the assumptions of cultural superiority ingrained so deeply in his so-called civilized society. This two-sidedness of the poet-accountant is a legacy of the powerful grip and the moral distancing of the modern-civilized-rational mind. Scott was completely modern in outlook; he was a reasonable man whose actions contributed directly to the demise of Indigenous peoples; and he was a romantic who, in spite of his own power in the bureaucratic machine, was able to mourn their loss.

The Accountant and the Poet

In 1879, a seventeen-year-old Ottawa man who had "grown to maturity in the shadow of parliament" and "as a small child ... was taken to hear Joseph Howe speak in the Commons" was given a position as a copy clerk in the Department of Indian Affairs by Sir John A. Macdonald, a friend of the family and Prime Minister of Canada (Brown 1944: 121). The young clerk, D.C. Scott, was, over the next thirty-four years, to work his way up to the highest civil service post in the department. In 1889, he was promoted to first-class clerk at $1400 a year, building himself a house at 108 Lisgar Street, Ottawa, in which he was to live the rest of his life. In 1891 he was appointed clerk in charge of the Accountants' Branch, where among his responsibilities was "the administration of the Indian Trust Fund which continued to expand as reserve lands were sold and leased" (Titley 1986: 25). In 1893, as Chief Clerk and Accountant, Scott monitored department expenditure, and in 1905 he was appointed one of the commissioners to negotiate Treaty Nine. From 1906 to 1913, he was Superintendent of Indian Education, and from 1913 to 1932, Deputy Superintendent of Indian Affairs, his immediate superior, the Superintendent General, being a cabinet post. As Deputy, Scott was given "considerable freedom in determining the direction of policy" (Titley 1986: 25). Thus it was that, from the very beginning of his career, D.C. Scott was attuned to the most central mechanism of the Indian Department's administration: accounting.

But the life of the bureaucrat represented only half of the enigma known as Duncan Campbell Scott. For many members of Ottawa's elite, D.C. Scott was a musician, an esteemed member of the Royal Society of Canada and a highly regarded poet, known especially for his sympathetic literary treatment of Aboriginals. To many within his cultural circle, to his peers and to his readers, his life as bureaucrat was practically nonexistent. In Robert L. McDougall's introduction to *The Poet and the Critic*, a collection of correspondence between Scott and the critic E.K. Brown, Scott is referred to as "poet and short-story writer, *sometime bureaucrat...*"(Scott et al. 1983: 1, emphasis added). The rare references to his government work tend to be coloured by the assumption that because he wrote sympathetically of the Indians, he must also be sympathetic to them in his capacity as a government official (cf. Brown 1944). E.K. Brown, in his essay *On Canadian Poetry*, says of Scott, his life-long friend, that during his tenure as Deputy Superintendent:

> and indeed ... before his formal accession to the post, he was the chief moulder of departmental policy, an administrator of rare imaginative sympathy and almost perfect wisdom [who spent time among his charges] both on the reservations and in the wild

> and remote areas where the Indians continue to lead a life which preserves much of the nomadic picturesque quality of the past. (Brown 1944: 130)

Scott was a president of the Ottawa Symphony Society and a founding member of Ottawa's Little Theatre. "Scott's house at 108 Lisgar Street, now torn down, became a favourite meeting place for writers, artists, and musicians in the Ottawa area," where the Hart House Quartet occasionally played, and numerous poetry readings took place, including Scott himself reading from is own work and the work of others (Titley 1986: 28). Murray and Frances Adaskin, Lawrence Harris, W.J. Phillips were frequent visitors (Scott et al. 1983: 2). The walls were adorned with original paintings—including the work of Emily Carr and Walter J. Phillips. Scott was the sales agent for the painter Clarence Gagnon and good friends with Edmond Morris.

In his introduction to *More Letters of Duncan Campbell Scott*, Arthur S. Bourinot, who grew up in the same Ottawa neighbourhood as Scott, describes the literary evenings held by his father, Sir John Bourinot, at their home—"and I can remember peering over the banisters at such literary figures as Wilfred Campbell, Pauline Johnstone, Gilbert Parker, John Reade and last but not least, Duncan Campbell Scott" (Scott and Bourinot 1960: 1). And later: "I remember when I worked in the Department of Indian Affairs under Scott, as a very junior clerk, he had a silent piano in his sumptuous office with the green baize door, and on this in his few leisure moments he would practice to keep his fingers in condition" (Scott and Bourinot 1960: 2). Scott kept a garden of wildflowers at 108 Lisgar Street, "which was overlooked from a window of the music room [and] he grew clumps of Trilliums, Bloodroots, violets, blue and yellow, and more particularly the lovely wood daffodil, a favorite of his...." The walls were hung with paintings by "Gagnon, Walker, Norwell and many others—in fact, a small, but outstanding private collection" (Scott and Bourinot 1960: 4). All of this is to demonstrate the impression of genteel, Victorian cultural life in colonial Ottawa, in direct contrast to the persona of the nature poet out in the wilds of the new world. Perhaps this is the sort of civility that Scott was trying to impose on his charges. While his poetry may have been reaching for an authentic voice, reflective of his untamed country, Scott's lifestyle was definitely British and clearly imperialistic. In defending this "intoxicating imperialism"—as exemplified by another Confederation poet, Wilfred Campbell, when he said Canada's destiny was to be a part of a "Vaster Britain"—E.K Brown relegated its source as "not so much loyalty to Britain, but sharing Britain's glories" (Brown 1944: 16).

Passion, Order and Control

> It is a curious fact that in nineteenth century Canada Literature became connected with the civil service in a way it has never been, one is inclined to think, in any other country except Tsarist Russia. Sangster, Mair, Lampman, W.W. Campbell, D.C. Scott and Tom MacInnes were all civil servants, and Sir Charles G.D. Roberts was one of the official historians of the First World War. There was also a strong connection with the clergy: Campbell was a clergyman before he entered the civil service ... and Roberts, D.C. Scott and Lampman were sons of clergymen.... They were an elite group, obviously: they were to a very large extent dependent upon public institutions for their living, and most of them came from "good families" of the old-fashioned kind." (Norman Newton, quoted in Woodcock 1974: 13)

Scott's poetic heritage was steeped in romanticism and influenced locally by the Confederation poets. He was, according to Gary Geddes (in Woodcock 1974: 148), "firmly rooted by age and temperament in the nineteenth century." His spiritual mentors were Coleridge, Tennyson and Arnold. He "responded to nature in the best traditions of romanticism" (148). Scott saw in nature a varied and complex life and "the means by which man's own important sensations are elicited and activated. *Nature remains subordinate to man*, a vast reservoir from which he draws at will; it is but one of the means by which man may penetrate to the truth of his own sensations" (149, emphasis added). In other words, nature is a way to truth. In poetry, this is best marked by the proper balance between emotion and form. Scott, says Geddes, had a deep respect for "the guiding and restraining influence of traditional forms and metres ... to hold in check the workings of passion" (152). Scott shared with Arnold and Coleridge "the classical balance between passion and order" (152).

Passion on the one hand and order on the other. In Scott's life passion was associated with nature, order with civilization and culture. Life in his poetry did not unfold as a dance between the two but as struggle for restraint, and it was for this restraint that he was praised. The poet and critic A.J.M. Smith writes that Scott was spared "excessive adulation" because he placed a "special kind of excellence ... before himself as a conscious aim. These are the classical virtues of restraint and precision" (quoted in Dragland 1974: 105). "In his work," writes E.K. Brown, "there is a mixture of restraint and intensity which rasps at one and will not let go" (1944: 122). The "emotional centre of Scott's work," he says, lies in a "search for the adequate theme and the adequate form in which restrained intensity may express itself" (126). And again, "Throughout almost all of the Indian poems the fusion of intensity and restraint is notable" (132).

We need not, however, go far beyond the borders of his poetry to see that, in Scott's own stated cosmology, the deck was stacked in favour of restraint—reason—over passion. Nature was subordinate to man, according to Scott, and man to civilization. In his work at Indian Affairs, civilization was represented by government and its offices—and therefore himself—and in his poetic treatment of Natives, Indians were represented as savage, pagan, wild, orgiastic. As a true Victorian in sensibility, the poet-accountant perceived nature as quite distinct from, and even anathema to, human beings. It is his placing of Aboriginals apart from and subordinate to civilized (i.e., European) people that directed Scott's policy-making initiatives. Natives were to be guided, restrained, bureaucratically manipulated and, in no uncertain terms, absorbed into Canadian-European culture.

The emphasis on order and control which was so evident in the poetry of D.C. Scott was also present in his handling of the Indian Department. Over the course of his tenure in the Indian Department, there was both a retrenchment of authority away from the field offices to the bureaucracy in Ottawa and an increasing pattern of control via spending restraints. For example, around the time that D.C. Scott was promoted to Chief Accountant, the decision was made to institute a program of spending restraint as a way of curbing the unexpected expenditures that resulted from the signing of the western treaties and the simultaneous devastation of the buffalo on the prairies. In contrast to later initiatives introduced by D.C. Scott, this first restraint program concentrated on non-targeted, across-the-board spending reductions. Salaries of agents, clerks and farming instructors were decreased by approximately 30 percent (Titley 1986: 17).

One of the consequences of these administrative changes was the centralization of authority in Ottawa, which in turn increased the influence of D.C. Scott. Titley (1986: 17) comments:

> The centralization of decision-making meant greater authority for head-quarters officials such as secretary J.D. McLean and accountant Duncan Campbell Scott. Neither had much experience in dealing directly with Indians, but they shared [Superintendent General of Indian Affairs Clifford] Sifton's concern that expenses be minimized.

The notion of restraint became an underlying departmental philosophy over the next forty years, with the continual upward ratcheting of the modes of restraint. The 1908 *Annual Report of the Department of Indian Affairs* captures this nicely. The task of the treaties, according to the report, was "that of converting helpless and ignorant savages into civilized and industrious members of the commonwealth." The cost of "affording just sufficient help necessary to enable Indians to help themselves" was brought consciously into check, reducing the $372,000 aggregate of 1887 to $182,700 by 1898, and in 1907–8, that was further reduced to $143,000 (Indian Affairs 1908: xx).

In his summary of the operation of the Department of Indian Affairs between 1867 and 1912, D.C. Scott (1914: 601) comments approvingly on this ratcheting of restraint:

> The system of rationing which thus began in a time of dire necessity, and which embraced the whole native population dependent upon the buffalo, has been continued to the present day. Each year has seen a diminution of the number of Indians rationed, until now some bands are independent of the government food supply. In no band are the whole of the members fed gratuitously.

Interestingly, D.C. Scott did not view this mode of control as a form of constraint but rather a quite consistent "spirit of generosity" toward Indigenous peoples by the government, which "was always anxious to fulfill the obligations which were laid upon it by these treaties" (Scott 1914: 600).

As in Scott's poetry, the imposition of restraint was viewed as a positive force, a favour toward Indigenous peoples. When Scott became Deputy Superintendent in 1913, the notion of spending restraint once again became a priority, adding "accountability" as a new watchword for departmental operations. A "growing and cumbersome bureaucracy was making increasing demands on the public purse" (Titley 1986: 38) and the new deputy superintendent "made clear a renewed emphasis on accountability and spending restraint. On 25 October 1913, he sent a circular to all agents for the purpose of assisting them in the "efficient management" of their agencies (Titley 1986: 38). Under this new regime, agents were required to maintain scrupulous accounts and to provide justification for the expenditure of departmental funds.

Throughout D.C. Scott's time in the Department of Indian Affairs, the dichotomy between passion and order was a subtext of departmental operations. As reflected in Scott's poetic aborigines, Natives were constructed as part of untamed nature, and departmental initiatives were a form of order that was necessary to allow them to realize their potential. Reminiscent of the 1830s, Scott instructed his Indian agents to encourage "habits of industry and thrift" as a way of curbing their nomadic passions (Titley 1986: 38). But in keeping with his emphasis on economy and accountability, agents were requested to encourage such habits but to minimize the expense to the department (by spending band funds if at all possible) and to "keep accurate accounts and to justify every penny" (Titley 1986: 38).

In his report of 1914, using the surrender of 115,000 acres of Blackfoot reserve in 1910 as an example of "an ideal land surrender" and showing how "Indians may be advised to make a prudent use of their estate," Scott describes the bureaucratic accounting mechanisms he employed. The "sale" was for $1,600,000, divided into three funds: $50,000 to be set aside for the purchase of agricultural implements—to be paid back from the proceeds of the harvest by each Indian within six years; $350,000 "was to be expended within five years in the interests of the reserve in general" (Scott 1914:605). Further expenditures were to go to one hundred and sixty cottages, furniture, one hundred stables, buildings for housing, machinery, boring wells, repairs to roads, culverts, and fences.

> The residue from the sale of the land was to be capitalized. The interest accruing from this capital, together with the interest on any deferred payments on surrendered land, was to be used to defray the expenses of operating the agricultural motors ... to meet such general expenses as should be in the interest of the band, and to pay the cost of blankets and food for the aged and infirm as well as a regular weekly ration to all members of the band.... In this surrender, as will be observed, *no cash is to be distributed to the Indians, and the whole expenditure is defined and controlled.* (Scott 1914: 605 emphasis added)

This passage documents how Scott, the accountant, thought about the problems of government associated with the Indian Department. To him, the proper structuring of financial transactions would encourage changed habits and patterns of behaviour. Through the attention to financial details—i.e., how many funds to set up, what would the monies be used for, what monies would be treated as capital and what as interest, and so on—Scott believed it possible to introduce order. Here was his accountant's dream of the perfect surrender.

The Conceptual Indian

> She stands full-throated and with careless pose,
> This woman of a weird and waning race,
> The tragic savage lurking in her face,
> Where all her pagan passion burns and glows;
> Her blood is mingled with her ancient foes,
> And thrills with war and wildness in her veins;
> Her rebel lips are dabbled with the stains
> Of feuds and forays and her father's woes.
>
> And closer in the shawl about her breast,

> The latest promise of her nation's doom,
> Paler than she her baby clings and lies,
> The primal warrior gleaming from his eyes,
> He sulks, and burdened with his infant gloom,
> He draws his heavy brows and will not rest.
> —D.C Scott, "The Onondaga Madonna" (Scott 1926: 230)

The term "Indian poetry" has been used to describe Scott's poems set in the wilderness using Native subjects, as distinct from his more pastoral and urban poetry. This does not, however, make them Indian poems any more than busts of generic Indian chiefs could be termed Indian art. That Scott was in the bureaucracy that controlled Natives and that he was able to add an air of authenticity to his writing by giving his characters Indian names and referring to actual historical events does not by necessity bring him any closer to the heart of Aboriginal existence, nor give him any advantaged perspective. His poetry came from the same pen as his departmental correspondence and was ordered by a Victorian mind enthralled and intimidated by a wilderness which he was unable to enter and experience from inside. The Natives he represented in his writing and in his job were only ever "Indians" in that wild intimidating wilderness.

The perception popular among his contemporaries and later literary critics that Scott spent a great deal of time among his charges may be an exaggeration. Though he was known as a nature poet and was fond of canoeing and hiking, it does not naturally follow that his time in the wilderness actually amounted to much contact, let alone personal interaction with, the Natives as individuals, as people. In his poems and writings, it is hard to find Natives with actual individual personalities, Natives who are not emblematic of the poet's existential struggles between light and dark, or civilization and wilderness. Take for example "The Onondaga Madonna," which is often used as an example of Scott's ability to exploit such tensions, to maintain a reasonable distance from his subjects. Here his deft use of elegiac portraiture is seductive: This "woman of a weird and waning race" has a baby at her breast, "primal warrior gleaming in his eyes" and "burdened with his infant gloom/He draws his heavy brows and will not rest."

If Scott's poetry exhibited a certain distance from its subject matter, this distance also permeated the bureaucratic initiatives that he introduced. Control of the Aboriginal population via legislation was a favourite method. However, in keeping with his accounting expertise, this legislation often included financial carrots and sticks. The legislation and other accounting techniques functioned as a de-coupling mechanism—between Natives as individual human beings and Natives as abstracted populations, bureaucratically defined and represented as numbers used in cost analysis and gain-loss in the rationalization process of the Department of Indian Affairs. This distancing effect between actual human beings and conceptual Indians resonated with the distancing effects found in Scott's romantic poetry, in which Indians were a subset of nature, which was, in his terms, clearly subordinate to civilization. The abstraction in the case of poetry lies in the reduction of individual human beings—Indigenous persons—as symbols within nature, which the civilized poet uses as a tool for reflecting Western social-philosophical-aesthetic preoccupations. It is our contention that Scott could not have possibly allowed himself to address the Native as is, as uniquely human, without throwing into question his entire *raison d'être,* as poet, as outspoken defender of civilized British-Canadian culture and as Indian Affairs Deputy Superintendent.

Between 1910 and 1930, the department introduced a series of legislative amendments to the *Indian Act* which tightened control over the expenditures of monies by Indian bands, provided the government with greater powers of land expropriation and sought to erase "Indian" as a distinct conceptual category. Expenditures of band funds were circumscribed by legislation in 1910, 1924 and 1927. The 1910 amendment stated:

> No contract or agreement binding ... made either by the chiefs or councilors of any band ... other than and except as authorized by and for the purposes of this Part of the Act, shall be valid or of any force or effect unless and until it has been approved in writing by the Superintendent General. (SC 1910, c.28, s.2)

In 1924 the *Indian Act* was amended to allow the Indian Department to "authorize and direct" the expenditure of band funds for capital projects which would promote "progress" (SC 1924, c.47, s.5). In 1924 Scott proposed that the Act be amended again to prohibit "lawyers and other agitators from collecting money from Indians for the pursuit of claims against the government without departmental approval" (Titley 1986: 59). This proposal was incorporated into the *Act* in 1927.

These legislative amendments had the effect of centralizing control of funds received by Indigenous peoples for land surrenders, annuity payments and other transactions at the level of the Indian Department. Through these mechanisms, bureaucrats were able to decide when, how and on what Indigenous peoples could spend their monies. The 1927 amendments, by controlling expenditures, made any challenge to the government's control over Indigenous affairs prohibitive.

The use of Indigenous lands were subject to similar controls. In 1911, two amendments were introduced which gave the Indian Department the authority to expropriate Indigenous lands when necessary. The first allowed for the expropriation of land for "the purpose of any railway, road, public work or any work designed for any public utility" (SC 1911 c.14, s.1). The second allowed for the expropriation of land near towns if such expropriation was "expedient" for the public and the Indians:

> In the case of an Indian reserve which adjoins or is situated wholly or partly within an incorporated town or city having a population of not less than eight thousand ... the Governor in Council may, upon the recommendation of the Superintendent General, refer to the judge of the Exchequer Court of Canada for inquiry and report the question as to whether it is expedient, having regard to the interest of the public and of the Indians of the band for whose use the reserve is held, that the Indians should be removed from the reserve or any part of it. (SC 1911, c.14, s.2)

Similar to the financial amendments, these amendments gave the Indian Department greater say in when and how Indigenous lands would be surrendered to settler society.

If control of land and monies was a central preoccupation of the Indian Department during Scott's tenure, so was the notion of what constituted an Indigenous person. For example, in 1919, an amendment was introduced that: "Any Indian woman who marries any person other than an Indian, or a non-treaty Indian, shall cease to be an Indian in every respect within the meaning of this Act" (SC 1919–20, c.50, s.2). The pervasiveness of Scott's bureaucratic power was increased even further in March 1920 with the introduction of Bill 14. The purpose of the bill was compulsory enfranchisement, the relinquishment of Indian status in return for voting privileges. The bill "allowed for the enfranchisement of an Indian against his will following a report by a person appointed by the Superintendent General on his suitability" (Titley 1986: 49–49). That person would inevitably be Scott himself or someone directly responsible to him, since the Superintendent General was a cabinet post completely divorced from the daily workings of the department, with no possible sense of continuity from one elected regime to another (48–49). In his testimony to the House of Commons to consider Bill 14, D.C. Scott stated:

> I want to get rid of the Indian problem. I do not think as a matter of fact, that this country ought to continuously protect a class of people who are able to stand alone. That is my whole point. Our objective is to continue until there is not a single Indian in Canada that has not been absorbed into the body politic, and there is no Indian question, and no Indian Department and that is the whole object of this Bill. (quoted in Titley 1986: 50)

Scott wanted to get rid of the Indian problem—but what exactly was the problem, if not the Indians themselves? On a practical level, progress and civilization meant settlement and agriculture. Increased settlement and real estate values clashed with nomadic usage values, a way of life that was inextricably bound to the free use of hunting grounds—the same territory needed for settlement. How, then, to separate the Natives and their way of life from the land without actually exterminating them? The solution was bureaucratic: to forcibly, through legislation, separate Indigenous peoples from their way of life, their hunting territory, their agency over their land and behaviours while at the same time rendering them "Indian-less" through initiatives like compulsory enfranchisement and marriage with non-Indians.

The symmetry between Scott's poetry and his bureaucratic endeavours is striking: in Scott's poetry Aboriginal peoples were but rhetorical tropes used to present themes of struggle between passion/order, darkness/light and pagan/civilized, whereas in his bureaucratic initiatives, Indigenous peoples were erased through a focus on population. The legislation introduced by Scott attempted to control the Indigenous population through the use of financial incentives. And like the preceding section on passion, order and control, the legislation was about order and control. It attempted to control the customs, habits and behaviours of the Indigenous population and to erase them as a conceptual category.

Civilized Solutions

> He crouches in his dwarf wigwam
> Wizened with fasting,
> Fierce with thirst,
> Making great medicine
> In memory of hated things dead
> Or in menace of hated things to come,
> And the universe listens
> To the throb—throb—throb—throb—
> Throbbing of Powassan's Drum.
> —D.C Scott, "Powassan's Drum" (Scott 1926: 59)

In "Powassan's Drum," we have a poem where the poet, the bureaucrat and history actually meet. In June of 1905, Duncan Campbell Scott and his entourage left Ottawa to go treat with the Ojibwa north of Lake Superior. The last leg of their trip would be up the Abitibi River into the Lac Seul and Lake St. Joseph systems. Treaty Nine was first signed at Osnaburgh Post on July 12; ninety thousand acres were ceded; the following year forty thousand were to be ceded. There is a photo of Scott taken on the trip, sitting in a long Peterborough canoe. He leans back, sitting low between the gunnels in the middle of the vessel while eight Natives do the paddling. The following summer, in a follow-up trip, he will be accompanied by Pelham Edgar and they will be reading *The Oxford Book of Poetry* out loud to each other. It was on these two trips that he wrote or was inspired to write many of his Indian poems, including "Spring on the Mattagami," "Vengeance is Mine," "Night Burial in the Forest," "The Half-breed Girl" and certainly "Powassan's Drum," though the latter was not actually completed until ten years later.

On July 9, 1905, the party heard a drumming coming across Lac Seul. Scott was obliged as commissioner to enforce one of the laws he'd had a hand in formulating; in an amendment to the *Indian Act* passed in 1895, "the government had outlawed certain religious and social ceremonies like the Sun Dance and the Potlatch." Across Lac Seul one such ceremony was taking place—the White Dog Feast—and Scott crossed the lake to shut it down. From this incident, "Powassan's Drum" emerged—"one of Scott's most powerful poems" (Dragland 1974: 22).

"Powassan's Drum" is too long to reproduce in full here. Its narrative tells of a drumbeat, "an ache in the air/pervasive as light/measured and inevitable." Scott imagines the shaman who beats the drum "wizened with fasting/fierce with thirst ... [crouching] under the poles covered with strips of birch bark/And branches of poplar and pine/Piled for shade and dying/In dense perfume/With closed eyelids/With eyes so fierce." Scott uses the recurring theme of the drum itself "throb—throb—throb—throbbing" throughout the poem as a menacing sound, to enliven what he imagines is the shaman's purpose, "Making great medicine/In memory of hated things dead/Or in menace of hated things to come." The poet wonders what the purpose of the drumming might be—a purge? a conjuring?—and asks, repeating the theme, "Is it a memory of hated things dead/That he beats—famished—/Or a menace of hated things to come/That he beats—parched with anger/And famished with hatred?" Scott then leads us to a vision, technically adept, poetically elegant, that is conceptually indistinguishable from the setting sun and a gathering storm—the vision of a spectral headless Indian in a "canoe ... noiseless as sleep/Noiseless as the trance of deep sleep" trailing "his severed head/Through the dead water."

There is no shortage of published criticism and interpretation for this poem, but inevitably what discursive reasoning is attempted can only end in guesswork. The poem is more a question—a series of questions—written in a style that creates a haunting and oppressive atmosphere. Scott's emphasis on the sheer physicality of the pervasive drumming, the darkness of the language, the infusing of the sound with anger, hatred, fierceness, prepares us for the end of the poem, the severed Indian head.

Scott's macabre rendering of Indigenous life is highlighted by the contrast to his vision of a new Victorian society, designed in Europe and grounded in Christianity, which marked his colonial prejudices. The theme of Christian belief is pervasive in much of Scott's poetry. For example, in "Night Burial in the Forest," in contrast to the motifs of darkness and wildness, synonymous with lust and deceit, and Indians, the Christian symbol provides relief, the sound of wings—"The wings of the Angel." Likewise "The Forsaken" ends with the impression that this "Chippawa woman ... gathered up by the hand of God and hid in His breast" was forsaken, as it turns out, by both her son and her own culture, but saved by the Christian God.

If these themes were present in Scott's poetry, they also permeated the initiatives of the Indian Department of this era. Writing in 1914, Scott (1914: 599) sets out his bureaucratic vision for his Indigenous charges:

> the happiest future for the Indian Race is absorption into the general population, and this is the object of the policy of our government. The great forces of intermarriage and education will finally overcome the lingering traces of native custom and tradition.

Scott and the Residential Schools

Scott's vision for the future clearly entailed the complete disappearance of the Indian as a cultural and biological entity. Though he was pessimistic about the plains Indians being able to turn from hunting to agriculture and held out some hope for the Indians of southern Ontario, he reserved his greatest optimism for the Natives of British Columbia, especially Northern B.C., where "a radical experiment in social engineering conducted by the Anglican missionary William Duncan" in Fort Simpson had taken place. Duncan had created the model village of Metlakatla, based exclusively on Victorian England in government and design. In order to save the Indians from themselves Duncan moved them away from Fort Simpson, where "heathen superstitions" and "savage atrocities" prevailed. These sentiments seemed to guide the introduction of residential schools (Fisher 1977: 133–34).

The emergence of residential schools in the post-Confederation period owed much to the belief that only Christianity, isolation and education could prepare the Indians for a life without Indian-ness. The involvement of missionary societies in educational activities, along with their active lobbying, encouraged the federal government to utilize them in the provision of Aboriginal education (Titley 1986: 75). By the end of the 1800s, there were 290 schools in operation (Indian Affairs 1902).

With the federal government providing the funds for residential schools, the missionary societies were quick to seize the opportunity to utilize state subsidies to expand their spheres of operations (Titley 1986:

76). The churches had been integral to pioneering efforts into remote areas, using missionary funds for construction and departmental funds for maintenance. As the system expanded, the missionary societies soon joined a "queue of determined church lobbyists, hands outstretched for operating grants" (Milloy 1999: 52–56). Education was seen as a method of inducing "pacification, an indispensable element in the creation of conditions for the peaceful occupation of the west" (Milloy 1999: 32). When he was Superintendent of Indian Education, Scott commented that "without education and with neglect the Indians would produce an undesirable and often dangerous element in society" (quoted in Milloy 1999: 33). Residential schools were envisioned as a "circle of civilized conditions" where one culture would be replaced with another, through the teaching of a set curriculum—a curriculum which emphasized European virtues and knowledges (Milloy 1999: 34–35).

By the early 1890s, there was concern about the mounting financial expenditures and the ambiguity of government-church relations in the area of residential schooling. Scott and others encouraged the department to introduce a general financial system for the schools, by an order-in-council in October 1892. This included a series of rules, which were meant to introduce order and economy into the system (Milloy 1999: 62).

As a tool to restrain the financial expenditures of the missionary societies and thus the financial obligations of the department, the new system was "for the close control of the *per capita* allowance placed in the hands of the various religious denominations" (Milloy 1999: 65). The order-in-council set a *per capita* funding rate (which was below then-current levels of expenditure) and stipulated that most expenses were to be paid out of this, except for books and appliances and the cost of building repairs, which would be borne by the government (Milloy 1999: 63).

The new system of financial controls did not fare any better than the previous one, however, in that the department had no control over maintenance expenditures, nor any sense of the associated costs until the repair bills were received. Furthermore, the churches refused to be bound by the terms of the system and continued to operate as always. And because of the political clout of the churches, the department continued to accept full financial responsibility for expenditures. This, as well as the failure of the schools in the area of assimilation, led Scott himself to conclude that, "the government's attempt between 1892 and 1894 to bring order, Departmental authority, economy and financial control to the system was ... a total failure" (quoted in Milloy 1999: 64–65).

The system of financial controls appeared to fail in other ways as well. The inadequate *per capita* funding amount encouraged school operators to concentrate on the recruiting and retention of students regardless of their physical health (Milloy 1999: 67). Within the department it was "well known that schools routinely admitted unhealthy students without any medical check" and although the 1892/94 orders-in-council stipulated that (a) a medical certificate was a condition of admission, and (b) that the department could inspect the schools, there was no regular inspection (Milloy 1999: 88–89). This intersection of an inadequate funding mechanism, the lack of enforcement of departmental rules and the substandard facilities resulted in mortality rates of around 40 percent for Aboriginal youth sent to such institutions. As Milloy (1999: 52) concludes:

> The method of funding the individual schools, the intricacies of the Department-church partnership in financing and managing schools and the failure of the Department to exercise effective oversight of the schools, led directly to their rapid deterioration and overcrowding. Those were the conditions within which, as in urban slums of the time, tubercular disease became endemic.

Around 1905, the department was forced to bail-out several schools because of their accumulated debts resulting, in part, from financial mismanagement (Titley 1986: 82). Around this same time, Dr. Bryce, the medical inspector to the Department of the Interior, examined the state of health within industrial and boarding schools on the prairies. His report became national news when he documented not only the appalling conditions in residential schools but how approximately 24 percent of students died while in attendance and another 18 percent as a result of illness shortly after leaving (Milloy 1999: 91). These two events provided the impetus for Scott to suggest the need to "reconstruct the whole school system." After he became Superintendent of Indian Education in 1909, Scott revamped the financial controls (Titley 1986: 82).

Though Bryce's report contained specific recommendations, Scott vetoed these because of cost considerations (Titley 1986: 85); his solutions remained administrative and accounting-based, emphasizing screening of individual student entrants, funding revisions to encourage better maintenance of facilities and a ceiling on student enrollment (Milloy 1999: 94). Presuming that operators of low-grade facilities would have incentives to upgrade facilities if they wanted more funding, differential *per capita* funding rates were provided depending on the quality of the facility. But these "administrative fictions," as Milloy calls them, failed to facilitate effective economical management. Political patronage and cheap construction materials played a large role in the building of schools, and low administrative follow-up meant business as usual in terms of school conditions and mortality rates (Milloy 1999: 90–101). In frustration over both the department's inaction regarding his recommendations and his subsequent dismissal by Scott, after Scott became Deputy Superintendent, ex-medical inspector Bryce wrote *The Story of a National Crime* in 1922. He laid the blame for the continuing death of children after 1907 squarely on the shoulders of "the dominating influence," Duncan Campbell Scott, who had become "the reactionary" Deputy Superintendent General in 1913 and prevented "even the simplest efforts to deal with the health problem of the Indians along modern scientific lines." Bryce went on to charge: "owing to Scott's active opposition ... no action was taken by the Department to give effect to the recommendations made in the 1911 contracts" (quoted in Milloy 1999: 95).

Initially, one of the objectives of residential schooling operated through a church-run system was assimilation, in the belief that this could be achieved through a combination of religious instruction, education and the isolation of Aboriginal youth from their communities. By the early 1890s, excess costs suggested that it was also necessary to govern the churches.

Macro policy objectives are often translated through accounting/numerical methods into numerical micro-level statements. In the case of Nazi Germany, for example, bureaucrats were concerned with the cost per kilometer of transporting human cargo (Bauman 1989: 101). For the Indian Department, the policy of assimilation was carried through a cost-effective minimalization of the percentage of the Aboriginal population that deviated from the norms of settler society. While Scott and many other whites viewed Indigenous peoples both in terms of a population and of a deviance, Victorian sensibilities prevented the outright elimination of Indigenous peoples. Social-engineering projects, however, in which Indigenous populations were manipulated as numerical and quantitative integers, were more acceptable and served the objectives of the Indian Department well.

Bauman describes the shift in outcomes that can occur when micro policies are constructed with bureaucratic/accounting techniques; efficiency can become an end-in-itself. Regardless of bureaucratic intentionality, it is important to note that high mortality rates were not inconsistent with an objective of decreasing the percentage of Aboriginal peoples who deviated from the norms of settler society. Thus while Victorian sensibilities may have precluded direct annihilation, genocide through indifference or a withholding of funds seemed acceptable.

Subsequent events during Scott's regime are consistent with this interpretation. The dominance of cost containment as a policy objective encouraged Scott to rationalize the department's medical budget during the 1914–1918 war years. In the same year that the war ended, Scott decided to dispense with the position of medical inspector "for reasons of economy"—this was the year of the Spanish influenza and the death of four thousand Indigenous people as a consequence (Milloy 1999: 97). Around this same time, Scott instituted measures designed to increase the scope of the residential school system and, hence, the numbers of Indigenous youth attending such schools. He introduced legislative amendments in 1920 and 1930 which strengthened compulsory attendance: "Bill 14 (1920) empowered the Superintendent General by means of truant officers and penalties to compel the attendance at school of all Indian children between the ages of seven and fifteen years" (Titley 1986: 90–103). Although conditions in the residential schools had not improved, Scott's emphasis was on increasing system efficiency—defined as the percentage/number of Aboriginal youth being subjected to social engineering techniques—rather than on correcting the problematic mortality outcomes.

During Duncan Campbell Scott's tenure, accounting solutions came to dominate the activities of the Indian Department. We conclude with one final example of this dominance—Scott's emphasis on annual report disclosures as a method to demonstrate progress and silence his critics. Following his promotion to Deputy Superintendent in 1913, Scott revamped the annual report to more clearly show the results of departmental activities:

> An attempt has been made to render the report of greater practical value by re-arrangement and consolidation.... The form of the statements has been revised, and a series of tables is presented, designed to show in a clear way the results of the various activities engaged in by the Indians. (Indian Affairs 1915: 1)

Subsequent annual reports contained statistical tables on the Aboriginal population, the value of crops under cultivation, the value of real property and total income, along with statistics on the number of schools in operation and the number of students.

Likewise, the annual reports also sought to counter concerns regarding not only the degree of control that the department was exercising over residential schools but also the condition of the schools themselves. For example, the 1915 Annual Report goes out of its way to make assurances that "almost all the schools are under the direct supervision of the different Indian agents, who are required to make monthly inspections and reports" (Indian Affairs 1915: xxiii). And the 1916 Annual Report describes "calisthenics ... fresh air ... and personal cleanliness" as instructions that "cannot fail to influence their later life upon the reserves" (Indian Affairs 1916: xxiii). These reassurances seem to foreshadow the impression-management activities of modern day corporations (Preston et al. 1996). With such public relations, it became less important for bureaucrats such as Scott to confront the impacts which governance-at-a-distance had on Native peoples.

Table 3

The value of land in the Indian reserves has been slightly augmented. The figures for provinces are as follows:

Alberta	$12,615,240
British Columbia	15,796,510
Manitoba	2,331,591
New Brunswick	71,589
Nova Scotia	82,985
Ontario	4,648,455
Prince Edward Island	19,914
Quebec	1,032,327
Saskatchewan	10,116,327
Total	46,765,011

THE FOLLOWING TABLE SHOWS THE VALUE PER CAPITA OF REAL AND PERSONAL PROPERTY:

Province	Population	Total Value of Real and Personal Property $	Value per Capita of Real and Personal Property $ cts
Alberta	8,500	14,252,454	1,676 76
British Columbia	25,399	19,950,924	785 50
Manitoba	10,798	3,110,670	288 08
New Brunswick	1,862	237,414	127 50
Nova Scotia	2,042	218,543	107 02
Ontario	26,162	8,509,217	325 48
Prince Edward Island	288	43,924	152 51
Quebec	13,174	2,410,230	182 95
Saskatchewan	9,775	11,705,834	1,197 52
Total	98,000[1]	60,439,210	616 72

1. Not including 5,531 Indians in Yukon and Northwest Territories

SOURCES AND VALUE OF INCOME

The table showing the sources and value of income of the Indians, may be summarized as follows:

Value of farm products, including hay	$1,813,619 00
Value of beef sold and consumed for food	309,506 00
Wages earned	1,419,244 00
Received from farm rentals	81,160 00
Earned by fishing	586,781 00
Earned by hunting	654,501 00
Earned by other industries and occupations	632,118 00
Annuities and interest on Indian trust funds	430,665 52
Total	$5,927,594 52

Source: Indian Affairs 1916: xxviii

She is free of the trap and the paddle,
The portage and the trail,
But something behind her savage life
Shines like a fragile veil.

Her dreams are undiscovered,
Shadows trouble her breast,
When the time for resting cometh
Then least is she at rest.
—D.C. Scott, "The Half-Breed Girl" (Scott 1926: 55)

By the end of Scott's tenure as Deputy Superintendent of Indian Affairs, Indigenous people were indeed "free of the trap and the paddle"—but they were also uneasy about this freedom, given the costs borne by individuals and communities in conforming to white visions of civilization (Hildebrandt et al. 1996). The vision of Native existence held by senior bureaucrats, voiced by Scott in "The Half-Breed Girl," rationalized bureaucratic interventions since these apparently freed Aboriginals from a savage existence. But as Zygmunt Bauman reminds us, such perceptions depend on one's vantage point. From the outside looking in, accounting techniques provided Scott with a method of translating government objectives into practice. This governance was directed toward the population of Indigenous peoples and sought to inculcate westernized modes of being. And like Scott's poetry, these initiatives were couched in romantic and humanistic verse even though the outcomes were genocidal. Beneath this veneer of humanism and romanticism was a series of techniques that stripped Indigenous peoples of their agency and centralized control of their lives in the Department of Indian Affairs. From their vantage point, these outcomes contributed to the unease experienced by Aboriginal peoples regarding their changed circumstances.

Chapter Seven

Funding "Citizens Plus"

Introduction

The development of government-Indigenous funding relations from the post-World War II era to the present follows two parallel narrative arcs that might be typified as an historically entrenched paradox. One arc represents the attempt to industrialize, urbanize and bureaucratize the Indigenous peoples; the other arc represents the self-education, organization and consciousness-raising radicalization of the First Nations movement towards sovereignty. The paradox, stemming from colonialism and its bureaucratic approach to cultural genocide, is inextricable from the funding relations between these two groups—both of which have a demonstrated need to be free of each other. From the Native perspective, the paradox may be stated as a question: Given that financial support has been contracted via several historical events and agreements, can there be both independence and continued (financial) support? From the government perspective it might be: Can we give up (legislated) control to a people that sees itself as sovereign and demands a nation-to-nation relationship, while maintaining our historically entrenched responsibilities towards it? Obviously, the paradox is dissolved if the Gordian knot, which is entirely political, is attacked with the sword of legal obligation—in other words, if it is not a question of support/independence but rather of legal obligation arising from treaty agreements. But, we are following the government's lead, a paper-trail of bureaucratic-political manipulation which seems to have arisen out of a persistent refusal to deal with its legal-moral obligations.

A thumbnail sketch of the parallel narrative arc described above would reveal its pinnacle in the hefty two-volume Hawthorn Report of 1966; that peak was preceded by the post-war awakening of government and the general population towards the dispossessed Native population, and followed by the organized and concerted determination of Indigenous peoples to receive what they considered their due. In 1951, the government responded to the growing awareness of Third-World living conditions in Native communities by retreating into the rhetoric of consultation, partnership and co-operation—but, as we see in this chapter, failed the test of making substantial legislative or funding arrangement changes. In 1969, the government responded to the same pressures by trying to wave the magic wand of self-government over the entire First Nations as a way of washing its hands of the whole affair. But the fall-out from that idealistic and radical failure—the infamous White Paper of then Indian Affairs Minister Jean Chretien—was soundly and almost universally rejected, and the White Paper of 1969 lives in present Indigenous-government negotiations; the event marks the point from which each side—but, arguably, more the Indigenous side—has been able to articulate its position more and more clearly.

In this chapter, we examine the mountains of paper, resolutions, organization flow-charts and accounting tables that have grown, since World War II, from the central paradox that is deeply entrenched in the historical struggle between "the keepers and the kept." Winding its way through these bureaucratic artifacts is the eternally fluctuating tension of the funding relations between the two parties—evoking questions which can perhaps be simply stated but whose answers have proven somewhat illusive: Can the shackles of racial oppression, cultural genocide and political hegemony finally be loosed and discarded through economic and bureaucratic means? How do two sovereign nations with a history of enforced dependency find political and economical solutions to a problem they essentially share?

A Gradual Awakening

On October 24, 1946, eleven men set out from Ottawa for Eastern Quebec and the Maritime Provinces to conduct an enquiry into Indian administration (Canada et al. 1947). It was, to say the least, a gargantuan task. The commissioners, who considered themselves to be a fact-finding body, were all members of the Special Joint Committee of the Senate and the House of Commons. Their final hearing was held at Quebec City on November 6, 1946. According to the report, "all Indians were given an opportunity to make representations at well-attended meetings" (Canada et al. 1947: 2). The commissioners had been appointed just thirteen days before they headed out. The report, sixteen pages in length, whose evidence took eighteen days to gather, would be tabled in the House of Commons on July 8, 1947, eight months later.

The Commission travelled 2850 miles in eighteen days, "by rail, land and water"—160 miles per day—and interviewed 170 witnesses—approximately ten per day—spread out over twenty reserves, or more than one reserve per day, if we assume that travel did not necessitate an interruption in consecutive work days. They visited homes, schools and infirmaries. Considering the extent to which their findings were to influence legislation, one cannot but wonder about the thoroughness of their information-gathering, and how it was possible for "all Indians" to participate in any meaningful manner.

The Joint Committee would stand for another two years, the result of a new awareness, after World War II, of the expanded role of government in the social welfare of citizens and the economy (Hawthorn and Canada 1966). The Indian department was not immune to this generally shifting attitude, and the role of enlisted Natives in the European battlefields and the plight of the Indian veterans who had returned, still wards of the government, contributed to public awareness of the obvious injustices. Concurrently, Aboriginal leaders were emerging, expressing their people's desire to gain their rightful place among Canadians. In British Columbia, Alberta, Saskatchewan and Ontario, organizations to protect and advance Native interests were being formed.

The central bureaucratic task of Indian Affairs has been, through all its nominal permutations, to define the term Indian and to calculate their numbers and costs for the government. The first definition of an Indian was formulated in the *Indian Act* of 1886. Because definition and funding were virtually inextricable, to those depending on funding for survival, lacking Indian status meant economic as well as social exclusion (see Paul 2000: 267–69 for an example of how this worked in the Maritimes). In the 1947 report, defining "band membership" was a priority. When the commissioners, in their hasty survey, asked the opinion of Native witnesses regarding the acceptance of more people under the Indian Status heading, their response, naturally, was cautious. "Inhabitants of some reserves," the report said, "are jealous of the 'privileges' which they enjoy at this present location and are not disposed to accept with good graces the infiltration from other reserves, by marriage or otherwise, of Indians of even the same racial origins" (Canada et al. 1947: 4). Their reticence and guard are understandable, given the precariousness of their own abilities to support themselves on their imposed reserves. But here, under the guise of following Aboriginal sentiment, the commission was excusing its power to exclude certain people from Indian status and thereby saving the additional costs of funding a larger population of Aboriginal people.

Band membership, whether living on or off reserve, has always been tied to the issue of taxes that, in a democracy, is reflected in having a vote. This issue, however, is side-stepped in the report, other than a mention that "generally speaking the Indian does not feel that he should pay any taxes." Although the commissioners stated those who paid taxes on income earned off reserve "feel that they should, for that reason, be given the right to vote," no recommendations are made (Canada et al. 1947: 6). The report glosses over a fundamental argument about the nature of democracy *vis-à-vis* Natives: Aboriginal people who pay taxes which are then allocated by a member of Parliament elected without Aboriginal input, are, in fact, funding a government that cannot represent their interests.

We have seen in previous chapters how residential schools were primarily a form of enforced acculturation. By the 1940s, indoctrination methods had gained in subtlety. Girls, for example, were "taught home-making and domestic sciences, weaving and other hand-crafts" (Canada et al. 1947: 9) —skills, to be sure, modelled on British ideals of domesticity. The commissioners also reported that "the institution of payment of family allowances has meant a decided improvement in school attendance" (11). While family allowances did not constitute, for non-Native families, anything but a small token amount, for Natives living in poverty, this same amount could mean an important increase to their income—payment, we might say, for sending their children to an institution designed to inculcate them with values contrary to those of their own culture. To the government and general population, however, this seemed to be the normal course of events—to improve, advance and civilize their Native charges was the whole point. The more civilized they became, the less they would cost the government. As the commissioners stated, it was their opinion, "based upon actual investigation," that much had been done to "improve the social and economic status of the Indians," so that one day, "the need for the special services now rendered to these wards of the Crown will gradually lessen" (10).

Bill 79: Consultation—or Not

On February 28 through March 3 of 1951, nineteen "representative Indians and officers of Indian associations" gathered in Ottawa and sat around a table with government representatives to discuss amendments (Bill 79) to the *Indian Act*. This was the first time since European incursions, including the entire treaty-making era, that such a conference had taken place. The chairperson was W.E. Harris, the Minister of Citizenship and Immigration. According to the *Summary of Proceedings*, all of the representatives agreed that the government "should *continue* to extend self government to the Indian band councils consistent with their demonstrated ability to exercise increasing responsibility" (*Hansard* 1951: 1364–67, emphasis added). Exactly which Indian band councils the Minister imagined were enjoying self-government at this juncture in history, the summary does not say.

It is worth noting that the conference—"an historic occasion for the Indians"(*Hansard* 1951: 714), according to Harris in his introduction of Bill 79 to the House, began the day *after* the Bill received first reading. Interestingly, the question which opened the House debate was concerned with the right of Indians to appeal decisions made by the ministry, or, as the questioner put it, "the arbitrary power of the Minister to determine nearly everything of importance in the life of the Indian, without appeal from the Minister's decision except in some cases to the Governor in

Council." Not granting the right of appeal to the courts, he said, "makes our adherence to the United Nations declaration of human rights and fundamental freedoms nothing more than a farce" (*Hansard* 1951: 715).

Self government implies sovereignty, which would put discussions of such far-reaching legislation on a government-to-government basis. But it is clear, following the procedural manoeuvring of the legislation through the House of Commons, that discussions with the representative Indians had no legislative and very little consultative effect on the process of making the amendments law. The ideals of consultation and self government, it seems, were more rhetorical than substantive.

With no input from the Indian representatives—waiting in the wings—the bill was given first reading on February 27, 1951. During the ensuing discussions, the official opposition lobbied for a delay of second reading so that a special committee could be struck, with which the Indian representatives now present in Ottawa for the conference could meet to give their responses to the proposed amendments. The delay in second reading would also allow those present to "acquaint the Indians in [MP's] own districts with the effects of the new legislation" (*Hansard* 1951: 731–34). Minister Harris, of course was reluctant, citing lack of time and procedural etiquette. To send the bill to a special committee would, in his opinion, mean scrapping the bill. But Winnipeg MP Stanley Knowles, on the opposite side of the House, cited historical precedents, demonstrating that consultation was possible without contravening legislative convention. The Minister dug in his heels: "Every Indian who is coming here" he said disingenuously "is a member of the public of Canada, and is represented by a member of the house. I am quite sure he would want to pay his respects to his member and to discuss with him the problems of Indian Affairs, and through him perhaps make representations" (*Hansard* 1951: 734). The fact is, being leaders on their respective reserves, hence paying no property taxes and being without voting privileges, the Indians had no representation in the House of Commons. Asked how long they would be "kept here," Harris responded that the work should be done in three days. End of discussion. Second reading went ahead, with no special committee, no substantive participation of the Native representatives.

Perhaps the sovereignty/responsibility paradox is most clearly illustrated by the question of enfranchisement and its relationship to funding. What the government thinks of as funding is, from the Native perspective, due payment and obligation. What Indigenous people might perceive as a way of enticing them from their ancestral land with entitlements that have little value and which give the government a way out of meeting its obligations, the government imagines as a great bounty for those who want, by natural instinct, to emulate Canadian values and lifestyle. Minister Harris, in the Bill 79 debates, admits as much:

> Heretofore we have thought of enfranchisement as being the ultimate role of Indian policy, and let us say frankly that we rather expected that the Indian would want to become enfranchised in order to be like us. Nothing can be further from the truth, Mr. Speaker. The Indian has no desire to become one of us, and all his representatives have said: I hope you are not going to take away from me the right to be an Indian. (*Hansard* 1951: 1352)

"Of course there is no such intention" Harris continues, and states what appears to be a radical proposal, that "our policy should be to extend self-government to all the reserves as soon as possible" (1352). He warns the members that some of the powers that could be turned over to individual bands may be "greater powers than are now held … by municipal authorities" (1352). But this is rhetoric. In the next breath he is describing the method of band election to be imposed—until such a time as the chiefs and councillors "might learn the procedure and methods of handling the money of their bands and dealing with property" (1353).

That the government hand intends to be a paternalistic and firm one, while its voice speaks of self-government and cooperation, becomes more evident as we examine closely the language used by the Minister. Harris describes enfranchisement as an act whereby the Indian is "released from the land" and "goes out into the world on his own" (1353). He does this with the aid of "funds that are due him and a small gratuity from the government." But for Natives, there may be no need or wish to be "released" from the place which has sustained their people for hundreds of years; they already live "in the world," and the funds and gratuities present a small portion of a withholding due and by which they are being pressured to leave home.

Having had his eyes opened to the Natives' reluctance towards enfranchisement, Harris magnanimously announces that in the new bill, upon being enfranchised, "the Indian may hold his land for a period of ten years" (1353). "Hold" in this case does not mean ownership. Only after ten years will the Native be given the option to buy, provided the ministry deems it is in the best interests of the band and individuals concerned. Meanwhile this land is land over which the ministry has complete and utter control, called ministerial discretion, especially in terms of any income that may be raised from it. And though its inclusion in previous legislation (Bill 267) was soundly criticized by the Indigenous community, Harris announces that it will be retained in Bill 79—though the discretion will be "very much limited." While the changes will be discussed in committee, he assures the House that:

> In particular the Minister is obliged to retain authority over the

> expenditure of band funds.... I would not want to mislead the house. The ministerial authority does extend to supervision of expenditure of band funds, but I want to assure the house that just as soon as a band demonstrates its ability to handle money it will be given an opportunity of doing so. (*Hansard* 1951: 1353)

"Demonstrates" means taking employment off reserve, becoming enfranchised, paying taxes and losing Indian status, thus contributing to the demise of traditional life on the reserve. In pushing his bill through, Mr. Harris enlightened the house on the good fortunes enjoyed by the Indians, especially in the matter of hunting and fishing. While admitting that treaty rights to hunt and fish had been restricted by provincial fish and game laws, Natives were getting healthier and richer. "Many people say that he lives a happier life than you or I do," and "may I also add that he is getting wealthy too" (1355).

Masters of their Destiny— Elections, Zoning and Garbage Disposal

The rhetoric so well demonstrated by Minister Harris in his Bill 79 was rampant within the department in the post-war years. It was an era of economic rebirth, high expectations and liberal ideals. New communications technology and increased higher education were tied to notions of economic progress, and it was impossible to keep the embarrassing plight of the Indigenous population out of the public eye. But Ottawa was not prepared to relinquish control of the monster they had created; rhetoric served to disguise the contradictions. In *The Review of Activities 1948–1958, Indian Affairs Branch of Citizenship and Immigration* (Canada 1958), we are offered a glimpse into the mechanistic-statistical construction of Indigenous peoples by the department and shown how rhetoric—i.e., "collaboration, consultation and partnership"—served to wrap this extremely coercive action-at-a-distance in a more palatable package.

While the administrative mandate of Indian Affairs, under the Department of Citizenship and Immigration, remained the same as it was under Mines and Resources, the change of bureaucratic location, effective January 1950, seemed to emphasize an ideological purpose:

> to administer the affairs of the Indians of Canada in a manner that will enable them to make the necessary adjustments to become fully participating and self-supporting members of the communities in which they live. (Canada 1958: 1)

One can only assume that the adjustments necessary were to adapt them, not to their actual home communities, to which no adaptation was necessary, but to the communities in which the government wished them to live. The review observed that increased emphasis was being given to consultation. However, as we saw in the case of the 1951 conference, the consultations were, in the end, without substance: the conference took place *after* the proposed legislation was tabled and any possible collaboration in the shaping of the amendments was effectively blocked by the parliamentary majority.

The rhetoric was broad; what it lacked in substance was easily made up for by the depth and weight of the bureaucracy. The review was a kind of organizational flow chart, with accompanying accounting tables and graphs, involving over fifty bureaus, starting from the Deputy Minister's office and spreading their way down in a sort of pyramidal contagion, to various supervisors, officers and inspectors—and this, before even reaching the level of Indian agent, to say nothing of the individuals on the reserve. Immediately under the Deputy Minister was the Director of Indian Affairs, who in turn had six separate offices under his wing, including an executive assistant, a special assistant and a secretariat. These administrators oversaw eight regional offices and eighty-nine Indian agencies. With "decentralization" as a key expression in the rhetorical lexicon, this would inevitably mean more, not less, bureaucracy—to fulfill "the necessity for intimate knowledge of regional conditions in relation to reserves and problems faced by Indians" (Canada 1958: 4).

Staff specialists—social workers, education officers, job placement experts—had to be hired for the "expansion of programs aimed at developing the economy of the Indian Reserves" (5). Field staff thus rose from 445 in 1945 to 597 in 1958. In the pyramid, they can be found near the bottom, just above the agencies themselves. And above them are approximately forty bureaucratic offices. The expansion of the department also included housing construction—not for the Natives but for field staff. By 1958, 157 residences were owned and maintained by the department.

Bureaucracy was not only occupied with staff infrastructure. To ensure that only entitled Aboriginals were receiving monies, lists were kept of these individuals (Canada 1958: 32). Government administrators also controlled the elections of band councillors. Here again we have the ironic interface of liberal rhetoric and, we might even assume, sincere concern, with paternalistic domination. Since the elected band councillors would presumably be Indigenous peoples, the department could boast of democratization—but where exactly is sovereignty being practised? What, specifically, were the councillors elected to *do*?

On paper, it appears that the councillors were indeed involved in the running of their own affairs. The review displays a set of tables as "an indication of the extent to which the Indians of Canada are assuming greater responsibility in the intelligent administration of their own affairs" (Canada 1958: 9). It shows the number and types of by-laws passed by various Indian band councils who "have been declared by the Governor-in-Council as having reached an advanced stage of development" and therefore were allowed to "make by-laws under Section 82 of the Act" (9).

By 1958, only 22 of the 571 bands under the department's administration were deemed to be in that elevated position. Between them they passed 208 by-laws, or an average of approximately 9 for each council. Of the 208 by-laws passed across the country, few dealt with matters of tribal import: 10 were classified under Fish and Game, 6 under Expenditure of Moneys, 2 under Zoning. The remainder had to do with such things as Sanitation and Conduct of Hawkers; the highest, 27 and 23, were concerned with Disorderly Conduct and Garbage Disposal, respectively.

It seems a dual purpose was served by this show of democratic puppetry. One was to present the general public and official history with the face of increasing democratic participation, and the other was to indoctrinate the Natives into their new improved culture. According to the review, the purpose of the revised 1951 Act had been "to provide uniform procedures closely following those used in municipal elections. These regulations have been a significant step in introducing band members to ordinary democratic election procedure" (Canada 1958: 8).

Procedure at council meetings was also regulated by the Act "so that their meetings could be conducted along generally accepted parliamentary lines for the proper despatch of band business" (Canada 1958: 8). The drafting of band council by-laws was modelled after municipal procedures, "existing [municipal] by-laws in various parts of Canada were obtained and used as a basis for drafting sample by-laws" (9).

In *The 18th Brumaire of Louis Bonaparte*, Karl Marx comments that history repeats itself, once as tragedy and once as farce (Marx 1963: 15). In looking back at earlier periods (see chapter five) we observe similar patterns. Once again we see the government holding out the carrot of greater Indigenous autonomy and financial control—however, only if "westernized" models of governance are adopted. And again even these apparent freedoms cannot withstand closer scrutiny since lurking in the background is government control over band elections and critical day-to-day operations.

In the 1958 flow chart for the Indian Affairs bureaucracy there is an office—four levels below the deputy minister and seven above the agency level—whose chief bureaucrat is directly answerable to the Assistant Regional Superintendent. This is the Reserves and Trusts Division, which in turn administers the bureaus known as Land Registry, Band Trust Funds, Estates, Resources and Band Membership. Were it not for the appellate "Band" in two of those sub-bureaus, we might be fooled into thinking we were looking at the flow-chart of a giant resource conglomerate with innumerable subsidiaries. Directly opposite the Reserves and Trusts Division, in a perfect mirror image of the organizational sub-

Table 4

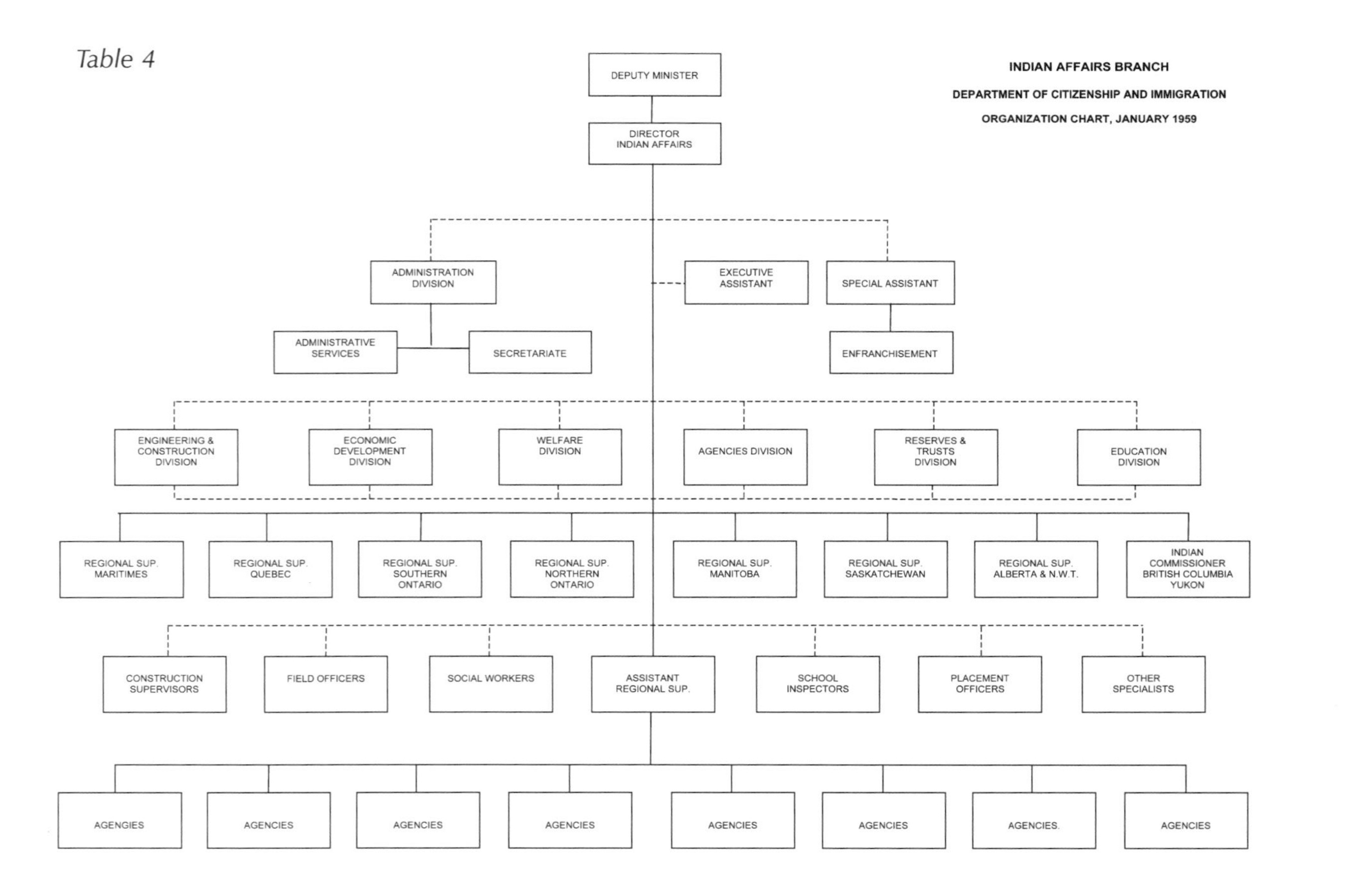

INDIAN AFFAIRS BRANCH
DEPARTMENT OF CITIZENSHIP AND IMMIGRATION
ORGANIZATION CHART, JANUARY 1959
DEPUTY MINISTER
DIRECTOR INDIAN AFFAIRS
ADMINISTRATION DIVISION
EXECUTIVE ASSISTANT
SPECIAL ASSISTANT
ADMINISTRATIVE SERVICES
SECRETARIATE
ENFRANCHISEMENT
ENGINEERING & CONSTRUCTION DIVISION
ECONOMIC DEVELOPMENT DIVISION
WELFARE DIVISION
AGENCIES DIVISION
RESERVES & TRUSTS DIVISION
EDUCATION DIVISION
REGIONAL SUP. MARITIMES
REGIONAL SUP. QUEBEC
REGIONAL SUP. SOUTHERN ONTARIO
REGIONAL SUP. NORTHERN ONTARIO
REGIONAL SUP. MANITOBA
REGIONAL SUP. SASKATCHEWAN
REGIONAL SUP. ALBERTA & N.W.T.
INDIAN COMMISSIONER BRITISH COLUMBIA YUKON
CONSTRUCTION SUPERVISORS
FIELD OFFICERS
SOCIAL WORKERS
ASSISTANT REGIONAL SUP.
SCHOOL INSPECTORS
PLACEMENT OFFICERS
OTHER SPECIALISTS
AGENGIES
AGENCIES
AGENCIES
AGENCIES
AGENCIES
AGENCIES
AGENCIES.
AGENCIES

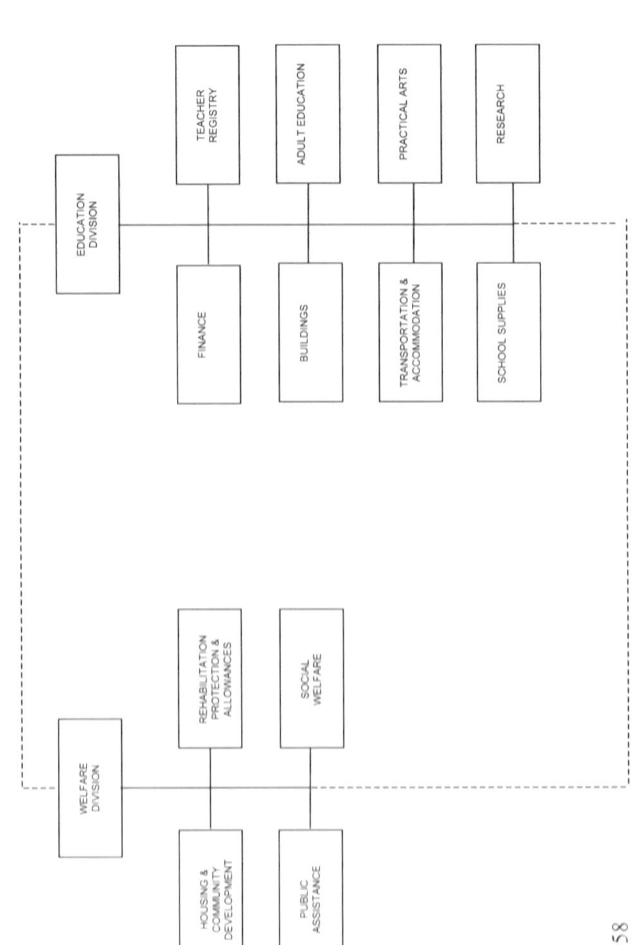

Source: Canada 1958

divisions, we have the Economic Development Division—with Wildlife and Fisheries, Projects and Credits, on the same level with Engineering and Construction. These brokers of administrative control, working through the Assistant Regional Superintendent, exercised real power over reserve life.

The Reserves and Trusts Division of the Indian Affairs Branch of the Department of Citizenship and Immigration was responsible for:

> the management of all reserves and the resources therein such as land, timber and minerals; the management of the Indian Trust Fund; the maintenance of a Land Registry system; the administration of the estates of deceased Indians, and the maintenance of a Band Membership Register. (Canada 1958: 29)

It is hard to imagine a more pervasive bureaucratic occupation of a people's community. After World War II, this pervasiveness became more pronounced as the bureaucracy reproduced itself. Business was picking up in the wake of country-wide economic development; there was an increasing awareness among the entrepreneurial class, municipalities and band councils of the desirability of unused reserve lands. In the 1948–1958 period, reserve land sales reached $4,000,000 and land leases totalled $7,870,000. Timber sales during the same period went from $300,000 to $580,000. Over the ten years, receipts totalled $5,500,000. These business activities "required a great deal of time and staff work to bring to completion and added substantially to the work of the division" (Canada 1958: 29–30).

Where was the money going? Why were Natives so poor? Not having demonstrated that they had achieved an adequate degree of responsibility, it was incumbent upon the government to put their revenues in trust. "The work of the Resources Section" of the Indian Affairs Branch, according to the review, "may be likened to that of a trust company managing valuable assets for a client. During the ten year period in review this section, through its management of reserve resources, has derived for the Indians over $30,000,000" (Canada 1958: 30).

But was the Resources Section actually managing valuable assets for a client, and who was that client? In chapter five, we examined how the affairs and lands of Indigenous peoples had been managed in prior periods—where proper management was synonymous with freeing up Indigenous lands for settlement activities. Furthermore, the proceeds that flowed into the trust accounts were dependent on government decisions regarding selling prices, administration fees and the rate of interest to be paid on trust funds. Thus, the term "trust account" belied the fact that trust account activities were used as instruments of government policy designed to accomplish settlement and economic objectives.

Has the trust account portion of the administration of Indigenous

Table 5
Band By-laws

In line with the policy of encouraging the Indians to take a greater interest and responsibility in the management of local affairs, assistance has been given band councils in drafting appropriate by-laws under Section 80 and 82 of the *Indian Act*. All band councils have authority under Section 80 to make by-laws dealing with such matters as regulation of traffic, control of livestock, zoning, conduct of businesses, and the preservation, protection and management of game, fish and fur on reserves, to cite a few examples. Existing municipal by-laws in various parts of Canada were obtained and used as a basis for drafting sample by-laws under Section 80, which are available to band councils as a guide when considering matters that might be dealt with by local legislation.

Only those bands which have been declared by the Governor-in-Council as having reached an advanced stage of development may make by-laws under Section 82 of the *Indian Act*. These by-laws have to do with raising of money, the appropriation and expenditure of moneys to defray band expenses, and the appointment of officials to conduct the business of the council and provide for their remuneration. To date 22 bands have been accorded this wider authority provided under Section 82.

An indication of the extent to which the Indians of Canada are assuming greater responsibility in the intelligent administration of their own affairs will be apparent from the following tables showing the number and types of by-laws passed by various band councils throughout the country since the new Act came into force.

No. of By-laws by Provinces	
British Columbia	121
Alberta	20
Saskatchewan	5
Manitoba	6
Southern Ontario	27
Northern Ontario	6
Quebec	19
Maritimes	4
Total	208

Types of By-laws	
Disorderly Conduct	27
Garbage Disposal	23
Traffic	21
Weed Control	19
Conduct of Hawkers	19
Water Supply	18
Licensing	19
Pounds	17
Sanitation	15
Fish and Game	10

Expenditures of Moneys	6
Fencing	4
Electric Power	3
Zoning	2
Other	5
Total	208
No. of Bands Passing By-Laws	
British Columbia	28
Alberta	14
Saskatchewan	3
Manitoba	4
Southern Ontario	10
Northern Ontario	5
Quebec	6
Maritimes	1
Total	71
No. of By-Laws by Years	
1951	nil
1952	9
1953	20
1954	49
1955	37
1956	35
1957	25
1958	33
Total	208

Source: Canada 1958: 9

affairs changed since the late 1800s? Unfortunately, the number and complexity of the transactions makes it impossible to provide a simple answer to this question. However, recent lawsuits filed against the federal government pertaining to their management of Indigenous land and resources suggest perhaps not. The Six Nations of Grand River is currently negotiating with the federal government over missing land and trust monies valued at over $30 billion (Barnsley 2000). After more than eleven years of preparation, in April 2000, the Samson and Ermineskin bands of Alberta initiated a $1.4 billion lawsuit against the federal government for the mismanagement of petroleum royalties over the preceding fifty years (Weir 2000). The lawyer for the Samson and Ermineskin bands comments that, "native trust account holders were always paid interest at the lowest possible rate ... allowing the government to benefit from the investment income generated by money which belonged to the band" (Barnsley 2000). And in the United States, a recent report by auditors Arthur Anderson found that the Bureau of Indian Affairs couldn't account for $2.4 billion, or one in seven dollars, that flowed through tribal trust accounts in the last twenty years (Brasher 1996).

The Hawthorn Report— Equality, Dignity and Social Engineering

It is a truism that Canadians tend to define themselves by comparison to the friendly giant living south of the border. In terms of Native policy, we are apt to focus on the American Indian massacres while congratulating ourselves on our kinder, gentler approach. But if we use the Hawthorn Report (Hawthorn and Canada 1966) as measurement, we might conclude that the Hollywood cliché, "the only good Indian is a dead Indian," could be translated north of the border as, "the only good Indian is a white Indian." The report, and the mindset it betrays, is a blueprint for rendering Native people indistinguishable from their non-Native counterparts. This blueprint indicates three key elements in constructing the economic viability of the Indigenous community: (1) the natural goodness of industrial urbanization and the destined demise of reserve life; (2) the quantification and numerical valuing of social ills and the economic cures for those ills; and (3) the social engineering necessary to move entire populations along their prescribed road to recovery (Hawthorn and Canada 1966: 5).

Ostensibly, the report was commissioned to address the skills that Aboriginals needed to manage their own affairs and resources (5). However both the construction of the problem and the analysis and recommendations are paternalistic in the extreme. The concern is not that the Native people live without equality or dignity, but that they lack the *knowledge* that "they live in equality and dignity." They want independence from special controls, the report implies, not from the dishonouring of treaty agreements and the institutional racism on which those controls are based. And those controls, somehow, represent "sponsorship and support" (5) rather than oppression. In spite of having no direct control over their own resources, attempts by the Indians to engage in economically viable endeavours are fine, but first they need "specialized assistance with the management of their resources" (5). Indeed, the need for such assistance is greater now than ever—perhaps, in reality because the demand for independence was louder and more organized than it had ever been before. But as we shall see, specialized assistance was to take the form of more bureaucracy.

It is bureaucracy which will fill the chasm that separated the government's rhetoric from its economic imperative of cultural dominance; its entry point was precisely where the Indigenous peoples' two conflicting needs came face to face: the need for legislative and economic protection from cultural dominance and the need for sovereignty. The bureaucratic incursion slipping in between those two needs came robed in the government's monetary mitigation of its historical undermining of Indigenous peoples' sustenance. The person "who lacks the shields and weapons of adequate schooling, rewarding employment, good health and fit housing; and the capital equipment, training and knowledge adequate for the enterprises he undertakes" will in today's world be rendered "completely helpless" (6). Thus, the Indian Department—the bureaucrats—came to the rescue. Indeed, more bureaucracy, more programs and hence more funding was the medicine prescribed for mitigating the damage already done. The promotion of bureaucracy as the solution is ironic given the roles played by bureaucracy in previous cultural genocides.

Economic Viability One: City Good, Reserve Bad

To understand the reasons for the economic ill health of the reserves, the commission "scrutinized a number of factors that economic theorists commonly associate with economic development," and came to the conclusion, among others, that

> such primary resource-based modes of livelihood as trapping, fishing, and farming exert a negative influence on Indian prosperity. This influence is contrasted to the great contribution to prosperity made by steady wage and salaried employment off the reserve. (Hawthorn and Canada 1966: 7).

The solution was just as obvious as the simplistically articulated problem: "vocational training and job placement services on a massive scale ... special assistance to those who choose to work off reserve ... and the creation of opportunities for industrial and other urban employment" (7).

The more Indians could be moved off the reserves and into urban centres, it seems, the better off they would be. In particular, "commercial farming, even in those reserves where relatively plentiful amounts of arable land are available" (7) should be *discouraged*. But "subsistence farming ... for households who do not wish to migrate to other areas, and who have no alternative opportunities for remunerative employment" (7) should be encouraged. The rationalization was strictly economic, transferring Third-World economic theory to the Canadian reserve. It was simply a question of efficiency. Unfortunately "there is no law or regulation ... which can force Indians to leave their reserve communities" (7). Some would choose to remain. The most that could be recommended was "to provide financial aid and other support for the large and increasing numbers who wish to do so [leave the reserves], where such measures are demonstrably the best means for improving their economic status and welfare generally" (7).

Economic Viability Two: Personal Disorganization and Kinship Handicaps

In examining welfare, the report stated that economic development "faces special difficulties because of widespread apathy, resignation and lack of motivation" brought about by "ready provisions of welfare grants" (31). The solution was "a new program of community development ... to help people to help themselves, to arouse and mobilize the latent and unused energies of people in various communities by inducing them, by one means or another, to undertake projects on their own that will contribute to their economic and social betterment" (31).

These programs of community development had to address the "personal disorganization" of Indigenous peoples. Personal disorganization was viewed as a symptom of poor economic development, with such examples as "drunkenness, sexual promiscuity, shiftlessness or laziness, irresponsibility, neglect of family and the like" (127). The report recognized that there was not necessarily a correlation between social disorganization and personal disorganization; however, in those bands that had lost their traditional means of livelihood and not "become engaged in new types of employment," poverty was the norm, and "social disorganization tends to be accompanied by personal disorganization" (127). Furthermore, this had a demoralizing effect which tended to be greater when the poor lived within or in close proximity to "a rapidly growing affluent society" (127).

From the "development" vantage point, activities outside of the utilitarian framework were of diminished value. Ceremonial events were seen as regressive, further isolating Indian bands from white society, rendering individuals "that much less able to participate effectively in a modern economy" (120). Alternatively, in the case of reducing ceremonial and useful objects into quaint handicrafts, ceremonies were seen as a sort of psychological antidote for their "apathy and defeatism" and might help them to "acquire the confidence to participate in the world around them and compete on a more equal basis" (120). But engaging in traditional Native activities also made "good tourist attractions, ranging from colourful pageants down to the sale of handicrafts [providing] a variable source of extra income" (121).

Traditional practices in the area of kinship obligations were, however, "generally held to be negative.... The mutual ties of rights and obligations act as deterrents to economic advancement in an industrial society" (121). The need of individuals in subsistence economies to take care of one another, especially in times of need, as well as being a fundamental organism in tribal cultures, was economically—in the strict capitalist sense of the word—simply unsound. The reserve system was seen as creating dependency and reinforcing "the more parasitic aspects of kin-

Table 6
Unwed Mothers

Band	Unwed Mothers as Percent of All Mothers
Skidegate	9.0
Caughnawaga	2.0
Walpole Is.	11.3
Sheshaht, V.I.	5.3
Lorette	nil
Squamish	10.1
Tyendinaga	5.0
Six Nations	9.1
Curve Lake	12.2
Mistassini	1.1
Masset	24.4
Dog Rib Rae	14.3
Port Simpson	16.1
Kamloops	22.8
Sarcee	13.2
Fort William	13.6
Williams Lake	27.5
Moose Factory	10.3
Fort Alexander	n/a
River Desert	10.7
St. Mary's	11.4
Attawapiskat	11.0
Pointe Bleue	1.2
Tobique	9.5
Pikangikum	4.6
Shubenacadie	15.7
Oak River	5.7
Rupert House	7.2
Cold Lake	8.3
Fort St. John	35.5
Deer Lake	2.3
The Pas	8.4
James Smith	7.8
Peguis	12.5
Big Cove	6.4
Piapot	9.5

Source: Hawthorne and Canada 1966: 129

ship." Change in the welfare and relief systems was needed to "free the individual and the immediate family from the burdens of supporting other kin, and thus encourage their independence and ambition to better themselves" (121).

Economic Viability Three: Social Engineering—A Massive Undertaking

In order to bring reserve life up to "White norms" (Hawthorne and Canada 1966: 14) more gathering of information to Ottawa will be needed, according to the report's recommendations:

> A working blueprint for a viable economic development program for Indians will require a more detailed cross-country survey to provide an inventory in terms of job aptitudes and capabilities, potential income-yielding resources, job opportunities locally available, and numbers in each community requiring special training and migration to other areas. Such a survey would be carried out jointly by the Indian Affairs Branch and the new Department of Manpower, with the aid of various experts in industry and resources. (14)

Like the recommendations of a series of reports more than a century earlier (see chapters three and four), the solution was more and better information about Indigenous peoples—in other words, more bureaucracy, more state(istics), more programs and more social engineering.

The commissioners see economic development as a process that moves through various stages, stages that can be applied to groups and individuals alike. This is an important factor of the report, demonstrating the manner in which statistical measurement translates integers into group behaviour and then substitutes the individual for the group. In this case—attempting to correlate personal disorganization with poor economic performance—the statistical quantification of such things as dependency and ambition could only be implied in the interpretation of numbers measuring group activity and its relationship to economic development. Thus, economic development "tends to be closely related with the degree of industrialization and urbanization in *work behaviour*, and way of life generally of individuals and groups" (140, emphasis added). Urbanization and industrialization, then, could be measured by the "characteristics of the job requirement" and the "degree of mechanization and size of capital investment per worker ... [and] rules and sanctions governing hours of work, punctuality, tardiness or absenteeism, pace of work ... and the like" (140). However, it is clear that the more important determination of industrialization and urbanization was "the degree of break from the reserve culture, and the attitudes, values and behaviour patterns that it tends to generate" (140).

The individual Native person, then, moving from subsistence existence on ancestral land to an urbanized industrial existence, follows the path of economic development "as a progression ... through a series of different types of industries and occupations." The progression, according to the report, was from subsistence activities to casual labour and, finally, to regular employment in "relatively high-wage, urban-located industries, particularly in small and medium-sized industrial towns" (140–41). Tirelessly, the report continued to drive the message home that "any substantial improvement" would come about only as a result of moving the Natives off the reserves, into "better-paid wage and salaried employment in other industries" (141). Marshalling the growing population of Indigenous peoples along their route of industrialization towards prosperity would require plenty of funding and even more bureaucracy. It would, the report confessed, "cost thousands of dollars per capita, and hundreds of millions per annum in the aggregate" (141).

Level upon level of bureaucracy heaped upon the Indian Affairs branch, all for the training and eventual well-being of the Indigenous people, might be read as a job-creation extravaganza—but we cannot help but notice that all the jobs would go to non-Natives, who were to be put in place for facilitating the movement of relatively large numbers, as rapidly as possible, through a series of industries and occupations having widely different job characteristics and requirements, with regard to such matters as skill, seasonality, punctuality, degree of mechanization, authority and supervision (Hawthorn and Canada 1966: 184). But the social engineering didn't stop there; in order that Indians might "live a style of life acceptable to their White neighbours in town," home economists were to be hired to offer counselling "in such matters as household management, clothing, food and sanitation" (185).

Juxtaposing the Hawthorn Report with prior reports and initiatives, it is clear that no matter how much things change, they remain the same. The Hawthorn Report echoes—both in terms of the paternalistic starting point and the selection of social engineering as the solution—a 1936 government report that examined the path to "self-sufficiency" for Maritime Aboriginals (Paul 2000: 269–73). Like the period prior to Confederation (chapter four), the collection of additional accounting numbers is viewed as the starting point for more targeted government interventions. Similarly in the post-Confederation period (chapter five), the coercive carrot of increased funding and increased autonomy is held out in return for the adoption of westernized modes of governance and behaviour. In the D.C. Scott era (chapter six), (vocational) education is viewed as the way to encourage assimilation and to erase "Indian-ness." And finally, all of the recommendations start from the presumption that social-engineering is not only necessary and acceptable but can be accomplished via the enlistment of a variety of professionalized expertises, managed by an all-pervasive bureaucracy. Of course, this numerization of Indigenous peoples within bureaucratic processes encouraged and facilitated the cultural genocides of the early twentieth century.

The White Paper: Perception is Everything

Only three years after the massive Hawthorn Report recommended extraordinary bureaucratic mobilization and heavy budget demands, the slow awakening of the public's awareness of the inequities between Native and non-Native, especially since World War II, had reached full flowering in the liberal ideas of Prime Minister Pierre Trudeau's "just society." The political mood seemed right for the devolution of administrative control over Indigenous peoples. In reaction, it seems, to the hefty and comprehensive Hawthorn Report, the White Paper, the Trudeau government's policy paper for Indian Affairs (Canada 1969), was short, concise and almost facile in its declaration of liberating the Native population from the bindings of the *Indian Act*—and, incidentally, from any protection of their Native rights. Minister Jean Chretien's paper took into account the essence of the Hawthorn Report—the unacceptable status quo of Native living conditions and the counterproductive funding arrangements between them and the government—but cut out the bureaucratic management of the transition from subsistence to industrialization—and attempted to declare the *Indian Act* no longer relevant. But—as Indigenous response to the White Paper clearly demonstrated—the government's comprehension of what Natives "really wanted" was far removed from the Natives' historical perception of Indigenous-government relations. This question of perception, of each culture's obligations towards the other, of the foundational concepts of land, treaties and sovereignty, and even of the meaning of history itself, was brought to light like never before in the bold and idealistic White Paper proposal of complete and radical devolution of Indian Affairs.

The policy paper followed the rhetoric of previous studies, recognizing, theoretically, that only with a policy based on equality would the Indians realize their needs and aspirations. As in previous papers, the government begins with the assumption of cultural and democratic equality, acknowledging the right of Indians as *Canadian citizens* to full participation in society—economically and socially: "To argue against this right is to argue for discrimination, isolation, and separation" (Canada 1969: 8).

But from the Indigenous perspective, the crux of the matter precedes the questions of equality and discrimination regarding individuals as Canadian citizens. The more salient matter is rather a nation-to-nation issue, and all the other problems stem from the government's refusal,

Table 7
Durable Consumer Goods: Percentage of Households in Thirty-five Sample Bands with Basic Home Facilities and Automobiles

Band	Per Capita Income	Indoor Toilets % h.h.	Baths % h.h.	Tele-phone % h.h.	Auto-mobiles % h.h.	Elec-tricity % h.h.
Skidegate	$1252	74	83	55.5	54	100
Caughnawaga	793	33	33	33	88.5	92
Walpole Is.	715	13	13	43	33	56
Sheshaht, V.I.	664	80	80	45	25	86
Lorette	630	100	100	100	17.5	100
Squamish	630	75	99	21	36	100
Tyendinaga	516	2	2	35	81	73.5
Curve Lake	350	11.2	2	18	66	95
Six Nations	350	4.5	4.5	31	68.5	72
Mistassini	341	2.5	2.5	2.5	7.3	2.5*
Dog Rib Rae	332	0	0	0	0	0
Port Simpson	325	21	88	0	1	87
Kamloops	314	3	3	11	25.5	100
Sarcee	302	6	6	23	48	0
Fort William	298	2	2	11	42.5	82
Williams Lake	291	3.3	3.3	10	8	100
Moose Factory	284	1.6	1.6	45	33	4
River Desert	250	7	5	35	30	41
Attawapiskat	247	0	0	32	14	0
St. Mary's	249	n/a	n/a	n/a	10	0
Pointe Bleue	222	20	12.7	51	22.5	70
Tobique	215	33	28	10	34.6	98
Fond du Lac	200	0	0	0	0	0
Pikangikum	197	0	0	0	12.3	0
Shubenacadie	180	6	4	10	30.1	0
Oak River	176	0	0	2	72.1	33
Rupert House	174	0	0	0	0	1.2
Cold Lake	165	1.7	1.7	1.7	13	1.7**
Fort St. John	161	0	0	0	0	0
Deer Lake	156	0	0	0	7	0
The Pas	140	0	0	8	9	7
James Smith	126	0	0	2	14	2
Peguis	99	1	1	0	12.5	40
Big Cove	61	4	4	4	38.6	40
Piapot	55	0	0	0	46	2
Coefficient of Correlation with Per capita Income		.72	.67	.64	.40	.55

* 1 household out of 41 **2 households

Source: Hawthorne and Canada 1966: 81

from the very beginning, to honour its promises and deliver on its treaty obligations. To begin from the liberal assumption of equality of individuals as defined by a European democratic convention, as the White Paper does, is to turn back the clock and ignore history; it is a mere continuation of the paternalistic attitudes that divest Indigenous peoples of their right to bargain on a nation-to-nation basis. This bargaining position is often viewed by non-Natives as "demanding special treatment." In recommending the abolition of the Indian Department, the Minister may also have been trying to do away with the whole question of special considerations for Indigenous peoples and in the process avoid facing the issue of treaty obligations.

Government-Indigenous relations had from the beginning of the treaty-making era been based on the unique legislative authority of government over the sovereignty of First Nations. The government's 1969 message of devolution was a mixed one. The White Paper says that the system of "exclusive legislative authority ... in relation to Indians, and lands reserved for the Indians under Head 24 of Section 90 of the *British North America Act*" had given birth to, over the years, "a network of administrative offices spread across the country" and admits that this "special legislation, a special land system and separate administration for the Indian Peoples ... has carried with it serious human and physical as well as administrative disabilities" (Canada 1969: 7). On the one hand, the special treatment is discriminatory and constitutes "a policy of treating Indian people as a race apart"; on the other hand, this special consideration has "saved for the Indian people places they can call home." There is a sense that the well-intentioned largesse of the government has simply gone wrong over the years and now, by washing its hands of its self-imposed guardianship role, the problems will get fixed. But nowhere is the question asked: How much to we *owe* these people for the millions of acres we now occupy and call Canada?

This is not to say that questions of land and treaty rights were ignored. "Many of the Indian people," it was admitted in the White Paper, "believe that lands have been taken from them in an improper manner, or without adequate compensation, that their funds have been improperly administered, that their treaty rights have been breached" (11). However treaties have been "widely misunderstood" (11). Whether the allegations that treaties have not been honoured is true or not, "the fact is the treaties affect only half the Indians of Canada" (11). Furthermore:

> The significance of the treaties in meeting the economic, educational, health and welfare needs of the Indian people has always been limited and will continue to decline. The services that have been provided go far beyond what could have been foreseen by those who signed the treaties. (11)

And besides, "many of the provisions and practices of another century may [now] be considered irrelevant" (11).

Thus, the problem from the perspective of the White Paper is not an equity matter or one of honouring agreements; admitting discrimination and abject poverty, it nonetheless persists in seeing the injustices as resulting from out-dated legislation and a bureaucracy which has served its purpose. The solution, then, is to rewrite the laws that constitute "the bases of discrimination"; while this may take some time, in the short term, "Repeal of the *Indian Act* and enactment of transitional legislation to ensure the orderly management of Indian land would do much to mitigate the problem" (8).

It was in its proposed transfer of control of lands that the White Paper took its boldest step. The government recognized that, though under the existing system, control of Indian lands is vested exclusively in the hands of the government, "full and true equality calls for Indian control and ownership of reserve land" (12). Handing over control of their own land to the Indians is rationalized economically; Crown ownership inhibits development. The process of devolution will take some time.

> In our society [ownership of land] carries with it the obligation to pay for certain services.... When the Indian people see that the only way they can own and fully control land is to accept taxation the way other Canadians do, they will make that decision. (12)

The offer the White Paper seems to be making is this: enter into a new legislative relationship with the provinces, who have no historical obligations towards Indigenous nations; pay taxes for the privilege of accepting control over the land that already belongs to you; and forego any hope of restitution for past wrongs or the protection of the *Indian Act* in pursuing your Native rights as set out in a succession of historical events and documents but rarely honoured. This new offer of autonomy and freedom, when looked at closely, resembles the enfranchisement of old. And the Native population turned it down resolutely.

The Evolution of Funding—Freedom or New Era Assimilation?

The rhetorical purpose of all studies, commissions and *Indian Act* amendments since shortly after World War II had been to enable the decision-making powers of the Indigenous peoples to increase, while devolving and decentralizing Ottawa's role. Until the late 1950s, Ottawa delivered programs and services directly, with a bureaucratic hands-on approach to follow-up and administration. In the late 1960s, First Nations began to administer their own government programs, and by the late 1980s, funding arrangements were ostensibly designed to give First Nations more autonomy. In the 1990s, the Department of Indian and Northern Development (DIAND) saw itself as basically a funding agency. "Accountability has changed," a 1993 DIAND report states, "reflecting the evolution in the government-to-government relationship with First Nations. The intent now is to share accountability" (DIAND 1993: i). Government-to-government, from the federal government's perspective, meant taking into account "the capacity of the government receiving the transfers [i.e., First Nations] to raise revenues" (ii).

The report acknowledges that the mix of conditional and unconditional funding affects dependency but suggests that conditional funding "is not inconsistent with government-to-government relations" (31). We know that the conditions are being set by the *funding agency*, though it now calls funds "transfers," and according to information gathered—statistics, accounting data—all tools of our familiar action-at-a-distance. Though the language has changed, is the story still the same? How much real difference is there between this new relationship and the old one?

To determine "the appropriate mix of conditional and unconditional funding" (DIAND 1993: 7), where the money comes from, and under whose auspices, must be taken into account. Consistent with prior periods, Parliament appears to rely on the same old tools to make these determinations—"resourcing formulas, which use much of the information collected from First Nations to justify resources from parliament" (7)—and "prioritization, whereby the department implements the priorities of cabinet" (7). These are political determinations then, set by a cabinet that does not and cannot—if indeed this is *government-to-government*—represent First Nations priorities. Decisions must be made, for example, "as to which communities ... receive funding to undertake large capital projects such as water and sewer, schools, roads, or other needs" (7).

"Consultation," naturally, is a key word in these reformulations. Since it still has the last word, the Government of Canada would appear to be high-handed if it proceeded to exercise its authority without consultation. Over forty years after the first so-called consultation with Native leaders in 1951, the department is still using that as its rhetorical example, a demonstration of its consultative approach (DIAND 1993: 41)—when in fact, as pointed out previously, the legislation was already before the House prior to any salient discussions having taken place, and it was rushed through to final reading without any substantive Indigenous input.

Though there were significant milestones in devolution during the seventies, especially the introduction of the Indian Local Government program in 1974 and the introduction of block funding for social and economic development, housing and education in 1975 (DIAND 1993: 43), the Penner Report (Canada and Penner 1983) was still able to report inadequate band input in budgetary decisions and that, as defined by the *Indian Act*, band councils had only limited powers. The report called for "a distinct order of government" for First Nations, rejecting "the department's notion of municipal governments" (quoted in DIAND 1993: 43).

Thus, the road to autonomy is surely a narrow and well-patrolled one. "Accounting," serving the function of policing, or guardianship, takes on all of its connotative meanings in this paradoxical government mission to *allow* as much Indigenous decision-making power as possible without losing its grip on the legislative and treasury board reins. The government put it succinctly in its Main Estimates 1992–93, stating that the objectives of the Inuit and Indian Affairs Program are:

> To support Indians and Inuit in achieving their self-government, economic, industrial, cultural, social, and community development needs and aspirations; to settle accepted Native claims through negotiations; and to ensure Canada's constitutional and statutory obligations and responsibilities to the Indian and Inuit peoples are fulfilled. (DIAND 1993: 44)

From the mid-eighties onward, this narrow passage would be negotiated with the help of bureaucratic inventions—subdivisions—of funding allocations, with various types of formulas for reporting and being held accountable. For example:

> Contribution Arrangements: arrangements used to fund specific programs or complex projects.... Contributions involve significant terms and conditions which stipulate matter such as what service is to be provided, to whom it is to be provided, and what expenses are eligible. (DIAND 1993: 12–13)

> Comprehensive Funding Arrangements: are the basic funding mechanism used with First Nations.... Program terms and conditions require recipients to administer programs in accordance with DIAND's policy and procedures manual. (12)

> Alternative Funding Arrangements: is an optional funding mechanism which increases the discretion of a First Nation beyond that available through a comprehensive funding arrangement. *Prior to entering into an afa, a First Nation must successfully complete an afa entry assessment, which is a joint review of the First Nation's accountability and management system.* (12, emphasis added)

> Self-Government Funding Arrangements: are negotiated under self-government legislation. They define a funding base for a set

> of programs or services, the standards which may apply, a process for adjusting the base, any requirements for reporting or evaluation, and a process for the periodic renegotiation of the agreement. (12)

DIAND notes that the degree of First Nations' control increases as we move from contribution arrangements toward self-government funding relations.

The DIAND report tells us that since 1983 "funds administered by First Nations have increased from 41 percent to 77 percent" of program funding (44). But the question must be asked, whether the administration of funds—insofar as the principles, formulas and specific practices of that administration are imposed—actually constitutes sovereignty over those funds? As of 1992, over 85 percent of funding was still administered via contribution arrangements and comprehensive funding arrangements, whereas only one percent was administered under self-government arrangements (13). Which prompts a second question: Concerning Native rights to pursue traditional practices, how do the mechanisms of accounting and reporting—the essential bureaucratic core of non-Native administration—affect the types of "self-government" decisions being made? DIAND speaks of the *delivery* of programs and services by Native leaders to their own people. But do these programs and services carry within them certain mechanisms endemic to the dominant bureaucratic culture, such as the need to have westernized systems of management and accountability in place? Is it possible that the so-called devolution of government control over Indigenous decision-making may actually be an evolution of Indigenous bureaucracy, accompanied by soft technologies similar to those used by the government? If so, might this not be considered assimilation, and couldn't we say that the government is still playing the same old game under a new name? Perhaps the slow, relentless historical assimilation of Native culture is taking a different form than was earlier feared. Cultural awareness among Indigenous individuals and groups is certainly high, and the Assembly of First Nations, which may or may not speak with a unified voice for grassroots First Nations people, has gained in political ascendancy. But when we examine the language of departmental studies and reports, we see that "government-to-government" does not necessarily equate with nation-to-nation.

The transitional phase, from the fifties to the nineties, between direct delivery and grant funding has had accountability and delivery systems as its central tenets. That language is very much alive today and prompts us to wonder whether the real transition might have occurred not as a response to the need of First Nations for sovereignty, nor as restitution for dishonoured treaty agreements, but as a transfer of bureaucracy from the Canadian government to the Indigenous "governments," i.e., government defined not by a continuity of tradition and leadership but through the (still) imperialistic power's definitions of what constitutes a responsible government. Thus, when the DIAND report quotes the Penner Report's recommendation that "federal payments ... be in the form of direct grants ... to First Nation governments recognized by the federal government as being accountable to their people" (10), the report also finds it necessary to "make explicit a point implicit in its advocacy of this arrangement" (10): only when the Indigenous government has been recognized as having "an adequate system of accountability in place" (10) would that government be entitled to the grant.

Chapter Eight

Ecocide and Changing Accountability Relations

Ecology, Ecocide and Sovereignty

Over the centuries and until relatively recently, the St. Lawrence River watershed provided bounty, meaning and sustenance to its Indigenous inhabitants, especially the Akwesasne Mohawks of the Haudenosaunee Confederacy, often referred to as Iroquois. The St. Lawrence was also the river from which the Europeans launched their trading routes. The fur trade initially fed a market driven almost entirely by fashion-conscious gentlemen on the streets of European capitals, demanding the weather-resistant and elegant beaver hats made from the pelts of *Castor Canadensis*. The fur trade eventually gave way to agriculture, lumber and mineral extraction and, over the last century in particular, to industrial development, which in turn brought a rising tide of chlorine, mercury, styrenes, polychlorinated biphenyls (PCBs) and fluorides. By the 1980s, these toxins had forced the Mohawk community to issue a fishing advisory, limiting fish consumption in the community and warning women of childbearing age and children under the age of fifteen to eat no fish from the St. Lawrence River. Backyard gardens were abandoned as residents in the Racquette Point area (the closest to the contamination) feared the airborne contamination of their vegetables.

More recently, the confluence of the Grasse and St. Lawrence rivers—the quaintly named "Contaminant Cove"—has been documented to contain sludge with 3,000 parts per million PCBs, which are known to cause brain nerve damage, liver and skin disorders, cancer and reproductive disorders.

While the Akwesasne were living in a toxic wasteland, under the shadow of the Alcoa and Reynolds aluminium plants and a General Motors foundry with a reputation as one of the most significant PCB dump sites in North America, their neighbours, the Ojibwa of Western Ontario, had been forced off their territories by the incursion of industrial interests. In the 1950s, camouflaged as an attempt to "modernize" the Ojibwa, the government removed them from their land so that Ontario Hydro could be developed. In their efforts at coping with this major blow, the

Ojibwa became more dependent on fish. The Wabigoon River, the major source of their fish diet, had since 1962 been used as a dumping ground by Reed Paper's chlor-alkili plant at Dryden, Ontario. The mercury used to bleach paper products, released into the fish-bearing river, in turn mixed with other pollutants to form methyl mercury. Between 1962 and 1970, an estimated twenty pounds of mercury were released into the river per day (Harding 1976; LaDuke 1998: 327). By the early seventies, the Natives living off the river began to show signs of mercury poisoning.

Meanwhile, as the twentieth century was drawing to a close, a Supreme Court decision in British Columbia shattered the lens of European colonization through which colonial history had, until then, been viewed. The *Delgamuukw* decision of December 11, 1997, which overturned an earlier court decision that Aboriginal title did not exist in law, while being ostensibly about land claims, was at a much deeper level about the very making of history itself—how language and stories *make* history—and as we demonstrate, about the indivisibility of ecology and culture.[1] *Delgamuukw,* in terms of land claims, might be seen as a rather narrow decision; while the court overturned the decision of the lower court that had denied the Gitxsan and Wet'suwet'en claim to Aboriginal title, it was unable to decide the case on its merits because of procedural errors in the plaintiff's pleadings. In broad terms, Justice Antonio Lamer, referring to section 43 of the decision, also cites examples of acceptable forms of infringement on Aboriginal title, such as "the development of agriculture, forestry, mining, and hydro-electric power (Perskey 1998: 20). The decision, however, makes a shift in the legal perception of Indigenous oral history and Native claims; it is this shift that is most relevant to our analysis. At first glance, the poisoning of traditional territories rationalized through economic mechanisms and government bureaucracies may seem a fair distance from the courtroom dramas—spanning several generations—which constitute the story of the *Delgamuukw* Supreme Court decision. And yet, if any reconciliation between Natives and non-Natives is possible, the hope may lie in new light shed by *Delgamuukw* on these relations—precisely because it is the lens of ecology that makes so clear how utterly dependent on nature's bounty—also known as resources—we all are and how this issue is critical to the survival of us all. The perpetrators of ecocide, we argue, undermine their own sustainability as much as that of the most obvious victims of this practice, those whose ancestral territories have become toxic dumping grounds. Although the *Delgamuukw* decision was not on the surface a case pertaining to ecology and ecocide, in examining the roots of the decision and the basic stand taken by the appellants, it becomes clear how the Supreme Court's acknowledgment of Indigenous history is, in fact, deeply ecological.

Before looking at *Delgamuukw,* we briefly examine the role of ecology in new-style colonialism. An examination of case studies of industrial pollution on traditional Indigenous territories, as well as the role played by accounting, takes us to a more detailed examination of the *Delgamuukw* decision and how it might shed light on the (dis)continuance of ecocide.

Ecology and New-Style Colonialism

Arne Næss, a pioneer in the philosophy of ecology, suggests that ecology is "the interdisciplinary scientific study of the living conditions of organisms in interaction with each other and with the surroundings, organic as well as inorganic" (Næss and Rothenberg 1989: 36). Ecology, Næss tells us, "is concerned first of all with relationships between entities as an essential component of what these entities are in themselves. These include both internal and external relations" (36). Næss points out that because of this dual relationship, ecology has applications in a variety of fields "outside its original biological domain" (36). This question of relationships/trangressions is salient to ecocide and new-style colonialism, since the latter employs new methods of incursion.

In earlier chapters we compared factors in the Holocaust to its predecessor, the cultural genocide of early Indigenous peoples. There we saw that the *U.N. Convention on the Prevention and Punishment of the Crime of Genocide* included a number of acts as part of the intent "to destroy, in whole or in part" a national, racial or religious group. These acts include, among others, "causing serious bodily harm to members of the group" and "imposing measures intended to prevent births within the group" (quoted in Andreopoulos 1994: 1). In chapter one we also examined Charny's typology of genocide, especially what he called "longer-term practices that ultimately have the same effect" (1994: 76–77), naming ecocide and cultural genocide as examples. Ecocide, we concluded, takes place as a result of criminal destruction or abuse of the environment or negligent failure to protect against known ecological and environmental hazards.

Robert Davis and Mark Zannis (1973: 19), using the development of the North as a prime example, demonstrate that "Genocide may be effected by means other than mass homicide." They point out that the United Nations secretariat's draft convention (United Nations Document A/362) of 1946 "is a powerful case for the recognition of biological and cultural methods of committing genocide as *bona fide* examples of genocide ... and not merely lesser crimes" (19, emphasis in original). While cultural genocide has gone hand in hand with the classical colonialism of old, a new style of colonialism has emerged with ecocide as one of its consequences.

Along with the *Indian Act*, Canadian colonialism, still maintained today through government bureaucracy, has rendered Native reserves vulnerable to industrial pollutants and weakened Natives' ability to protect themselves. While the ecocidal results befalling Indigenous communities were not designed specifically for introducing toxins into the bodies and bloodstreams of Natives, ecologically speaking the pollutants do not cease their interactivity at the borders of the reserves. Racist attitudes inherited from the old-style colonialism appear to have facilitated the government processes which allow industrial development to blossom alongside, and in some cases within, the boundaries of Native land.

At the turn of our new century, however, the exploitation imperative of the elites is meeting head on with the increased education and activism of Indigenous populations, as well as a burgeoning in both Native and non-Native ecological discourses. In reaction, the rhetoric of exploitation is forced to become more sensitive to the voices of opposition. This more subtle incursion is typical of new-style colonialism, under cover of which ecocidal government policies and corporate hegemony take place. The direct territorial conquests of old have shifted over time to indirect "land use" appropriation by multinational corporations (Davis and Zannis 1973: 37–38). "Development" and "progress" become the key words in new-style colonialism, and "few of the old national territorial colonial structures can stand up to the economic pressures of the multinational giants" (37). Where old-style colonialism simply settled territorial land, dispersing and containing targeted populations, new-style colonialism targets the natural resources contained within the land base of Native traditional territories. The struggle over territory becomes a struggle over the very substance and (ab)use of the land itself and the lives upon whose survival its inhabitants depend.

In chapter two, we defined accounting as the system of numerical techniques, financial mechanisms and accountability relations that mediate relations between individuals, groups and institutions. Under new-style colonialism, where the objective is resource extraction from Indigenous land, the emphasis is on financial incentives and changed accountability mechanisms. Here the governments' roles are: one, to provide financial incentives to corporations to appropriate wealth, while buffering them from absorbing the economic costs of their activities; and two, to downgrade accountability mechanisms for corporations, particularly regarding the environmental impact of their actions. As chapter five indicated, the use of financial incentives to encourage the extraction of natural resources from Indigenous lands has always been a government concern. However under new-style colonialism, it has become even more important.

Shifting Accountability—Consequences and Continuance

The shift to new-style colonialism could not have happened without accounting-bureaucratic mechanisms, most evident in changing accountability relations—environmental deregulation, increased subsidies for resource extraction companies and the minimization of accountability processes—that have a negative impact on the natural environments of Indigenous territories.

In 1974, for example, British Columbia relaxed its pollution standards to encourage the multinational mining corporation, AMAX, to develop a mine in the Alice Arm area, which hosted a significant Indigenous population. In order to permit the company to "discharge up to 400,000 milligrams per litre of suspended solids into the waters of Alice Arm" (Weyler 1992: 291), an increase 8,000 times the normal limit of 50 milligrams, the cabinet amended the *Fisheries Act* to clear the way for AMAX. Thus are costs externalized, the burden carried by Indigenous peoples who depend on fish and wildlife for their subsistence lifestyle. As we see in our case studies below, this same scenario was played out in the case of James Bay Hydro Quebec—with dire environmental consequences.

As we track these shifts in accountability we begin to see how the distance in "action-at-a-distance" is substantially closing, so that it now looks like "action-by-stealth"—through the proxy use of corporations by government in disenfranchising First Nations—or, as it increasingly appears, the proxy use of governments by corporations. In old-style colonialism, populations had been reduced to integers so they could more easily be moved around. In the new style, there is no longer anywhere to move them. Since, ironically, they have been displaced to what is now perceived as resource-rich territories in an increasingly resource-poor world, colonization—of the economic variety—becomes part and parcel of government-corporate partnerships as they move into Indigenous territories under the camouflage of economic development.

Resource extraction is linked with social development through numbers; the success of the exploitation of land and its resources is measured numerically in the same terms which determine standard of living. This is pure accounting, linking socialization with the bookkeeper's ledger. Variations on the same theme are used to link economic development with nationalism. Economic summits are held by the elite nations whose wealth is narrowly defined in economic terms. When politicians boast of representing the world's greatest nations, they mean the world's richest nations—and the pursuit of such riches has always meant a visible downgrading of Indigenous people to secondary citizens. This rhetoric has no doubt paved the way for new-style colonialism, in which the free-trade rights of transnational corporations take precedence over human and Aboriginal rights and ecological sustainability.

In the cases that follow, we illustrate three variations of new-style colonialism: 1) modern-day nation building, inextricably bound up with resource extraction and under heavy globalization pressures; 2) industrialization, which in the new global economy can be seen as migrating across national borders, from used Native territories to newly discovered resource-rich territories; and 3) resource extraction, with its false promises of job creation and blatant exporting of raw material, impoverishing local economies by undermining all potential for value-added enterprises. The cases show how these objectives were facilitated via the use of financial incentives, along with changed accountability relations, and how these changes have left local communities with the burden of long-term social and environmental effects.

Nation-building—From the Ground Up, to the Multinational Beyond

In old-style colonialism, governments undertook activities designed to support national interests, with economic development underpinning that nationalism. The benefits, history tells us, went largely to settler societies and the costs mostly to Indigenous peoples. To preserve the impression to the taxpayer that the government is at least calling some of the shots, governments are fond of embarking on mega-project partnerships with industry, which are rationalized as boosting development and stimulating the economy, all in the name of national interest. Often these projects are developed on or adjacent to Indigenous land, and they are usually framed in a manner that sets up a pair of false dichotomies: (1) resource extraction or harnessing water power for electricity are the only modes of attaining economic benefits and that these economic benefits serve the national interest; while locally controlled, more traditional land uses with long-term sustainability do not bring in large revenues and do not serve the national interest, and (2) industry, by embarking on these government-industry mega-project partnerships, is somehow doing the public a favour (though in fact government subsidies, tax breaks and low fees normally underwrite the developments), while similar partnerships between government and Native communities are hand-outs from the taxpayer to the needy Indian.

One of the earliest examples was in Akwesasne—"the land where the partridge drums." Being historically critical, in central Canada, and situated along the country's major waterway, Akwesasne serves as a good example of nation-building on the backs of the first peoples. Industrial inroads into the territory made by timber, railroad and mining industries intensified in the modern era with the construction of the St. Lawrence Seaway by the American and Canadian governments in the 1950s. Construction of the Cornwall-Massena International Bridge and the St. Lawrence Power Project soon followed (Goodman-Draper 1994). The network of locks and dams provided international shipping routes to the great lakes—soon to become the pollution centre of Canada—and the creation of cheap power attracted industry from North America and abroad (Schell and Tarbell 1998). The ensuing rapid industrialization further escalated encroachment on Akwesasne territory.

Hydroelectric projects, by their mere presence and size and their central position in a vast grid that supplies power to the most far-flung communities, are easy showpieces for industry-government nation-building collaborations. In 1971, Quebec Premier Robert Bourassa announced plans for the largest hydroelectric project in the world—the La Grande project. His government and the power utility Hydro-Quebec "committed to harnessing 28,000 megawatts of hydroelectric capacity from northern rivers whose total catchment area covers almost 400,000 square kilometres" (Weyler 1992: 292). Like many of these projects, financial numbers were used to both demonstrate the expected economic benefits from development and to downplay the financial costs. However, like most of these estimates, while the project was to cost $6 billion over twelve years, by the mid-80s, it was already $22 billion in debt, with a new estimated cost of $50 billion (Weyler 1992: 292).

"The James Bay I project was intended to produce 10,000 megawatts of electricity by putting eleven and one-half square kilometres of land under water" (LaDuke 1998: 328). According to LaDuke, the project, "concentrated along the East Main and Rupert Rivers, had ruined the ecology of some 176,000 square kilometres, an area about two-thirds the size of West Germany" (328). The development was to affect the environment of about 12,000 Cree and 6,000 Inuit who were living in Opinaca, Kanaaupscow and other river valleys in Quebec and Labrador (Weyler 1992: 292), as well as a small population of about 450 Naskapi (Barker and Soyez 1994). Additionally, ten thousand migrating caribou, as important to the Inuit as buffalo had been to the Plains Cree, were trapped and killed in the new river course" (Weyler 1992: 292).

By the early nineties, mercury levels found in local inhabitants rose dramatically. Depending on the distance and proximity of the community to the modified fishing area, some individuals downstream from the reservoirs were found to have mercury contamination in their bodies as high as thirty times the allowable level (Roebuck 1999). Two thirds of the population were found to have contamination to some degree; six times the safe level was commonly found. A 1984 study showed that 64 percent of the Cree down-river from La Grande dams had been contaminated with mercury at levels known to cause birth defects, retardation, still births and convulsions. Hydro-Quebec's response was to suggest to the Cree "that medication and limits on fish consumption would solve the problem," but fish is a very important part of the Cree's diet, and it was difficult to change, especially for the elders (quoted in Weyler 1992: 292–93).

Within such nation-building exercises, accounting is important. Selective financial numbers are used to justify the expected financial benefits and to demonstrate that these benefits exceed the costs. Techniques such as net present value and rate of return calculations—which attempt to quantify the value of monetary benefits—are the favoured devices of government bureaucrats (Miller and Rose 1990). Not surprisingly, the calculations almost always suffer from the eternal optimism of financial planning in that cost overruns are the norm. Furthermore, the numbers are always partial in that there is little attempt to quantify in monetary terms the social and environmental costs of the project. It is easier to ignore these costs, because they are not included in the "bottom-line" number. While clearly there are problems associated with quantifying these consequences, their absence implies that they do not count.

Industrialization: Akwesasne—Health and Development Trade-offs

The rhetoric that precedes industrial activity on or near Aboriginal land often uses reassuring green language that signals the potential for weakened accountability relations between government and industry. The pragmatists speak of a trade-off between jobs and environmental risks. The government assures the people that standards will be put in place. When these standards turn out to be vague or inadequate, environmental critics are branded anti-progress or special-interest. Indigenous populations, because their economies are so often fragile, are particularly vulnerable to promises of jobs and economic stimulation. When ecological problems develop, the slowness of the bureaucracy in responding and the often outright refusal of government to enforce accountability benefit the polluters and take their toll on the health of the local population.

Through the latter half of the twentieth century, the General Motors Foundry, located on its 258-acre property adjacent to the Akwesasne Reserve, bordered on the north by the St. Lawrence River and the south by the Raquette River, was emptying PCBs into five lagoons and a number of sludge pits. The foundry is an aluminium casting plant that has been in operation since 1959 for the purpose of die-casting aluminium automotive parts. From 1959 until 1974, the facility used fire-resistant PCB-based hydraulic fluids in the die-casting machines. Leakage of the hydraulic fluid into the facility's wastewater treatment system produced PCB-contaminated sludge that was disposed of at several sites near the plant. These PCBs and other toxic wastes have contaminated the St. Lawrence River, the Raquette River and Turtle Creek. The Reynolds Aluminium Plant is located one mile north of the Akwesasne Mohawk Nation. This plant, which started operations in 1959, has been listed as a New York State Superfund site for improper disposal of hazardous wastes on the plant's property. Contaminants from the plant have impacted the St. Lawrence and the Raquette rivers. The Alcoa Aluminium Plant is located in Massena, New York, on the Grasse River. Contaminants at this site include PCBs, cyanide, polychlorinated aromatic hydrocarbons (PAHs), fluoride and arsenic.

While the government was operating in classic new-style colonialism in their collaboration with Alcoa, General Motors (GM), and others in dumping cyanide, fluoride, arsenic and polychlorinated aromatic hydrocarbons into the river systems, they were also using the bureaucratic-scientific community as a buffer in what minimal accountability there was. Not only was accountability downgraded, when the naked eye, common sense and actual human suffering made toxicity painfully obvious, GM and the New York Department of Environmental Conservation (DEC) assured the Mohawks that there was little to worry about. A water quality expert explained that the hazardous waste dumps on the GM property were separated from the reservation by geographical and geological barriers unlikely to permit the spread of pollutants. Hugh Kaufman, assistant director of the Environmental Protection Association's (EPA) Hazardous Waste Site Control Division, said in October of 1983 at a Clarkson University conference, *Managing Environmental Risk*, "that while technology existed to avoid many toxic-dump problems, the government and industry were not putting in the necessary time and money to use it" (Grinde and Johansen 1995: 182).

Like the preceding example, this case illustrates the dance of economic development in that selective numbers are used to justify the benefits of development. Although the economic benefits were not quantified to the same extent as in the hydro example, the promise of jobs along with the downplaying of environmental and social costs made it easier for government officials to sell the deal.

Resource Extraction: The Lubicon Cree—New-style Colonialism at Work

The ecocidal outcomes of economic development projects visited upon the Lubicon Cree of northern Alberta paint a prototypical picture of new-style colonialism at work, in particular how the promise of tax revenues in the form of oil royalty payments and timber stumpage fees encourage governments to disregard issues such as Aboriginal title and due process.

The Lubicon Lake Band of Bush Cree, numbering approximately five hundred members, reside in the boreal forest of northern Alberta, in the Peace River area, surrounding Lubicon Lake, 250 miles north of Edmonton. For hundreds of years, the Lubicon have inhabited the territory north of Lesser Slave Lake, southwest of Lake Athabasca, between Wabasca and Peace rivers, sustained by hunting, fishing and trapping since before Europeans arrived to the continent. With the exception of their marginal participation in the fur trade, the Lubicon Cree were very isolated and experienced minimal contact or influences from Europeans or their institutions, compared to other Native peoples in Canada (Goddard 1991; Tollefson 1996). The Lubicon had been missed by the treaty commissioners in the latter days of the nineteenth century, and they remained relatively unaffected by developments in the southern parts of Canada. In the late 1930s, the Lubicon were recognized as a distinct society and promised a reserve.

But this promise went unfulfilled. In the mid-1950s, oil exploration and well-drilling came to Lubicon territory. By the 1960s, twenty-three wells had been drilled on land that had never been ceded by the Lubicon, extracting oil for which there had been no negotiations. Doubling exploration to nearly fifty wells in the 1970s, oil companies were being enabled and encouraged by the provincial government's road-building programs in the North Peace area, on traditional Lubicon territory. Hunting trails and trap lines were being converted to company roads. Without a treaty agreement, without environmental impact studies or social impact assessments, with no regard for the people whose livelihoods depended on a healthy wilderness, the Alberta government issued exploration permits as soon as applications were made (Goddard 1991; Espiritu 1997: 55).

Fifty wells may seem like a relatively small number in so large an area. But the well itself is only the end product of a complex—and heavily industrial—process. A wide straight path must be cleared through the dense bush in winter while the muskeg is still frozen. This twenty-foot swath is cleared by a bulldozer at a rate of a mile per day. Besides the noise, pollution and attendant food, shelter and sanitation needs of the workers, the clear-cut trees, underbrush, topsoil and debris must be piled and burned. Along with the road-building crew, there are survey crews and seismic crews—often up to twenty-five people—in an assortment of trucks, plus the drilling trucks which bore holes sixty feet deep and approximately twenty per mile.

In the early 1980s, ten transnational energy giants, including Royal Dutch Shell, Shell Canada, Exxon, Gulf and Standard Oil of California—a consortium enlisted by the federal government's crown corporation Petro-Canada—were exploring and developing the area. During the winter of 1979–80, thirty wells were drilled, at least forty the following year, and "by 1984, more than four hundred oil and gas wells had been drilled within a fifteen-mile radius of Little Buffalo [a central settlement in Lubicon territory], and more than one hundred companies and subcontractors were working in the area" (Goddard 1991: 76; Espiritu 1997: 51). According to Goddard (1991: 76–77):

> Suddenly the bush was colonized by nodding pump jacks, clusters of trailer camps, No Trespassing signs and burn-off flares lighting at night.... Bulldozers pushed up snow and debris, block-

> ing animal trails and burying dozens of traps and snares at a time. A probation officer in Peace River told [Bernard] Ominayak, Lubicon's Chief, that several oil-company and forestry workers under his supervision were destroying traps on direct instructions from employers.

Road and seismic line construction had a dramatic effect on the Lubicon fur harvest (Espiritu 1997: 55). Trapping returns, the main source of income for the band, decreased from more than $5000 per trapper to less than $400 (Goddard 1991). The Lubicon's exposure and vulnerability to health problems such as alcoholism and tuberculosis were greatly increased. Welfare dependence among the Lubicon soared from 10 percent in 1980 to 95 percent in 1993. Meanwhile, an estimated one million dollars worth of oil had been extracted daily from their land (LaDuke 1998: 327).

Through a series of bureaucratic and legal manipulations, the Canadian and Alberta governments attempted first to relocate the Lubicon, and when that didn't work, the Alberta Government had the land in question designated as a provincial hamlet. Petro-Canada, a crown corporation, was protected against injunctions that might have been filed to stop oil production. As tensions increased, the Lubicon gained support from other Indigenous nations and grassroots organizations. To demonstrate their seriousness, the Lubicon claimed their whole traditional territory, encompassing 25,000 square miles, and organized blockades and protests, including demonstrations at the 1988 Winter Olympics in Calgary. Negotiations with the government were re-instituted. The Alberta Government used a divide-and-conquer tactic by offering some Lubicon a separate reserve—The Woodland Cree reserve—and funding (Churchill 1999). Finally, due to pressure and support from Natives across Canada, Premier Don Getty met with Lubicon Chief Bernard Ominayak and agreed that "95 square miles of land would be transferred to the Lubicons" and that negotiations would begin to resolve the outstanding issues (Churchill 1999: 207).

Ironically, at that very moment, the Alberta government was escalating the development of the province's northern resources—beginning with the Japanese company, Daishowa, which had its sights set on the province's boreal forest. The government offered them access to large timber supply areas and a "generous subsidy package to assist in the construction of new mills" (Tollefson 1996). By the late 1980s, the Alberta government had concluded two separate development agreements with major Japanese paper producers: in the northwest of the province with Daishowa and in the northeast, in a venture known as ALPAC, with the Mitsubishi and Honshu companies (Tollefson 1996: 122). Diashowa obtained approval to construct a pulp mill ten kilometres north of the village of Peace River (LaDuke 1998: 327). Under the agreement, Daishowa was also granted a forest management licence to a twenty-year leasehold of 25,000 square kilometres adjacent to the Peace River area, to provide fibre for the proposed mill, and an additional 15,000 square kilometres plus money for roads, rail lines and a bridge. The company also purchased the rights to log Wood Buffalo National Park, the last great stand of old-growth spruce in Alberta. The land leased to Diashowa, which was set to expire in 2002, encompasses the 10,000 square kilometres which the Lubicon regard as their unceded traditional lands. The mill, with a capacity to process eleven thousand trees per day (Tollefson 1996: 122) was prepared to dump five thousand tons of chlorinated organic compounds into the Peace River annually. Thus, in February of 1988, when the agreement between Daishowa and the Alberta government was announced, the Lubicon Cree not only had to deal with the impact of oil development, estimated at more than a million dollars per day (Espiritu 1997; Tollefson 1996), but also with a major pulp mill.

Stories such as these of the Mohawks, Cree and Inuit have been told in many locations with many different variations. As we mentioned in the introduction, similar events have occurred in Nigeria and Colombia, to name but two countries. The lure of royalty revenues and/or tax dollars from economic development encourages governments to rush forward with financial incentives, to downgrade accountability mechanisms and to use whatever other bureaucratic-legal mechanisms are available to minimize dissent. Conveniently, the costs associated with these projects are either not quantified or they are externalities, which will be borne by groups with less political capital. As we noted in earlier chapters, this "hierarchy of humans" makes it easier to ignore these costs. However as Matthew Coon-Come, former Grand Chief of the Grand Council of the Cree of Quebec, stated, it is important to name these activities for what they are: "environmental racism" that sacrifices "our way of life, our lands, our communities, and our people" (quoted in Gedicks 1994: 19). The resultant ecocide might result from externalities—i.e., pollution which destroys fish and wildlife stocks; or it might result from less-than-adequate safety procedures utilized by corporations operating on the Indigenous lands. However, the result is often a situation where the lands and the reproductive ability and long-term health of the Indigenous population are irreparably damaged.

Delgamuukw—We Are Who We Say We Are

Canadians are generally aware of the social, economic and personal price paid by Indigenous peoples for colonial incursions into their territories; this view tends to be focused on the obvious social and economic ills that have arisen as a result of colonial policies. But we are much less aware of the historically rooted cultures upon which colonialism was impressed. From the colonial side of the government-Indigenous interface, we have examined the accounting-supported and -driven governmentalities and bureaucratic manipulations designed to change the behaviour of Indigenous peoples. For the most part, our examination has remained within this purview, with the pre-contact status quo being beyond our scope. The *Delgamuukw* decision of the Supreme Court of Canada, in 1997, however, prompts us to peer into the reality of a healthy, unmolested society; for the first time since contact we are given a hint of how the question, "What if we had entered into nation-to-nation dialogue from the beginning?" might be answered. As mentioned earlier there is a strong ecological component to *Delgamuukw*, which may have serious repercussions in future Canadian-Indigenous relations. Another way of framing the above "what if" question is: "If not ecocide, what?"

Central to the Supreme Court's decision is the recognition that in further negotiations, the oral histories of the Gitxsan and Wet'suwet'en constitute definitive evidence of prior occupation of land out of which Aboriginal rights arise (Persky 1998: 99). The centrepiece of the decision, according to Chief Negotiator 'Mass Gaak (Don Ryan) was precisely "our laws, oral histories, songs, crests, dances, social institutions that govern us, language, and notions of land title" (Persky 1998: v).

The entrenchment into law that "stories matter" (Persky 1998: 13) did more than alter a single strand in the weave that bound European-Indigenous relations, bringing into sharp focus two nearly irreconcilable views of history; it also unveiled the extent to which an oral culture incorporates all levels of being—perceptual, ecological, social, spiritual—in its web of life. This web is neither a nature-conservation euphemism nor a romantic "noble savage " notion. It has at its centre what the Gitxsan and Wet'suwet'en people call, respectively, *adaawk* and *kunqax*, commonly referred to as "storytelling" in European terms. These oral histories, fixed in the common spirit of the people through ritual and ceremony, contain the territorial foundations of the ancestors' place in the created world, further strengthened by the particular totem poles and regalia, as historical representations, which identify, for example, a Gitxsan House (Persky 1998: 45–46).

From an ecological perspective, it is worth noting that these histories, the *adaawk* and *qunkax*, are told and retold as a constant reminder of the inviolable connection of the people with the land, in a feast hall where Wet'suwet'en and Gitxsan gather in ceremony and celebration. In other words, storytelling, ritual dance *and the food they eat* come together in a manner that acts as both law and history. This holism supports the view that honouring the web of life involves a religious praxis that is foundational in both transcendent and imminent senses; it is both about land and food, and about *more* than land and food. To compare, for example, the Christian ceremony of ingesting the Host, or body of Christ, as spiritual sustenance; no supplicant ever died from starvation because of a lack of sacred Hosts. But many Natives have died from the lack of, or poisoning of, their medicine— a term analogous to the sacred Host but which is inseparable from their sustaining nutrient source—food. To perhaps stretch the comparison, we might say that dumping known toxins into the Wabigoon River, for example, can be viewed as an act not very different from, say, lacing the communicants' wine with rat poison. This ecological unity between actual nutrient-rich food and sacred, power-endowed medicine holds in exactly the same manner between the traditional elders' storytelling and the revelations of history. Their stories *are* their recorded law and history.

In delivering the third annual LaFontaine-Baldwin Lecture on March 8, 2002, Georges Erasmus, former President of the Indian Brotherhood of Northwest Territories/Dene Nation and former National Chief of the Assembly of First Nations, went to great lengths, both in the lecture and in the following discussions, to point out that the key to future peaceful coexistence between Indigenous people and non-Indigenous people does not lie in litigation but in developing relationships based on trust and dialogue. From this basis, real treaty-making would be possible. But Erasmus warns, "It is difficult to establish trust when the person sitting across the negotiating table from you begins by saying: You are not who you say you are."[2]

Delgamuukw addresses this fundamental barrier head on. Though hindsight is not always helpful, in this case it may provide a useful background; had the principle of Indigenous oral-historical veracity implicit in *Delgamuukw* been entrenched in Canadian law earlier, the horrific ecocidal scenarios we have described either would not have been allowed or would have been considered acts of aggression comparable to military attacks on a sovereign nation. For our purposes, *Delgamuukw* is relevant because the case centres on the apparent conflict between history based on oral tradition and European law based on the written word. At stake is nothing less than who may do what, on and to the land in dispute. The argument is essentially ecological in that both its history and its outcome centre on the question of nature-human relationships in the context of land usage. Defenders of European industrial culture, viewing nature-human relationships through the narrow lens of economic outcome, may point to the civilized benefits of industrialization on the one hand and unemployment in the Native population on the other.

In an industrial culture, the incontrovertible human dependence on natural resources is mediated through capitalization and industrialization, with the greatest benefit going to those who wield those mediative tools—the entrepreneurs—so that extraction and commodification in themselves seem to create wealth. In this case, the relationship between human need and extraction of resources serves corporate ownership before—and sometimes to the exclusion of—individual or societal needs. In the context of land-based traditional cultures, human dependence on nature (natural resources) is mediated through collective ritual and ceremony, incorporating laws which govern hunting and usage (extraction and distribution) through storytelling, ritual and song, and ensuring ecological balance—i.e., the continued propagation of the host species (resources)—and hence sustainability of the interdependent relationships between people and their natural environment.

It is important to note the role of government bureaucracy and accounting mechanisms in the entrepreneurial function. The historic trajectory of the transfer of land—from Indigenous to Crown possession to individual title to industrial land-use—can be described as a continuous series of government-bureaucratic transactions, dependent upon and rationalized through accounting mechanisms. Refusing to treat accounting as a neutral technique, in other words of neutral morality, we have contextualized accounting techniques in the field of colonial and neocolonial policies and shown that such techniques can have genocidal outcomes. By including *Delgamuukw* in this context, the questions of consequence, equity and morality are further highlighted against the most basic background of Indigenous sovereignty—i.e., nationhood—that *Delgamuukw* gave us. It so happens that the Supreme Court decision includes a perspective of Aboriginal rights that is land-based—implying land usage—and therefore ecological.

Following the paper trail from original usurpation to continuing corporate exploitation, government and business become virtually indistinguishable. This bureaucratic-entrepreneurial partnership between government and corporation is threatened by any other form of mediation between land base and final user—especially a form of mediation as all-encompassing, traditionally sound and sustainable as that once practised, and in some but not all cases continued, by Indigenous cultures.

A word of caution here: we are not suggesting that Indigenous exercise of their sovereignty precludes their adaptation to European-type extraction and distribution, nor that, by virtue of their traditional culture, any economic activity practised on their land is automatically environmentally benign. We are merely arguing that in the clash of cultures that is colonialism, the rights of the settler culture cannot be determined by an assumption of superiority based on economic success, with a blind eye turned to the benefits—and ecologically speaking, the need for—a land-centred, sustainable world view.

Cultures often mix and adapt, sometimes happily, sometimes not. European and Native cultures have historically had occasional overlapping interests and solutions to their economic needs. Even today, the principle of *usufruct* still obtains in some Native communities, while others have done well in adapting to capital and technology. Often an ingenious blend of the two world views serves well. In some cases, Indigenous communities have been enrolled in activities that have damaged the environment and their own people. In some industrial and corporate projects, they have benefitted; in others, they have been pawns in the assimilative and extractive strategies of developers. But in many cases, Natives have conserved their traditions, culture and beliefs and, in a continual battle to defend them, have been ignored, deliberately undermined or outrightly persecuted. Others have found a way to mobilize and use public relations to pressure governments and corporations. While most of these activist goals are aimed at preserving their environment, land, animals and fishing and hunting rights, the underlying and most volatile issue is their right to determine their own futures in a relationship with the land and in manner they see fit to exercise. This sovereignty of practice and usage, this incontrovertible connection to their traditional territories is what constitutes their very existence as Indigenous peoples, and it is this question that the *Delgamuukw* decision brought to light.

Because Indigenous history, sovereignty and land are inseparable, and are now *seen* to be inseparable, in practice as well as in law, it enables us to see with much more clarity how the contamination of earth, air and water by the settler society is an indirect attack on the rights of Indigenous people to survive as a sovereign culture. Industrial development projects have been and continue to be the major contributors to what we term ecocide—the genocide, in whole or in part, of a people, via the destruction of their sustaining environment. Furthermore, as both Justice Lamer in his decision and Georges Erasmus in his lecture warn, litigation is not the most efficacious route to conciliation. But the force of bureaucratic-accounting rationalization for further incursions into resource-rich Aboriginal territories may be significantly weakened by the Supreme Court's definite broadening of the historical and deeply ecological contexts for territorial rights.

Notes

1. In *Delgamuukw* v. *British Columbia*, the appellants, Delgamuukw (Earl Muldoe) and other members and representatives of the Gitxsan and Wet'suwet'en Houses, of Northern British Columbia, appealed a previous decision by the Court of Appeal of British Columbia, in which the apppellants were laying claim to various portions of 85,000 square kilometres of land in the province. The unanimous decision in favour of Delgamuukw ruled that the appeal should be allowed; however Chief Justice Lamer, in his written decision, made it clear that he was not encouraging the parties to go back to court. *Delgamuukw* v. *British Columbia* was considered a landmark decision primarily because, in reversing the lower court decision, it allowed the inclusion of oral histories as bona fide

evidence and established Aboriginal title as a right in land.

2. Remarks made in discussion; from author's notes at attendance; George Erasmus Third Annual LaFontaine-Baldwin Lecture, Wosk Centre for Dialogue, Vancouver, B.C., March 8, 2002, presented by the Dominion Institute.

Chapter Nine

Accounting for Resistance

Oka, Quebec, July 1990: A barricade has been erected to prevent expansion of a golf course over ancestral Mohawk burial grounds. The Mohawks are trying to prevent the construction of a golf course on their traditional burial grounds, part of a larger land dispute that has been going on for decades. In turn the Quebec Provincial Police have executed a raid on Mohawk warriors. The camouflaged and masked warriors, and the Canadian soldiers in full battle regalia are telegenic and startling in the middle of a civilized Canadian summer. The Natives have the attention of the entire country.

Fast forward four years: Chiapas Mexico, January 1994. Dark eyes stare out of a black balaclava—and from the mouthpiece juts the trademark pipe of photogenic, videogenic, media-wise Subcommandante Marcos of the Zapatista Army for National Liberation (EZLN). The message is clear: enough is enough, the people of Chiapas have been denied the most basic services for too long, the rich will "pillage the wealth of our country" no more (EZLN 1994). The date for the first uprising of the EZLN, January 1994, has been strategically chosen to coincide with the implementation of the North America Free Trade Agreement (NAFTA). In response, the Mexican government sends in the army. Twelve thousand troops are deployed into Chiapas, supported by artillery, armour, helicopter gun ships and rocket-equipped aircraft (Stephenson 1995: 17).

Back to Canada: Ipperwash, Ontario, September 1995. Aboriginal protesters occupy a military base and a nearby provincial park. The military base sits on land that was expropriated during World War II but never returned. The provincial park contains a sacred burial ground. Despite the fact that there has been no violence and the protest group contains only thirty to forty people, including women and children, the Ontario Provincial Police begin a buildup of 200 officers, including a heavily armed tactical unit. Feeling threatened, police open fire, killing one of the protesters—Anthony Dudley George (Platiel 1997: A1, A6). He becomes the first Native person killed in a land dispute in Canada during the century. Commenting on police tactics, then premier Mike Harris acknowledges that he authorized the police to remove the protesters: in his words, "the Ministry of Natural Resources staff were not able to access their property to do whatever work they had to do … we felt, the Ministry felt, they'd like to have their park back. I think that's a normal reaction" (quoted in Mittelstaedt 1997b: A5).

These images, broadcast worldwide via a multitude of media, bring us vivid illustrations of how monetary relations intersect with the hardwares and softwares of force. Throughout North America, centuries of attempted governance of Indigenous peoples by colonizing forces came to a head—after the fall of the Berlin wall, after the disintegration of the Soviet Union, after the formation of the European Union, after the Free Trade Agreement between the U.S. and Canada—at precisely the historical moment when economic globalization was being internationally mobilized, volubly, and with great fanfare. These examples are merely the most visible of a multitude of Indigenous resistances to corporate colonization aided and abetted by international organizations and governments. They reveal a continuum in the techniques of governmentality and force that were first brought to the shores of the New World six centuries ago. The fact that Indigenous movements and their relatively small populations should be such visible opponents of globalization signifies that the new-style colonialism discussed in chapter eight is not much different in forceful tactics than the old-style colonialism that preceded it.

Previous chapters examined how bureaucratic and accounting methods were used against Indigenous cultures; this chapter moves from governance to resistance. Starting from the events at Oka in the summer of 1990, we pose the questions: How was it that Indigenous peoples arrived at the position where they felt they had no choice but to take matters into their hands? What was the role of accounting and bureaucracy in placing them in this no-win position? We then move beyond Canada, using the case of Chiapas, to argue that military force is the prop that allows governments to use soft techniques such as accounting.

Our understanding of the dynamic between governance and force is deepened by looking at those subaltern voices that are usually lost in the official histories of progress and development. This perspective allows us to view how the colonized who dare attempt to secure their own freedom are met with barriers—forceful, often violent and always bureaucratically controlled (Guha 2000: 7). Subaltern groups perpetually struggle against the types of technologies of governance previously discussed: "we see them engaged in a struggle with the courts of law, with bureaucracy or the police—all signs of the new forms of domination that have been established over them" (Das 1989: 313). After these forms of sanctioned resistance are exhausted, militant uprising—peasant praxis—occurs (Guha 1983). And while these resistances are usually repressed, they are not in vain. For they demonstrate that underlying the rhetoric of liberty and equality, lies a different reality—a reality where the will to power and military force reign supreme. Perhaps it is easier to resist a visible opponent than a bureaucratic structure where nobody seems to be responsible.

Accounting for Force

In previous chapters we have hinted at how the process of governing stateless populations is essentially ideological. Discussions about appropriate modes of governance are inseparable from a wider discursive field in which conceptions of the proper ends and means of government are articulated, including discourses about the inferiority of Native peoples. These discourses permitted governments to view Native peoples as less-than-human, thereby paving the way for the types of social engineering projects that we have observed as recently as the 1960s. But military and police forces continue to be integral to these processes. Fanon (1963: 38), for example, notes that force is part of the history of colonial relations:

> the policeman and the soldier, by their immediate presence and their frequent and direct action maintain contact with the native and advise him by means of rifle butts and napalm not to budge. It is obvious here that the agents of government speak the language of pure force. The intermediary does not lighten the oppression, nor seek to hide the domination; he shows them up and puts them into practice with the clear conscience of an upholder of the peace.

The relations between ideological constructions, accounting techniques and military force have been symbiotic, permitting governments to back up their talk and their accounting techniques with tanks when targeted people dare to question them.

Indigenous America and Europe: Gold and Subjugation

An industrial-civil society in which the spiritual and political are ostensibly uncoupled encounters a culture organized around strongly integrated spiritual and political principles—and calls it savage; an autochthonous culture encounters an alien people with unimagined, mysterious technologies—and welcomes it. European colonial institutions and Native American traditions are as disparate from one another as are golf courses and traditional burial sites. The inevitable clash of the two cultures is exemplified by their divergent views of land: to the industrial culture, a wilderness to be subdued and commodified; to the other, a bountiful legacy to be inhabited, shared and cherished, an attitude which allies individuals and communities with the natural world. Central to the Iroquois culture, for example, was a celebration commonly known as the Thanksgiving Ceremony, which lasted for days—an expression of gratitude for the sun, the winds, the rain, the earth and everything that grows:

> Natural phenomena are addressed, not in some abstract manner but in their immediate physical presence. Especially impressive is the final exhortation of gratitude offered to each component of the natural world and that the people should remember as an integral community saying "Now our minds are one." The full significance of this ceremony can only be understood if we appreciate that this celebration was the binding ritual whereby the five original tribes of the Iroquois confederacy established their unity. (Berry 1999: 40)

To those whose spiritual and social identities were fixed elsewhere, however, seeking political refuge and a decent living in the new land, this pagan relationship to land was regarded as inferior. Natives were simply viewed as unable to manage their potential richness (Dickason 1993), and thus subjugation of the "savages" was justified. The Europeans had their own cosmology, descended from the Greco-Roman culture to the European monotheistic traditions; there was no new knowledge here for them to discover, and most importantly, private property was an absolute human right. The natural world, of which Indigenous people were simply an extension, had no rights whatsoever. This discontinuity between the human world and the natural world meant the inevitable economic exploitation of the New Land.

At the time of European contact, the Iroquois were one of the most complex civilizations in the Americas. In spite of this, the Europeans either destroyed their legacies or co-opted them, and this imposition of values, in particular regarding land, remains the fundamental conflict in subsequent disputes over territory and sovereignty.

The establishment of colonial institutions as the framework for the subjugation and exploitation of Indigenous peoples was driven by the imperative to accumulate wealth and land. Feudal social relations imposed in the Americas were based on relations over land, its production and the rights over that production (Cuevas 1993). The capital from land production indentured the peasants who worked the soil without owning it, supported the nobility who owned it without working it, and enriched the church and monarchy who assumed its possession by divine right. Seventeenth-century European norms were exported to the New Land, which was there to be depredated, guided by the principles of capitalism as it had emerged from feudalism, turning land and labour into commodities (Trigger 1977).

Thus, the practices in the Americas reflected the attitude of European elites: possession of land meant power and wealth. Institutions such as the state, church and seigneuries accumulated land, found Natives to work it, mobilized capital and attracted settlers to their concessions. Collecting dues and tithes became a profitable business. Concessions became written contracts, possessed by a privileged few (Hamilton 1988). Capital and its motivations came to the Americas to control and take advantage of land and people. The presence of money, market and trade in the Americas was the reflection of "a society afflicted with a mania for prestige and an atavistic attachment to the soil" (Hamilton 1988: 81).

Oka: The Seminary as Corporation

In 1535 when Cartier arrived in North America, he encountered Mohawk hospitality (Parent 1887). The Iroquois were one of the most politically and militarily powerful Native organizations in North America. Kanehsatake Natives belong to the Mohawk Nation, People of the Flint, one of the Iroquois Six Nations. The Confederacy of the Iroquois, much of which was to later inspire the United States Constitution, embraced the concept of Peacemakers and gatherings as a means of peaceful coexistence. As Parker asserts, "An Iroquois man must be generous and give to every one who asked for his arms or his meat" (1968: 22) Everything a man had or brought to the village became public property (Parker 1968: 22). The Iroquois Constitution established that the soil of the earth was the property of the people who inhabited and used it (Morgan and Lloyd 1901).

The Iroquois were located in the most productive areas by the Great Lakes and the St. Lawrence River. They lived off agriculture, hunting, fishing and, later, fur trading. Iroquois lineal descendants run in the female line. Women, the progenitor of the nation, oversaw land usage. The clan mothers chose the chiefs of the league, who in turn represented the clan at confederacy meetings. Iroquois knowledge was transmitted orally from one generation to another and preserved by a collection of wampum belts and strings whose symbols recalled laws, regulations and treaties (Blanchard 1980).

The Mohawks and the French agreed to co-exist amicably: as a sign, they created a belt, the Two Dog Wampum, a symbol of peace signifying two roads running parallel, distinctly different, yet in harmony with one-another. However, this state of affairs was short-lived. Driven by commercial objectives, Champlain, about seventy years after the arrival of Cartier, travelled to North America. As a strategy for strengthening France's hold on the fur trade, he persuaded two other Native civilizations, the Huron and the Algonquin, to confront the Iroquois. Equipped with arms supplied by Champlain, they defeated the Iroquois. This was the first in a series of attempts by the French to dominate the Iroquois people and territory (Hall 1991).

In Oka, the main struggles over land started in 1717, when the King of France gave a land grant to the Seminary of St. Sulpice to establish a Catholic mission and to provide education for the Indians. The ecclesiastics of the Seminary were assigned the land, known as the Seigneury of Two Mountains, "under the charge of paying Fealty and Homage to the King" (Lacan and Prévost 1876: 11). Under Royal Law, the inhabitants of the concession were obligated to sell their territories at an established price.

The purpose of this assignation was to encourage the assimilation of the Mohawks. As an indirect agent of the French crown, the Seminary received land in return for providing moral and religious instruction, and for maintaining places of education, such as convents and schoolhouses, where children were prohibited from using their own language and practising their traditional ways. Guaranteeing Indigenous well-being was part of the bargain, and this included introducing the Mohawks to European agricultural practices. The land for this agriculture—deemed a present with no determined expiration date—was prohibited from sale, which allowed the elites, especially the Catholic Seminary, to use the land for their own purposes. Even though the land assignations provided Natives with a place to live, the land base was not sufficient for self-sustenance. As a result, the Mohawks were totally dependent on the Seminary's charity and *miséricorde* (to pardon the conquered).

Crown mandates and laws allowed the Seminary to establish its own corporation. For example, the priests blessed normal activities of the Mohawks in exchange for payment. According to the Reverend Parent, Natives paid priests nominal amounts to get their children baptized, to have someone buried or married, and for a variety of ceremonial ways to protect themselves from the devil. To pay for the church, Indians gave fifty-pound packs of beaver skins, worth seven or eight dollars a pound. Natives also paid for masses said to make the land productive or to rescue the deceased from Purgatory. Tithing—"every twenty sixth bushel of grain went to the priest"—was common (Parent 1887: 193).

The Seminary as corporation was a perfect example of how the imposition of European institutions encouraged the shift from feudalism to capitalism, with the resultant subjugation of the poor (Young 1986). The high ongoing income of the profitable enterprise allowed priests to pay the King rent and taxes and to fulfill France's social investment expectations. The priests encouraged religiosity and warned Natives of penalties if they did not behave according to instructions.

After France's withdrawal, legal and economic support for seminary activities continued under British control. The business enterprise of the St. Sulpice Seminary included offices, managers, accounting and sales professionals, and other workers. After 1859, the state helped capitalize the rural seigneuries. Property privileges were assigned to the Seminary. Priests were legally approved to impose their prerogatives and business interests. Land use was squarely in the hands of the church. During the mid-1800s, for example, the Seminary seized land being used by the

Mohawks and sold part of it to finance its investments, that is, to pay for the construction of office buildings and housing for rental revenue. Any titles received by the Mohawks were precarious at best. The Seminary authorized all land usage, dictated who could make use of it, as well as how, and prohibited the unauthorized sale of the land itself, including the timber cut from it. Like the web of regulations surrounding the use of natural resources discussed in chapters seven and eight, these dictates were rationalized as part of the program to help Natives administer, conserve and use land properly.

The Seminary, rather than solve the problems wrought by landlessness and poverty, actively opposed Native efforts to control their own territories. By 1869, Natives were living under hard conditions, without autonomy, money or land. They were not allowed to be active in commerce, to hunt or to develop any of their traditional activities. Consistent with the federal government's emphasis on agriculture, the only support that Natives received was to implement agriculture.

After repeated protests, Native peoples received guarantees regarding their right to stay on the land without being disturbed. The disputes, however, continued. The asymmetry between a seminary endowed with great economic, social and political power, and the abject existence of Indigenous peoples, prompted the Mohawks to ask the Methodist Church for financial help. The Protestant Defense Association in Montreal raised funds for the Oka Question, to protect civil rights and land claims (Murray 1886). These events marked both a mass conversion to Protestantism amongst Indigenous peoples and the beginning of religious discrepancies toward Native's rights.

This initial period in Oka history illustrates the tentative introduction of governance via indirect agents—in this case the Seminary. Like the examples provided in chapter three, these mechanisms were directed toward changing the day-to-day habits and customs: the Seminary—with the support of the government—was able to influence the minutiae of Indigenous peoples' lives. This was accomplished through its control of land and any financial transactions pertaining to the land (i.e., the sale of timber), along with its role as educator. These initiatives foreshadowed the manner in which such policies would become institutionalized at the national level, both in terms of specific *Indian Act* legislation (see chapter five) and the creation of a residential schooling system, operated by religious orders (see chapter six). These same assimilative strategies continued up until the more recent Oka land disputes.

Looking for a way out of its intractable land disputes, the St. Sulpice Seminary in 1905 offered to sell to the federal government its land holdings. When this strategy failed—in part because the Mohawks challenged in court the right of the Seminary to sell the land—the Seminary agreed not to interfere with the lands that the Mohawks were using. In spite of this agreement, the pine forests and adjacent cultivated land were sold in 1936 to private investors, effectively transferring the land dispute to the new owners. In 1945, the remaining land (approximately 1 percent of the original grant) was sold by the Sulpicians back to the federal government, for Mohawk use, provided that the annual property rights be paid by the parish and township.

However, the land that was of concern to the Mohawks—the common lands traditionally used for gatherings and religious ceremonial purposes—was part of the parcel still owned privately. These common lands, located in the vicinity of Mohawk burial grounds, were later expropriated from the private owners for the development of the Oka Golf Club. Another portion of the traditional common lands was subsequently resold for the development of a sawmill.

Throughout this period, settlement activities and economic development were privileged by federal, provincial and municipal levels of government. For example, during the 1950s, the federal government expropriated five hundred hectares of Mohawk land to build the St. Lawrence Seaway. The seaway continues to be a visible reminder of federal government intrusions and helped to revive the nationalist movement amongst Indigenous peoples that, in turn, contributed to the Oka stand-off (York and Pindera 1992: 122).

Oka: Economic Development and Indian Souvenirs

The Oka confrontation was also foreshadowed by the encouragement of economic development schemes, which privileged settlement activities over Aboriginal sovereignty. For example, although the federal courts acknowledged that the Sulpicians had some responsibilities to the Mohawks (York and Pindera 1992: 102), these obligations did not prevent the Sulpicians from subsequently selling the land. In turn, the municipal government was willing to expropriate some of this land for recreation and economic development and to rezone some for housing. Whenever the Mohawks challenged these activities using methods acceptable to settler society, they were stonewalled by yet more administrative apparatuses.

As in many other Aboriginal communities, the land base held by the Mohawks was insufficient for subsistence activities. Thus, Indigenous peoples were forced to migrate to urban areas to try to find work. In nearby Kahnawake, the Mohawks pandered to settler images of Natives:

> Lacking any natural resources on their reserve, the Mohawks of Kahnawake began catering to tourists who wanted to see the Hollywood image of a western frontier Indian. They entered the entertainment industry in a big way, adopting the look of Sioux Indians and joining white-owned "Wild West" shows that traveled

> across the United States and Europe.... Many of the Mohawks had ramshackle booths in their front yards to sell souvenirs, mostly made in Japan, to tourists who visited the reserve.... In reality, teepees and totem poles were completely foreign to the Mohawk culture, but their phony image was a money-making enterprise in a community that had few other economic opportunities. (York and Pindera 1992: 121)

Perhaps this was the type of economic development that the Hawthorn Report (discussed in chapter seven) envisioned for those people who were unwilling to migrate to the cities.

While the selling of Indian culture did not threaten the established order, other economic activities did. For example, in 1986, opposition by non-Native neighbours who feared that a drug and alcohol treatment centre in Oka would devalue their property almost truncated its creation. Likewise, in 1990, a project to construct a steel manufacturing plant was refused by Indian Affairs because the Natives could not get the appropriate permissions from the municipality (York and Pindera 1992: 112). And like other Indigenous groups, the Mohawks of Kahnawake/Kanehsatake have been involved in a long-standing dispute with the federal government over whether they can sell tax-free cigarettes and operate gambling casinos on their lands. In all of these cases, regulations external to the Mohawk peoples have been used to define appropriate economic activities on their lands. And when these approved economic activities were too oppressive or anathema to Indigenous principles and cultural practices, rebellion and organized resistance were the result.

Oka: The Stand-Off

The stand-off itself brought into sharp focus the differing rationalities of the participants, along with the irony of financial relations as a mode of governance. The confrontation centred on different notions of value: the exchange value to the municipality versus the use value to the Mohawks. The municipality supported the expansion project because of the expected monetary benefits: an increase in tourism along with an increased tax base (York and Pindera 1992). And while the municipality possessed the legal deed title to support the clearing of the Pines, the Mohawks affirmed that they had never sold or given up this land and that the land had symbolic value. For Oka, the area was a municipal park, and for the Kanehsatake Mohawks, it was part of the common lands where they gathered to develop activities, share their traditions and honour their ancestors (MacLaine et al. 1990).

When the developer began construction on the golf course expansion, the Kanehsatake Mohawks erected barricades, blocking access to the

Pines, the Mercier Bridge to Montreal and other important highways. The problems caused by the barricades—in terms of traffic congestion and economic losses—prompted the Oka authorities to ask for the mobilization, first, of the provincial police, Sûreté du Québec, and then the Canadian army. These requests for police and armed forces presence introduced the threat of force into the negotiations (Dallaire 1991). This threat of force was self-fulfilling in that it resulted in the death of a Quebec police officer during the initial confrontation and the deaths of two elderly Mohawks, who were confronted by a mob while trying to leave Oka during the height of the stand-off. While the introduction of the army/police was a way of confronting the Mohawks and re-establishing law and order (Pertusati 1997), the mere presence of the army did not precipitate an immediate solution.

Accounting for Violence

The events at Oka illustrate the irony and limits of financial governance. Technologies of governance are efficient in that the social relations they inculcate become both self-monitoring and internalized (Rabinow 1984: 20). In contrast to techniques of force (Fanon 1963), technologies of governance can operate without the specific presence of government agents. However, when technologies of governance fail—in this case when Indigenous peoples resist their subjugation—an excess of force is often required to re-establish order.

The cost of the Oka crisis ran into the hundreds of million of dollars. The Quebec government, which sent fifteen hundred police officers to the barricades, spent $91.6 million on overtime bills and other expenses for the police, who set up round-the-clock surveillance during the seventy-seven-day confrontation; $23.5 million was paid in compensation to nearby homeowners and business people whose lives were disrupted by the crisis; and $13.5 million was spent on a highway extension to bypass the Kahnawake reserve. These costs are separate from the $83 million spent by the Canadian Armed Forces for more than three thousand soldiers involved in the military intervention. Also, local businesses lost an estimated $25,000 a day. These figures total more than $200 million.

The *Edmonton Journal* (May 6, 1991, Editorial) comments that:

> To put the cost of the crisis in some sort of context, it was about 10 times what the federal government budgeted for land claims settlements each year and more than half the $355 million that Prime Minister Mulroney grandly promised recently to spend over five years to speed up the land claims settlements. It is, needless to say, far more than the land claimed by the Mohawks (and sought by the town of Oka for a golf course) is worth on the market.

Not only were the immediate costs enormous, the crisis influenced the establishment of a Royal Commission on Aboriginal Peoples (RCAP 1996).

Beyond Canada

Canada is a former British colony that still prides itself for having Victorian sensibilities. Thus, the presence of military force usually remains well hidden, only appearing in those moments when the government feels it appropriate to remind Indigenous peoples of their place and to demonstrate to its constituents that it has the political will to aggressively deal with lawless actions of Indigenous protesters (Mittelstaedt 1997a: A8). In settings like Chiapas, Mexico, accounting and other bureaucratic mechanisms have a role to play in the appropriation of Indigenous labour and resources. But violence has been not so much a backdrop or a potential force as a constant series of eruptions—the military is always at hand as simply another agent, with business and government bureaucracies, in keeping the Natives down. The rhythm of subaltern activity, protests, marches and popular mobilizations, followed by military action, is part of the political landscape.

What is now called the Chiapas state of Mexico was, until 1824, a part of Guatemala occupied by the advanced civilization known as Maya. The Mayan cities were very well developed and organized, and included large buildings, pyramids—which still rise two hundred feet into the air—and places of worship: "Maya's achievements in arts, writing, architecture, astronomy and mathematics, rivaled those of Egypt or Classical Europe" (Wright 1992: 50). The Mayans invented the concepts of zero and place-system numerals, which allowed them to develop a perfect calendar, able to measure precisely over a billion years (Wright 1992: 50). Europeans, who diminished their measurement of culture to the use of metallic tools, classified the Mayans as savages who had not passed the Stone Age. The Mayans, however, were far superior in social and political structure, knowledge of the Universe—including plants, animals, weather and environment—the sciences and use of the intellect.

The Chiapas uprising of 1994 had roots that are clearly visible back to the sixteenth century. Throughout this unfolding, military violence accompanied governmentality and corporatism. The background against which this violence took place is multi-layered. Migration, labour exploitation and mixed-blood politics have all been factors (Womack 1999: 5–7), as have been the activities of the church. The Vatican-controlled upper echelons supported the Spanish Crown while the apostolic clergy were committed to the Indigenous communities. Peasant and labour organizations also played key roles in the politics of the country, as a counterforce to the elites and the business class.

Accounting and other bureaucratic techniques were introduced during the 1800s. By the middle of the 1800s, these technologies had changed the economic and social landscape of Chiapas. Liberal policies and constitutional reforms had contributed to the increased privatization of church and communal Indigenous lands, accumulating wealth and land in *caciques*, a type of rural bossism, for the ladino elites, against whom Indigenous peoples were in constant struggle. The increased privatization of land brought higher levels of conflict between landlords, the church and Indigenous peoples. In some regions, even as their land and labour continued to be exploited, Natives still had to pay taxes to the churches. They were caught in a *peonaje* relationship, where they were forced to labour for a landowner in exchange for a small plot of land within the plantation. The frustration of being prohibited from practising their religion and their subjection to the landlords often brought resistance. The response to these resistances was primarily military, organized by the merchant ladino class of San Cristobal in Chiapas, finally erupting in the Rebellion of 1867–1870 (Russell 1995) and culminating in the Caste War of 1869. Armed with little more than digging sticks and machetes, the Indigenous rebels lost over eight hundred men; the war also created thousands of migrants (Harvey 1998: 93–96).

During the last decade of the nineteenth century, new laws were introduced which increased taxes and reduced the authority and autonomy of Indigenous communities. For example, regulations separated Indigenous people from the land source of their traditional subsistence living and forced them to participate in the market economy by being employed at different times of the year. Furthermore, land reforms assigned large territories to coffee and cacao plantations, thereby encouraging the development of a modern, market-based agrarian economy (Harvey 1998: 47). This land-use legislation and social engineering parallel similar trends on other continents (i.e., Africa) to encourage assimilation via the enforcement of market relations (Bush and Maltby forthcoming).

At the beginning of the twentieth century modernization reforms established new laws and policies encouraging economic development. In the name of progress, these reforms increased foreign investment, imported new technologies and incorporated parts of Chiapas into the international economy, while political and economic control became even more concentrated, thereby increasing the financial dependence of the peasantry on the elite and the government (Villafuentes et al. 1999: 70).

Under this new-style colonialism, transnational corporations were given incentives, through government programs, to locate in Chiapas. Self-subsistence for the Natives and peasants became next to impossible with the loss of their land, and the only opportunities for employment were on the new large plantations. Natives were paid in tokens that could only be redeemed at stores known as *tiendas de atarralla*. And because payment did not meet their minimum living expenses, they were obligated to borrow money from their employer—known as the *patrón*. In this life-long commitment to, and dependence on, the *patrón*, we witness indirect government incentives given to transnationals effectively governing the day-to-day activities of Indigenous people—in this case displacing them from communal lands and forcing them into the plantation economy, much as they had been forced off the communal *ejidos* fifty years previously.

Over the next ninety years, the dance of modernization reforms and economic development, Indigenous resistance and military repression played itself out at numerous junctures. By 1980, Chiapas had become perhaps the most important source of natural resources for Mexico. Yet, despite the fact that it provided half the country's hydroelectric power and a significant amount of gas and petroleum, and was first of all Mexican states in coffee and banana production, second in cacao and beef and third in corn production, Chiapas remained the least electrified, least schooled, least literate agricultural state in the country (Hernandez 1994). This did not change during the 1980s, when the Mexico government, facing a major debt crisis, responded by developing large oil exploration and hydroelectric projects in Chiapas. The subsequent flooding forced the elimination of subsistence activities on the 200,000 hectares of flooded land. After the plunge in oil prices in 1982, support for agriculture was reduced as the government cut spending in an effort to balance its budget (Russell 1995: 14).

During the 1980s, peasant and Indigenous demonstrations were a common response to the exploitative situations Indigenous peoples and peasants found themselves facing. Not surprisingly, the government response was military. In September of 1983, the March for Dignity and Freedom from Chiapas to Mexico City made demands on the government to release activists from prison and for land reform. With much media coverage, some of the demands were met—but, afraid of the emerging grassroots movements, "local land-owners and cacique stepped up the number of attacks against activists" (Harvey 1998: 158)

As the rise in demonstrations continued throughout the eighties, so did government militarization. In 1984, nine members of the Casa del Pueblo (municipal centre) were massacred. In October of 1985, a deputy for the Unified Socialist Party of Mexico was assassinated. Nearing the end of the decade, when it became abundantly clear that social reform could not happen without displacing landowners and *caciques*, violence escalated, and death threats abounded (Harvey 1998: 160–61). From this bloody turmoil, the Zapatista Army of National Liberation (EZLN) was born.

On January 1, 1994, the *Ejercito Zapatista de Liberacion Nacional* (Zapatista Army for National Liberation) seized five towns and six villages in Chiapas state. They closed the main access highways and occupied governmental offices to support their demands for the abolition of big haciendas and the redistribution of land to local peasants. The statement contained in the Mexican Constitution, land for those who work it, was one of the rallying cries: a reference to the fact that in Chiapas, everything, including justice, progress, etc., always arrives late (Tello 1995).

In March 1994, the EZLN made public its thirty-four demands: economic demands relating to the poverty of Indians in Chiapas, social demands stemming from racism, political demands relating to democratic liberties throughout Mexico, and issues relating to the formal cessation of hostilities (Stephenson 1995: 12–13). This peasant praxis reinvigorated the resistance to government policies in that "the independent peasant movements gained a new lease on life, occupying over 50,000 hectares of land in the first six months of 1994 and forcing the government to recognize the continued need for land redistribution" (Harvey 1998: 2).

In Chiapas, after the appearance of the EZLN in January 1994, the government responded in a similar manner to the Canadian government when faced with Native resistance. Financial carrots were used in the attempt to divide Indigenous peoples: "the government swiftly attempted to divide the Indian movement even further by trying to buy off and co-opt the leadership of numerous organizations through a combination of financial incentives and coercion" (Stavenhagen 2000). But the stick of military force was not far behind. After the uprising in San Cristobal, twelve thousand troops were deployed into Chiapas (Stephenson 1995: 17). As in Oka, the amount of force deployed by the government was in excess of any real threat on the part of Indigenous peoples. The zapatistas had .22 calibre rifles, and the soldiers were armed with the latest in military technology (Tello 1995: 29). Like the Oka case, the case of Chiapas demonstrates that military force and accounting technologies are often inseparable.

Chapter Ten

The Fourth World

A Cree warrior from northern Quebec paddles a canoe down the Hudson River. In the bush country of his ancestors, his elders had taught him to track moose and shoot geese. Later, he had crossed the educational and cultural divide, transcended the racial barriers and committed himself to regaining the Indigenous rights of his people. His journey has taken him into the boardrooms of Geneva and the Hague and the halls of international justice at the United Nations. Now, as the sun sets on the twentieth century, he is moving into the heart of the battlefield. Mathew Coon-Come, Grand Chief of the Crees of northern Quebec, is paddling into the Big Apple—publicity machine in tandem—to push for the shelving of the Great Whale project, whose hydroelectric power is earmarked for consumption south of the border and whose development will bring ruin to his homeland. This is the way of modern treaty-making; this is Grand Chief Mathew Coon-Come's sophisticated Fourth-World tactical approach to the Native sovereignty that he knows is bound to come. Hydro-Quebec and the government of Quebec will indeed shelve the deal in 1995. In 2001, a new deal with the Crees will be struck, a deal that will be hailed as the beginning of a new era in Indigenous-Canadian relations.

> The hardest task in the struggle for the Fourth World is to learn to produce that new reality that reconstructs a tradition in which people can hold a common belief, and which uses all the benefits of a global technology. (Manuel and Posluns 1974: 245)

Running concurrently with the northern Quebec Cree struggle, another giant step was being taken at the other end of the country—a groundbreaking treaty involving nearly two thousand square kilometres of land, between the Nisga'a and the Province of British Columbia. These modern deals, appearing on the surface to be a far cry from the genocidal practices of previous governments, still raise questions about the on-going relationship between accounting/bureaucracy and emerging Native sovereignty. Where has the trajectory of governmental bureaucratic management of Indigenous peoples gone? Has it all but disappeared? How do the new agreements differ from the old ones? How are economic globalization and the pressures of ecological brinkmanship and dwindling resources relevant to these new agreements?

We have, in this study, traced the historical roots of heterophobia from the demonization of primal cultures in the middle ages and linked cultural genocide with modernity; we have examined accounting and bureaucracy as the key mechanisms—softwares of annihilation—in framing individuals as moveable statistical integers within a European imperialistically defined hierarchy of populations; and we have viewed modern global economics as a new form of imperialism, increasing the pressure by First-World appetite on increasingly scarce resources found within Indigenous ancestral lands. In relation to early treaties, we have examined the distinct world views of the European and Indigenous communities and looked at how those world views affected the understanding of the treaties; we have seen how the basic elements of treaty-making—collective memory and sealing the deal—were so disparate as to yield in essence two completely different historical perspectives.We have shown how those misapprehensions worked in favour of the European-Canadian society economically, but we have also seen how the *Delgamuukw* decision in British Columbia, in spite of its judicial limitations, has forever altered the perspective of Native rights and land rights.

In examining the historical trajectory of funding relationships, we have discovered that these relations have essentially defined the interactions between government agencies and their targeted populations; we have seen that, in spite of the covert intentions of Indigenous extinguishment as a bureaucratically driven, generations-long bleeding, the middle of the twentieth century witnessed a resurgence of the Native sovereignty movement and a heightened rhetoric of cooperation and consultation on the government side. But this resurgence and government shift also evinced an entrenched paradox, one whose shadow still falls on the layered and complex processes of modern treaty-making. A nation-to-nation relationship demands self-government, the only marker of sovereignty for each nation. The road to self-government—or rather, the *return* road to self-government—for Indigenous nations has been a long process of disentangling the bureaucratic strings attached to the funding mechanisms based on the *Indian Act* and treaty obligations—money, in simplest terms, in exchange for land appropriation and cultural decimation.

The strings attached, tied to the ascendancy of "economic viability" as defined by those providing the funding, have essentially bound the decision-making and leadership processes of those receiving the funding, resulting in the erosion of traditional leadership practices. The rhetoric of progress and development has also included accountability and self-sufficiency, as viewed through the lens of non-Indigenous global economics. Thus, the paradox: if sovereign, then why the funding? And if no funding, then how to gain access to the resources that define, nurture and cultivate independence? How, in other words, can government-to-government talks take place when one self-defined but unrecognized government appears to be dependent on the other; when the other is empowered by law to make decisions for the one; when the culturally dominated counterpart is prevented by the laws of the culturally dominant from making its own decisions? It is no wonder the 1969 White Paper tried to wash the government's hands of the whole affair. And no wonder that to this day negotiations hearken back to that radical, though ill-fated, government initiative and the constitutional package of 1982—including the Charter of Rights—the Meech Lake Accord, and later constitutional negotiations, all of which bear the fingerprints of the Native question.

Resistance to the concerted bureaucratic removal of traditional Native leadership and the ecocidal results of the Euro-Canadian incursion onto ancestral territories for economic gain have been exemplified by the Oka standoff in Quebec and the Zapatista insurgency in Mexico on the one hand and the types of agreements struck by the Nisga'a in British Columbia and the James Bay Cree in northern Quebec on the other hand. At the centre of these latter activities is resources—lumber and fishing in B.C. and hydro-electricity in Quebec. In relation to modern agreements, questions arise: What is the role of bureaucratic-accounting mechanisms? Have these mechanisms been dissipated; have they shifted? Are they masked? Is there co-option involved, and who is co-opting whom? Where do the two cultures meet economically and ecologically—are the ecological fallouts tempered by the Indigenous role in the partnerships? How are the conditions that brought about the earlier treaties similar or different than the new-era treaties? And finally, what are the links between self-government, land rights, sovereignty and economic development? In this final chapter we cannot possibly give definitive answers to all these questions; it is our intention however to pose them in the light of our previous investigations and to focus them through the lens of Fourth World Theory.

Globalization may be seen as an attempt to extend the circumference of First-World capitalist success far and wide without shifting its centre or having to accommodate other organisms of livelihood and statecraft. This extension of the centre-feeding organism into the farthest reaches of the world's economic frontiers necessitates the integration of the developing Second World and the undeveloped Third World into an even more monolithic hierarchy of nations. From this perspective, the world's Indigenous cultures may be barely observable, beyond the pale. If Indigenous cultures are barely visible at the outer fringes, waiting to get sucked into the global economy, they are also free enough of the monolith and its dominant economic machinations to be exercising that most common human propensity: identification in the most fundamental way, where geography, spirituality and survival find meaning through the collective images of selfhood and nationhood. In the face of globalization, the struggle for self-determination can only be intensified. Indigenous peoples from around the world are linked by their historical identification with their land, water and oral traditions. Their self-identity is linked neither through statehood nor through nation-states; they are "internationally unrecognized nations" (Seton 1999: unpaginated) representing a third of the world's population, and constitute the Fourth World, which "predates and continues to resist the encroachment of the 192 recognized states now in existence" (Seton 1999). According to Seton, "Fourth World Theory scrutinizes how colonial empires and modern states invaded and now encapsulate most of the world's enduring nations and peoples." Expansion of colonialism and modern statehood has further consequences on the biological and cultural diversity of the planet, as well as being responsible, according to Nietschmann, for producing "most of the world's wars, refugees, genocide, human rights violations, and environmental destruction" (Nietschmann 1994: 226).

Fourth World Theory distinguishes between nation and state. A state, according to the theory, enforces one set of institutions, laws and sometimes language and religion within its boundaries. The state is a legal creation which comes into being on a specific date and may contain within it more than one nation (Seton 1999). A nation, on the other hand, is less tangible; it has developed over time and is self-defining, held together by "a sense of solidarity, a common culture, an historically common territory and a national consciousness" (Seton 1999). Because nations do not voluntarily give up territory, resources or identity, nations tend to be an enduring form of organization, people and territory. Finally because states are artificial creations, "state breakdown occurs when new internal boundaries permit greater autonomy for nations within a state" (Seton 1999). Reconstruction usually occurs along "cultural fault lines," where group-identification and persistent cultural activity have continued regardless of political-legal boundaries.

In the present Canadian era of modern treaty-making, we have two recent agreements that may be illuminated by this concept of cultural fault lines: the Nisga'a treaty in British Columbia, and the northern Quebec Cree hydro deal. Both may be seen as examples of state breakdown—precisely along the cultural fault lines first laid down in the era of settlement and land-grants. Conversely, these agreements may be seen as a further entrenchment of new-style colonialism, motivated by resource-extraction interests, under the guise of necessary economic development and nation-to-nation cooperation. Which of these two perspectives is most accurate remains for the future to reveal.

Fourth World Theory postulates that Indigenous peoples seek balance and limited growth as essential to their continued livelihood, whereas political states strive for uncontrolled growth and economic progress. In the hierarchy of nation-states, with economic pressure applied downward, Third-World nations are often put in the position of being used by those above them in the pyramid of nation-states to exploit those below, Fourth-World nations, who, as it turns out, are the planet's remaining fundamental stewards and protectors of local ecosystems.

The Nisga'a Treaty

In 1887, Nisga'a and Tsimshian chiefs travelled to Victoria seeking a treaty and self-rule. They were turned away. On May 11, 2000, at the end of a persistent battle that took one hundred and thirteen years, Nisga'a chiefs representing approximately 5,500 people signed a treaty recognizing approximately two thousand square kilometres of the Nass River watershed in the northeastern corner of British Columbia as their homeland. The deal spelled out their rights to govern themselves and gave them the right to levy taxes (British Columbia 1999). According to Phil Fontaine, then National Chief of the Assembly of First Nations (AFN):

> For the first time in Canadian history, the jurisdiction of First Nations government has been affirmed and recognized by the federal and provincial governments of this land. (AFN 2000)

During third reading in Ottawa, the Reform (now the Canadian Alliance) Party introduced 471 amendments as a delaying tactic, pushed for the implementation of a B.C.-wide referendum and urged removal of Nisga'a self-government from protection under the *Charter of Rights and Freedoms*.

In April 2001, the treaty was ratified in Ottawa, while a B.C. Liberal Opposition went to the B.C. Supreme Court to challenge the constitutional right of the Nisga'a to self-government. In July 2001, the treaty was upheld by Supreme Court Justice Paul Williamson, who declared that Section 35 (1) of the Canadian Constitution:

> provides the solid constitutional framework within which Aboriginal rights in British Columbia may be defined by the negotiation of treaties in a manner compatible with the sovereignty of the Canadian state. I conclude that what Canada, British Columbia and the Nisga'a have achieved in the Nisga'a Final Agreement is consistent both with what the Supreme Court of Canada has encouraged, and consistent with the purpose of Section 35 of the Constitution Act, 1982.... The legislation and the Treaty are constitutionally valid. (Canadian News Wire, July 24, 2000)

Following the Canadian Parliament's ratification of the treaty, Chief Joseph Gosnell said, "The Royal Assent of our Treaty signifies the end of the colonial era for the Nisga'a people. It is a great and historic day for all

Canadians, and this achievement is a beacon of hope for colonized people in our own country and throughout the world" (Canadian News Wire, April 13, 2000).

While opponents of Indigenous sovereignty like to characterize treaties as tax-payer-funded giveaways by over-generous governments and Native rights as a return to fishing and trapping and multicultural festivities, Chief Gosnell's words point directly to the more fundamental issue: "The government of this country clearly recognizes that the Nisga'a were a self-governing people since well before European contact. We remain self-governing today, and we are proud to say that this inherent right is now clearly recognized and protected in the Constitution of Canada" (Canadian News Wire, April 13, 2000).

The inherent right to self-government is precisely what the B.C. Liberal opposition had challenged in court. Their argument was entirely constitutional. Confederation, they argued, had extinguished self-government. Only Parliament and the provinces could make laws; self government signified a change in the constitution. "I think frankly if the decision stands" Gordon Campbell, then leader of the Opposition (now premier) of B.C. said, "we'll be living in a profoundly different country tomorrow than we did today" (Canadian News Wire, July 25, 2000). At least he and Chief Gosnell agreed on the profound import of this change in the status quo. For Gosnell and the Indigenous people, replacing colonialism with sovereignty meant self-rule and hope for the future; for Campbell and the anti-sovereignty movement, it meant a loss of legislative and jurisdictional power for provincial and federal governments.

James Bay

The "Agreement Concerning a New Relationship" between the Cree of northern Quebec and the Quebec government reflects the difficult choices to be made by Indigenous leaders negotiating their future in an economic climate that in essence is a complete anathema to their cultural roots. Their battle was thrust upon the Cree suddenly in 1971, when Quebec Premier Robert Bourassa announced the development of the James Bay hydro project, without consulting or even informing the six thousand Cree who lived in the area. Their subsistence hunting and trapping had so far managed to co-exist with the encroaching forestry interests, their language base was fundamentally intact, and their lives were still primarily dictated by the cycle of the seasons. But they were not prepared for hydro-electric dams, an industrial behemoth that is as visibly destructive as any, one that is built on the actual re-construction of the landscape, diverting and damming waterways, destroying habitat for roads and workers' camps, flooding huge tracts of land and displacing countless populations, human and otherwise. Where there is hydro, there can be no return to wilderness. Bringing such a complex to Cree territory, without their permission, in the seventies, awakened the population to a future vastly different than what had gone before. The future leaders that would one day be taking their battle to the world courts were young then, youths taking instruction from unilingual elders who still lived traditional ways. These young people educated themselves, learned their second language, got their secondary and university educations, and spent the next twenty five years of their lives in pursuit of justice. Their organizing, militancy, dedication and courtroom challenges would culminate, at the turn of the century, in the Final Agreement—if indeed there can be such a thing. Between 1971 and 1975, this small band of neophyte activists had managed to lead their people to court and a victory, of sorts, against the Quebec government, in the form of the 1975 James Bay and Northern Quebec Agreement (Grand Council of the Crees 1975). Since 1975, they have repeatedly been forced to challenge the government and Hydro-Quebec in court and to take their issues to the court of public opinion, in order to enforce compliance with the agreement, especially in the area of environmental protection.

It is the question of the degree of compromise necessary to reach agreement and honouring agreements and protecting the environment that is still hotly debated within the Cree community itself. Compromise is always difficult to rationalize to those not present during the negotiations; it is a process of subtle language use and intricate balance-work that is necessary to keep the process from breaking down. The Final Agreement is definitely a compromise—for which the Cree leaders have been both criticized and praised. The language is clearly industrial-economic. There are no illusions about the Cree maintaining a pre-hydro lifestyle; their corporate interests are front and centre—but they are also inextricably tied to their Indigenous rights. Sovereignty, it is clear on paper and presumably in the hearts of the Cree negotiators, means control over the development of their traditional territories. And development, we see in the Agreement, regardless of whose control it is under, is primarily the manufacturing of hydro-electricity—i.e., diversion of waterways and rivers, flooding and the re-organization of the natural landscape.

For the critics of the deal, the Cree have been sold down the river; for the supporters, it is both a realistic assurance that they will get their rightful share of the inevitable development of the North, without giving up their sovereignty, and a recognition that the economic alternatives are scarce. George Wapachee, Chief of Namaska, states: "We have to look at the future, we have lots of young people with nothing to do" (Roslin 2001). To Chief Ted Moses, the trade-off was clear. "Our people" he said, "are realistic and practical. We don't romanticize the hardship associated with our traditional economies.... Our Cree concern has always been to obtain the most sustainable approach to development" (AEIQ 2001).

The Anti-Sovereignty Movement

Though apparently driven by a single fuel—the fear of a collapsing nation-state and what that does to the new corporate colonialism—the anti-sovereignty forces that focused on the Nisga'a treaty seemed to travel in three different vehicles: the constitution vehicle, driven by constitutional experts such as Melvin H. Smith; the accounting vehicle, driven by the Canadian Taxpayers Association and the Canadian Alliance (formerly the Reform) Party, Official Opposition in Ottawa; and the corporate-interest vehicle, driven by the esteemed right-wing think-tank and lobbyist, the Fraser Institute. These bodies appear to be part of a larger continental effort; their links with fishing and hunting lobby groups give them a patina of grassroots involvement, but in fact they often serve the resource-extraction business sector. Anti-sovereignty groups often give themselves names that imply a claim to the very rights that Indigenous groups have been fighting for over the last several hundred years, insinuating that Native sovereignty is somehow anti-democratic and a threat to property and individual rights. FIRE, the Federation for Individual Rights and Equality, in Ontario and British Columbia, argues that self-government should be restricted to the municipal model of government, under the power of the province and the federal government. The Fraser Institute posts its anti-sovereignty diatribes on something called The Economic Freedom Network. The Canadian Taxpayers Association has a Centre For Aboriginal Policy Change. In the U.S., such groups as ACE (All Citizens Equal) and SPEAR (Sportsmen Protecting Every American's Right) focus their rhetoric on the loss of property rights and the special rights received by Natives. In Canada, ON FIRE (Ontario Federation for Individual Rights and Equity) relies on slogans such as "One nation—One set of laws" and "Compensation for loss." The focus on equal rights for non-Natives, access to natural resources and Indian welfare dependency is universal amongst these groups, and their rhetoric is often indistinguishable from the Opposition Alliance Party in Canada and the Liberals in British Columbia.

There is common cause between the Fraser Institute, the B.C. Liberal Party, the Canadian Taxpayers Association and other anti-sovereignty groups such as ON FIRE. The recognition of Indigenous self-government seems, to them, to mean an attack on Canadian sovereignty. It is curious that pro-business activists and institutions such as the Fraser Institute and the Canadian Taxpayer's Association have so little to say when Canadian sovereignty is attacked from without—say, by U.S. incursions into Canadian security policy after September 11, or the flagrant abuses of NAFTA in softwood lumber, steel and agriculture. Perhaps it isn't fear of Native rights *per se* that frightens them but rather that self-government means the exercise of power and control over lumber, hydro and mineral rights within traditional territories. The federal Alliance Party, the B.C. provincial Liberals (formerly Reform and Social Credit), the Canadian Taxpayer's Association (indistinguishable from Alliance/Reform), FIRE (grassroots Reform/Alliance) and the Fraser Institute are all big-business fronts. And in British Columbia, big business means resource extraction. Only at the economic level does the notion that sovereignty is a zero-sum game ("if you gain more sovereignty, I have less") hold water. The anti-sovereignty movement seems incapable of seeing the burgeoning Fourth World as anything but a threat to business interests. Historically, Canadian governments have served the corporations. The fur trade, the railroads, mining, oil, lumber—all have benefitted from corporate welfare, all were built upon the largesse of the Crown at the cost of Aboriginal sustenance. What the reactionary anti-sovereignty right sees when it sees Indigenous self-government is an end to hand-outs, huge tax incentives and bargain-basement licence fees to corporations. If the activists of the global Indigenous cultural survival movement are prophetic, then it is truly a new day for the Fourth World. And in this new day—it is hoped—non-Indigenous business interests are finally going to be forced to play on a level playing field.

Back to the Numbers

To the anti-sovereignty forces, notions such as self-government, treaty rights and protection of traditional ways appear to be simply rhetoric that masks the real Aboriginal agenda: to use the taxpayers' money to gain control of resource-rich territory and, in the process, lining the pockets of Native leaders while keeping their own people in poverty and on welfare. The Canadian Taxpayers Association, the Alliance Party and the B.C Liberals share this stance. Having pushed for a province-wide referendum on the Nisga'a Treaty while in opposition and having challenged the constitutionality of the treaty in the Supreme Court, the first item on the B.C. Liberal agenda upon being elected in 2001 was to put in place a province-wide treaty referendum. The ballot contained eight questions, most of them regarding issues that had already been covered in previous agreements, questions which hearkened back to the most ignorant assumptions about Native life in Canada. The subtext of the questions in total was that non-Natives have much to fear from Indigenous sovereignty, especially expropriation and the loss of individual property rights, the right to enjoy national and provincial parks, the right to make a living, the right to fish and hunt and the right to affect decision-making in the use of Crown land. The key referendum question—and likely the question that will be most focused on when the parties get back to the negotiating table, buried in the middle of the ballot, surrounded by "motherhood" questions—is question #6: "Aboriginal self-government should have the characteristics of local government, with powers delegated from Canada and British Columbia." In other words, a complete refutation of nationhood, the very basis of all Indigenous rights claims.

In March of 2002, the Canadian Taxpayers Association, under the imprint of its Centre for Aboriginal Policy Change, put out a circular entitled, "Analysis of the British Columbia Treaty Referendum Questions." The Centre's mission statement speaks clearly:

> The Centre for Aboriginal Policy Change was founded in 2002 to provide a permanent and professional taxpayer and democratic advocacy presence to monitor, research and offer alternatives to current Aboriginal policy and court decisions under the guiding principles of support for individual property rights, equality, self-sufficiency, and democratic and financial accountability. (Canadian Taxpayers Association 2002)

This is a new improved language of colonialism, in a political climate where the worst accusation is one of anti-democracy, where terrorism lurks around every corner. The implication is that treaty rights are somehow undemocratic. It is the new nomenclature for what old-style colonialism called uncivilized and savage. "Self-sufficiency," implying by contrast dependency, when spoken in the same breath as "individual property rights" and "equality," leads the reader back to the worst European conceptions of "tribal." To drive home the point, "democratic" is used again in the same paragraph, coupled with "financial accountability." The implications are clear. Attempts at Native self-government, with tribal, anti-democratic, financially irresponsible Native leadership—like those Third-World countries attempting western-style democracy in order to please Washington, Wall Street and the World Bank—must be closely monitored. Property rights and Canadians' sovereignty are being threatened while the taxpayer is being bled dry. "Land ownership and resources," the pamphlet tells us, are, as new treaties are being signed, "increasingly becoming a Pandora's Box." And "Fishing, paying taxes and voting are increasingly being assigned on the basis of racial history."

In a tidy summing up, the Centre's propaganda pamphlet conflates two hot-button issues for average citizens, who recognize in an economically troubled province their dependence on fishing, forestry and mining and who are not in general knowledgeable about Indigenous-government history: benefits on the one hand and control over resource-rich (and job-rich) land, on the other. Fear of unemployment, heightened by the skewed spectre of Indians not paying taxes and living on government grants and welfare, casts a long shadow over the very idea of self-government—which has nothing to do with the latter and is in fact a remedy for it. When, in the context of Indigenous control over hundreds of thousands of acres, the words "billions of tax dollars are spent" are linked with "not finding [their] way to the people it was intended to help," they conjure up pictures of corrupt Native leaders, welfare fraud and destitute or drunken Indians. Again, we are taken to the worst stereotypes, where financial incompetence begs for the incursion of the federal government into the financial affairs of Indigenous peoples.

Clearly, these stereotypes have not disappeared because they are useful, as are the accounting concepts and numbers that are used to justify the status quo. Pro-business organizations such as the Fraser Institute and political parties such as the Alliance/Reform Party consistently recycle the historical stereotypes and numerical calculations that have been illustrated throughout the preceding chapters to defend a particular set of business interests and a particular vision of Canada. Take, for example *On-Reserve Welfare Dependency: An Accountability and Affordability Crisis,* a report prepared by the Reform Audit and Evaluation Team, for Mike Scott, MP, Opposition Critic for Indian Affairs and Northern Development (Reform Party of Canada 1997b). In essence, it is a political diatribe masked as an auditor's report, claiming that DIAND is attempting to hide the truth about how much taxpayers' money goes to support on-reserve residents and that corruption is rife on reserves. Or the study, *Aboriginal Benefits in Canada,* which uses the same dehumanized, integer-driven, ahistorical tactics to drive home the same claim: Natives are sucking the taxpayer dry (Reform Party of Canada 1997a). Even the neutral-sounding title belies its bias. Benefits (remember presents?) could have been called Compensations—or the title could have been: *Honouring Canada's Treaty Obligations.* The fifty-nine-page document contains eighteen charts and graphs. Its focus seems to be the amount of revenue loss generated by Indigenous tax exemptions, coupled with departmental spending and programs. In 1995–96, these totalled $8.7 billion, with $7.8 billion, or 89.7 percent, going to status Indians on reserves and Inuit living on Crown land. Seniors, according to the report, received an estimated $158.7 million in 1995–96, amounting to $10,420 per senior Indian. Post-secondary education grants are "potentially" worth up to $42,000 per applicant. Total benefits per status Indian were estimated at $19,903 for the same period. The report offers solutions—though the problem itself is not made entirely clear—unless it is that these payments in exchange for the entire northern half of the continent, taken without permission from its inhabitants, is somehow too high a price to pay. "Replace existing federal and provincial programs for Aboriginals" the report recommends, "with the full range of federal and provincial programs enjoyed by all other Canadians" (2). This is reminiscent of the infamous White Paper of 1969—no Indian status, no Indians, no Indian problem. And, while the "phasing out" (phasing out what, or *whom,* exactly?) period "would take as long as twenty years ... the massive benefits identified in this study would be better applied in most cases if directed to individual Indians rather than to band administrators" (2). No leadership, no bands, no nations, no problem.

Not only does the rule of quantification in such a study as this one narrow the perspective to almost suffocating levels, by virtue of its accounting language, it ignores history and the *Indian Act* itself and in the process avoids any discussion of interpretation. In the section, "The Need For Accountability," for example, it informs us that "over 80% of DIAND's total expenditures have been devolved and are managed by Indian bands. How these funds are dispersed is decided by the Chiefs and their Band Councils" (21). However, as we saw in chapter seven, this is disingenuous. Certain questions are missing from the equation: Under which non-Indigenous regulations, parameters and expectations were these funds disbursed? What limitations were imposed, without Indigenous input, on the devolution of said funding? Within which *Indian Act* restrictions are these so-called management decisions made? And most realistically: How does the dependence of livelihood on the largesse of the Crown and the continued disbursement of funds, in an *imposed* dependency relationship, affect behaviours, decisions and politically necessary considerations in managing such funds? No amount of sophisticated charting and graphing can answer these questions, and without the answers, the numbers hold no value. They do, however, lead to other types of questions, of an a-historical, "common-sense" bent. Why, for example, should we be paying taxes for these services which are normally found in a wide range of federal, provincial and municipal governments? The study's answers take us back at least half a century, to documents such as the Hawthorn Report. This observation echoes exactly one of that report's recommendations: Most of the programs are restricted to reserve Indians, who therefore have no incentive to move to the industrial-urban centres where the jobs are; they choose instead to live in virtual quarantine in reserve communities which have no real economic base and, in a number of instances, a disintegrating social and cultural fabric (Hawthorn and Canada 1966: 13).

The Changing Landscape

The status quo relationship between Indigenous peoples and those with whom they share their territories is unacceptable on both sides. New relationships are being forged. The Nisga'a and the British Columbia government are working out their differences on a nation-to-nation basis. The James Bay Cree have worked out a development deal on a nation-to-nation basis. Nunavut has defined its traditional territory and is self-governing. Retrograde, culturally presumptuous, anti-sovereignty interests in pursuit of the last resource-rich territories occupied by the remaining Indigenous nations of the world are fighting a battle that has already expired. Fear-mongering has run its course. Indigenous sovereignty, however it is configured between governments, is not without problems and risks, but negotiations between peoples are bound to be more productive when both sides recognize the nationhood of the other. Of course, there may be instances of corruption and unaccountability within a small percentage of Indigenous communities, as there is throughout Canadian society; should we expect more from them than we do from our other leaders? Of course, modern treaties are changing the landscape of our nation-states; is this something to fear?

As this book has shown, the racial genocidal use of the softwares of governmentality, especially accounting, have served colonialism well, but the emergence of the Fourth World—which has undoubtedly absorbed many of the problems inherent in the European tools it has learned to use for its own cultural survival—indicates that the machinery of cultural genocide is sputtering and failing. The new colonialism—as practised by the global transnational corporate empire—is exerting extreme pressure on the Indigenous peoples occupying the remaining resource-rich territories on the planet. However, Indigenous peoples are meeting that pressure with a concerted effort that is gaining support as the planetary game of ecological brinkmanship proves more and more nihilistic. While corporations, with their agenda of global dominance, undermine the geopolitical borders of nation-states, the advance movement of the Fourth World is eating away at them from inside. Changing times, changing landscapes, indeed.

> As we view the North American Indian world today, we must keep in mind two things: Indians have not yet left the Aboriginal universe in which they have always dwelt emotionally and intellectually, and the Western world is gradually working its way out of its former value system and into the value system of the Aboriginal World.
>
> Our celebration honours the emergence of the Fourth World: the utilization of technology and its life-enhancing potential within the framework of the values of the peoples of the Aboriginal World—not a single messianic moment after which there will never be another raging storm, but the free use of power by natural human groupings, immediate communities, people who are in direct contact with one another, to harness the strength of the torrent for the growth of their own community. Neither apartheid nor assimilation can be allowed to discolour the community of man in the Fourth World. An integration of free communities and the free exchange of people between those communities according to their talents and temperaments is the only kind of confederation that is not an imperial domination. (Manuel and Posluns 1974: 235)

References

Every effort has been made to ensure that the website addresses listed here are correct. They were accessed just before publication (in November 2002).

AEIQ. 2001. Available at http://www.aieq.net/aieq/communiques/pdf/2001_12_18_TMoses.PDF

Akwesasne Task Force on the Environment (ATFE). 2002. Available at http://www.slic.com/atfe/atfe.htm.

Amin, S. 2001 (Sept.). "Globalización o Apartheid a Escala Global?" Available at http://www.rcci.net/globalizacion/2001/fg193.htm.

Andreopoulos, G. 1994. *Genocide: Conceptual and Historical Dimensions*. Philadelphia: University of Pennsylvania.

Anon. 1983. "Royal Proclamation of 7 October 1763." In L. Getty and A. Lussier.

Arendt, H. 1951. *The Origins of Totalitarianism*. New York: Harcourt Brace.

Assembly of First Nations (AFN). 2000. Available at http://www.afn.ca/Press%20Realeses%20&%20Speeches/national_chief_fontaine_applauds.htm. Note typo Realeses [sic]

Barker, M.L., and D. Soyez. 1994. "Think locally, act globally? The transnationalization of Canadian resource-use conflicts." *Environment* 36, 12.

Barlow, M., and J. P. Winter. 1997. *The Big Black Book: The Essential Views of Conrad Black and Barbara Amiel*. Toronto: Stoddart.

Barnsley, P. 2000. "U.S. court rules trust funds mismanaged." Available at http://www.ammsa.com/windspeaker/WINDNEWSFEB2000.html#anchor3098906.

Barta, T. 1987. "Relations of Genocide: Land and Lives in the Colonization of Australia." In I. Wallimann and M. Dobkowski (eds.), *Genocide and the Modern Age*. Westport, CT: Greenwood.

Bartlett, R. 1980. *The Indian Act of Canada*. Saskatoon, SK: University of Saskatchewan, Native Law Centre.

Bauman, Z. 1989. *Modernity and the Holocaust*. Ithaca, NY: Cornell University Press.

Bell, M., R. Butlin and M. Heffernan. 1995. *Geography and Imperialism: 1820–1940*. Manchester: Manchester University Press.

Berry, T. M. 1999. *The Great Work: Our Way into the Future*. New York, NY: Bell Tower.

Blanchard, D. 1980. *Seven Generations: A History of Kanenkehaka*. Kanahwake: Kanahwake Survival School.

Boldt, M. 1993. *Surviving as Indians: The Challenge of Self-Government*. Toronto: University of Toronto Press.

Boldt, M., J.A. Long and L. Little Bear. 1985. *The Quest for Justice: Aboriginal Peoples and Aboriginal Rights*. Toronto: University of Toronto Press.

Brasher, P. 1996. "BIA Loses 2.4 Billion." *Seattle Post-Intelligencer*. Feb. 26.

British Columbia, Government of. 1999. *B.C. Treaty Commission Annual Report, 1999*. Available at http://www.bctreaty.net/annuals/99publicinformation.html.

Brown, E. K. 1944. *On Canadian Poetry*. Toronto: Ryerson Press.

Bryce, P. 1922. *The Story of a National Crime: Being an Appeal for Justice for the Indians of Canada*. Ottawa: James Hope & Sons.

Burchell, S., C. Clubb, A. Hopwood, J. Hughes and J. Nahapiet. 1980. "The Roles of Accounting in Organizations and Society." *Accounting, Organizations and Society* 5, 1.

Burroughs, P. 1969. *The Colonial Reformers and Canada, 1830–1849: Selections from Documents and Publications of the Times*. Toronto: McClelland and Stewart.

Bush, B., and J. Maltby. forthcoming. "Taxation in West Africa and the 'governable person.'" *Critical Perspectives on Accounting*.

Canada.1958. *Review of Activities 1948–1958, Indian Affairs Branch of Citizenship and Immigration*. Ottawa: Government of Canada.

Canada, 1969. *Statement of Government of Canada on Indian Policy*. Ottawa, Government of Canada.

Canada. Commission on Indian Affairs., J.F. Johnston and D.F. Brown. 1947. *Report of Commission on Indian Affairs, 1946*. Ottawa: The Commission.

Canada, House of Commons, Special Committee on Indian Self-Government. and K. Penner. 1983. *Indian Self-government in Canada: Report of the Special Committee*. Ottawa: Government of Canada.

Canada and the World Backgrounder. 1998. "Downsizing: Across Canada, the education system is being reformed and almost nowhere is that reform going smoothly." *Canada and the World Backgrounder* 64, 3.

Canadian Taxpayers Association. 2002. *Analysis of the British Columbia Treaty Referendum Questions*. http://www.taxpayer.com/studies/AboriginalCentre/Ref%20Analysis(April2002).pdf

Chalk, F. 1994. "Redefining Genocide." In G. Andreopoulus.

Charny, I. 1994. "Toward a Generic Definition of Genocide." In G. Andreopoulus.

Churchill, W. 1994. *Indians Are Us? Culture and Genocide in Native North America*. Toronto: Between the Lines.

———. 1999. *Struggle for the Land: Native North American Resistance to Genocide, Ecocide and Colonization*. Winnipeg: Arbeiter Ring.

Colonial Magazine. 1840. London: Fisher and Sons & Company.

Cook, R., and K. McNaught. 1963. *Canada and the United States: A Modern History*. Toronto: Clarke Irwin.

Cooper, D., and M. Sherer. 1984. "The Value of Corporate Accounting Reports: Arguments for a Political Economy of Accounting." *Accounting, Organizations and Society* 9, 2.

Creighton, D.G. 1958. *A History of Canada: Dominion of the North*. Boston: Houghton Mifflin.

Cuevas, H. 1993. *Introduction to Economy*. Columbia: University Externado de Columbia.

Dallaire, F. 1991. *Oka: la hache de guerre*. Ste-Foy, Québec: Éditions La Liberté.

Das, V. 1989. "Subaltern as Perspective." In *Subaltern Studies* No.6, Writings on South Asian History and Society, edited by Ranajit Guha. Dehli: Oxford University Press.

Davis, R., and M. Zannis. 1973. *The Genocide Machine in Canada*. Montreal: Black Rose.

Dickason, O.P. 1993. *Canada's First Nations: A History of Founding Peoples from Earliest Times*. Toronto: McClelland & Stewart.

Dragland, S.L. 1974. *Duncan Campbell Scott: A Book of Criticism*. Ottawa: Tecumseh Press.

Durham, J.G.L., and R. Coupland. 1946. *The Durham Report*. Oxford: Clarendon Press.

Dyck, N., and Institute of Social and Economic Research. 1991. *What is the Indian "problem"?: Tutelage and Resistance in Canadian Indian Administration*. St. John's, NF: Institute of Social and Economic Research, Memorial University of Newfoundland.

Edmonton Jounal. 1991. "The high cost of Oka." Monday, May 6, Editorial, A5.

Espiritu, A. 1997. "Aboriginal Nations: Natives in Northwest Siberia and Northern Alberta." In E.A. Smith and J. McCarter (eds.), *Contested Arctic*. Seattle: Russian East European and Central Asian Studies Center at the Henry M. Jackson School of International Studies in association with University of Washington Press.

EZLN (Zapatista Army for National Liberation). 1994. *First Declaration of the Lacandon Jungle*. General Command of the EZLN, Mexico. (quoted in full in Womack 1999, p.247, and available at http://www.exln.org/documentos/1994/199312xx.en.htm)

Fanon, F. 1963. *The Wretched of the Earth*. New York: Grove Press.

Fisher, Robin. 1977. *Contact and Conflict: Indian-European Relations in British Columbia, 1874–1890*. Vancouver: University of British Columbia Press.

Foucault, M. 1984. "Nietzche, Geneology, History." In P. Rabinow (ed.), *The Foucault Reader*. New York: Pantheon.

———. 1991. "Governmentality." In G. Burchell, C. Gordon and P. Miller (eds), *The Foucault Effect*. Chicago: University of Chicago Press.

Francis, D., R. Jones and D. Smith. 1988. *Origins: Canadian History to Confederation*. Toronto: Holt Rinehart and Winston.

Frideres, J. 1990. " Native Rights and the 21st Century: The Making of Red Power." *Canadian Ethnic Studies* 22, 3.

Frideres, J., and L.E. Krosenbrink-Gelissen. 1993. *Native Peoples in Canada: Contemporary Conflicts*. Scarborough, ON: Prentice-Hall Canada.

Funnel, W. 1998. "Accounting in the Service of the Holocaust." *Critical Perspectives on Accounting* 9, 4.

Galeano, E.H. 1997. *Open Veins of Latin America: Five Centuries of the Pillage of a Continent*. New York: Monthly Review Press.

Gedicks, A. 1994. *The New Resource Wars: Native and Environmental Struggles Against Multinational Corporations*. Montreal: Black Rose.

Getty, L., and A. Lussier (eds.). 1983. *As Long as the Sun Shines and Water Flows*. Vancouver: University of British Columbia Press.

Glenelg, L. 1836. "Copy of a Dispatch from Lord Glenelg to the Earl of Gosford." In *British Parliamentary Papers*. Shannon: Irish University Press.

Goddard, J. 1991. *The Last Stand of the Lubicon Cree*. Vancouver: Douglas and McIntyre.

Goodman-Draper, Jacqueline. 1994. "The Development and Underdevelopment at Akwesasne: Cultural and economic subversion."*Academic Journal of Economics and Sociology* 53, 1.

Gordon, C. 1991. "Government Rationality: An Introduction." In G. Burchell, C. Gordon and P. Miller (eds.), *The Foucault Effect*. Chicago: University of Chicago Press.

Great Britain, Government of. 1835. *Report from the Select Committee on the Colonial Military Expenditure with the Minutes of Evidence*. London: House of Commons.

———. 1845. *Report on the Affairs of the Indians in Canada. Sections I and II*. London: House of Commons.

———. 1847. *Report on the Affairs of the Indians in Canada, Section III*. London: House of Commons.

———. 1857–1858. *Report of the Special Commission to Investigate Indian Affairs in Canada*. Toronto: Steward Derbyshire & George Desbarats.

Grand Council of the Crees. 1975. *James Bay and Northern Quebec Agreement*. Available at http://www.gcc.ca/Political-Issues/jbnqa/jbnqa_menu.htm.

Grinde, D.A., and B. E. Johansen. 1995. *Ecocide of Native America: Environmental Destruction of Indian Lands and Peoples*. Sante Fe, NM: Clear Light.

Guha, R. 1983. "The Prose of Counter-Insurgency." In R. Guha (ed.), *Subaltern Studies II*. Dehli: Oxford.

———. 2000. "On Some Aspects of the Historiography of Colonial India." In V. Chaturvedi (ed.), *Mapping Subaltern Studies and the Postcolonial*. London: Verso.

Hall, L. 1991. "A Short History of the Montreal Mohawk." In C. MacLaine and M. Baxendale (ed.), *This Land is Our Land: The Mohawk Revolt in Quebec*. Montreal: Optimum Publishing.

Hamilton, R. 1988. *Feudal Society and Colonization: The Historiography of New France*. Gananoque, ON: Langdale Press.

Hanke, L. 1970. *Aristotle and the American Indians: A Study in Race Prejudice in the Modern World*. Bloomington: Indiana University Press.

Hansard. 1951. Ottawa: House of Commons.

Harding, J. 1976. "Mercury Poisoning." *Canadian Dimension* 11, 7.

Harvey, N. 1998. *The Chiapas Rebellion: The Struggle for Land and Democracy*. Durham, NC: Duke University Press.

Hawthorn, H.B., and Canada. Indian Affairs Branch. 1966. *A survey of the contemporary Indians of Canada: A report on economic, political, educational needs and policies*. Ottawa: Indian Affairs Branch.

Head, B.F. 1836. "Correspondence to Lord Glenelg: 20th Nov. 1836." In *British Parliamentary Papers*. Shannon: Irish University Press.

Headrick, D. 1981. *The Tools of Empire*. Oxford: Oxford University Press.

———. 1988. *The Tentacles of Progess*. Oxford:: Oxford University Press.

Hernandez, L. 1994. "Chiapas: la gestacion de la rebeldia." In *Chiapas: la rebellion de los pobres*. Nafarroa: Hirugarren Prentsa.

Hilberg, R. 1985. *The Destruction of the European Jews*. New York: Holmes & Meier.

Hildebrandt, W., S. Carter and D. F. Rider. 1996. *The True Spirit and Original*

Intent of Treaty 7. Montreal: McGill-Queen's University Press.
Indian Affairs, Department of. 1885. *Annual Report*. Ottawa: Government of Canada.
———. 1887. *Annual Report*. Ottawa: Government of Canada.
———. 1900. *Annual Report*. Ottawa: Government of Canada.
———. 1902. *Annual Report*. Ottawa: Government of Canada.
———. 1908. *Annual Report*. Ottawa: Government of Canada.
———. 1915. *Annual Report*. Ottawa: Government of Canada.
———. 1916. *Annual Report*. Ottawa: Government of Canada.
Indian Affairs and Northern Development, Department of (DIAND). 1993. *diand's Evolution from Direct Service Delivery to a Funding Agency*. Ottawa: DIAND.
Kieso, D., J. Weygandt and T. Warfield. 1991. *Intermediate Accounting*. Toronto: Wiley & Sons.
Knudston , Peter and David Suzuki. 1992. *Wisdom of the Elders; Honouring Sacred Native Visions of Nature*. Toronto, Stoddard.
Lacan, J., and W. Prévost. 1876. *An Historical Notice on the Difficulties Arisen between the Seminary of St. Sulpice of Montreal and Certain Indians, at Oka, Lake of Two Mountains [micorform]: A mere case of right of property*. Montreal: s.n.
LaDuke, W. 1998. *Indigenous Environmental Perspectives: A North American Primer*. New York: Longman.
Langevin, H. 1869. *Annual Report of the Secretary of State*. Ottawa, Government of Canada.
Leighton, D. 1983. "A Victorian Civil Servant at Work: Lawrence Vankoughnet and the Canadian Indian Department, 1874–1893." In I. Getty and A. Lussier.
Lemkin, R. 1947. "Genocide as a Crime Under International Law." *American Journal of International Law* 41, 1 (January).
Leslie, J., R. Maguire, R. G. Moore, K.T. Miller, 1978. *The Historical Development of the Indian Act*. Ottawa: Treaties and Historical Research Centre Research Branch Corporate Policy, Indian and Northern Affairs Canada.
MacLaine, C., M. S. Baxendale and R. Galbraith. 1990. *This Land is our Land: The Mohawk Revolt at Oka*. Montreal: Optimum.
Manuel, G., and M. Posluns. 1974. *The Fourth World: An Indian Reality*. New York: Free Press.
Marx, K. 1963. *The 18th Brumaire of Louis Bonaparte*. New York: International Publishers Co. Inc.
Maybury-Lewis, D. 2001. "Cultural Survival." Available at http://www.cs.org/.
McNab, D. 1983. "Herman Merivale and Colonial Office Indian Policy in the Mid-Nineteenth Century." In L. Getty and A. Lussier.
Mercredi, O., and M.E. Turpel. 1993. *In the Rapids, Navigating the Future of First Nations*. Toronto: Viking.
Merivale, H. 1967. *Lectures on Colonization and Colonies*. New York: A.M. Kelley.
Milchman, A., and A. Rosenberg. 1992. "Hannah Arendt and the Etiology of the Desk Killer: The Holocaust as Portent." *History of European Ideas* 14, 2.
Miller, P., and C. Napier. 1993. "Genealogies of Calculation." *Accounting, Organizations and Society* 18, 7.
Miller, P., and N. Rose. 1990. "Governing Economic Life." *Economy and Society*

19, 1 (February).

Milloy, J.S. 1983. "The Early Indian Acts: Developmental Strategy and Constitutional Change." In L. Getty and A. Lussier.

———. 1999. *A National Crime: The Canadian Government and the Residential School System, 1879 to 1986*. Winnipeg: University of Manitoba Press.

Mittelstaedt, M. 1997a. "MPP resisted Ippewash fall-guy role: Beaubien warned of not taking responsibility in fax to Premier's Office during native occupation." *Globe and Mail* January 14, A8.

———. 1997b. "Harris confirms role of ministry in Ipperwash park clash." *Globe and Mail* April 1, A5.

Morgan, L.H., and H.M. Lloyd. 1901. *League of the Ho-dé-no-sau-nee, or Iroquois*. New York: Dodd Mead.

Morris, A. 1991. *The treaties of Canada with the Indians of Manitoba and the North-West Territories: Including the negotiations on which they were based, and other information relating thereto.* Saskatoon: Fifth House.

Murray, Norman. 1886. *The Oka question containing the original title, and a brief account of the feudal system of seigniorial tenure in Canada, and its abolition in 1854: with a general review of the Oka question in particular and Roman agression in general.* [Microfiche, sl: sn 1981].

Myers, G. 1914. *History of Canadian Wealth*. Montreal: C.H. Kerr & Company.

Næss, A., and D. Rothenberg. 1989. *Ecology, Community, and Lifestyle: Outline of an Ecosophy*. New York: Cambridge University Press.

National Institute of Environmental Health Sciences (NIEHS). N.D. "Restoration, Basic Research on Hazardous Chemical Wastes." Available at http://www.albany.edu/sph/superfund/restor.html.

Neu, D., 1999. "'Discovering' Indigenous Peoples: Accounting and the Machinery of Empire." *Accounting Historians Journal* 26, 1.

———. 2000a. "'Presents' for the Indians: Land, Colonialism and Accounting in Canada." *Accounting, Organizations and Society* 25, 2.

———. 2000b. "Locating Accounting." *Accounting, Auditing and Accountability Journal* 13, 3.

Neu, D., and A. Taylor. 1996. "Accounting and the Politics of Divestment." *Critical Perspectives on Accounting* 7, 4.

Nietschmann, Bernard Q. 1994. "The Fourth World: Nations vs States." In G.J. Demko and W.R. Wood (eds.), *Reordering the World: Geopolitical Perspectives in the Twenty-first Century.* Boulder, Colorado: Westview Press.

Parent, A. 1887. *The Life of Rev. Amand Parent*. Toronto: William Briggs 1981.

Parker, Arthur C. 1968. *Iroquois Uses of Maize and Other Food Plants*. Edited with an introd. by William N. Fenton. Syracuse, NY: Syracuse University Press.

Parker, A.C., and S. Newhouse. 1916. *The Constitution of the Five Nations; or, The Iroquois Book of the Great Law.* Albany, NY: University of the State of New York.

Paul, D. 2000. *We Were Not the Savages*. Halifax: Fernwood.

Persky, S. 1998. *Delgamuukw: The Supreme Court of Canada Decision on Aboriginal Title*. Vancouver: Greystone Books.

Pertusati, L. 1997. *In Defense of Mohawk land: Ethnopolitical Conflict in Native North America.* Albany, NY: State University of New York Press.

Peters, E. 1999. "Native People and the Environmental Regime in the James Bay and Northern Quebec Agreement." *Arctic* 52, 4.

Platiel, R. 1997. "Ipperwash statements contradictory: Police officer reportedly fired first." *Globe and Mail*. March 3, A1.
Postman, N. 1993. *Technopoly: The Surrender of Culture to Technology*. New York: Vintage Books.
Power, M. 1992. "After Calculation? Reflections on Critique of Economic Reason by Andre Gorz." *Accounting, Organizations and Society* 17, 5.
Preston, A., C. Wright and J. Young. 1996. "Imag(in)ing Annual Reports."*Accounting, Organizations and Society* 21.
Preston, A., W. Chua and D. Neu. 1997. "The Diagnosis-Related Group Prospective Payment System and the Problem of Government Rationing Health Care to the Elderly." *Accounting, Organizations and Society* 22, 1.
Price, R., Indian Association of Alberta, and Treaty and Aboriginal Rights Research Centre of Manitoba. 1975. *Spirit and Terms of Treaties 6, 7 & 8: Alberta Indian Perspectives*. Edmonton: Indian Association of Alberta.
Programme, F. P. 2001. "Guyana Government Grants 5.1 Million Acre Mining Concession on Indigenous Lands." Available at http://www.wrm.org.uy/bulletin/17.html#Guyana
Rabinow, P. (ed.). 1984. *The Foucault Reader*. New York: Pantheon.
Royal Commission on Aboriginal Peoples (RCAP). 1996. *Report of the Royal Commission on Aboriginal Peoples*. Ottawa: Canada Communications Group.
Reform Party of Canada. 1997a. *Aboriginal Benefits in Canada*. Ottawa: Reform Party.
———. 1997b. *On-Reserve Welfare Dependency: An Accountability and Affordability Crisis*. Ottawa: Reform Party.
Roebuck, B.D. 1999. *Elevated Mercury in Fish as a Result of the James Bay Hydroelectric Project*. Montreal and Kingston: McGill-Queens University Press.
Roslin, A. 2001. "Cree Deal: A Model or Betrayal?" (Nov. 10). Available at www.ottertooth.com/Reports/Rupert/News/rupert-surrender4.htm
Ross, J. 1995. *Rebellion from the Roots: Indian uprising in Chiapas*. Monroe, ME: Common Courage Press.
Rubenstein, R.L. 1978. *The Cunning of History: The Holocaust and the American Future*. New York: Harper & Row.
Russell, G. 1998. Acteal Massacre—December 22, 1997. Available at http://www.rightsaction.org/articles/0398.htm
Russell, P. 1995. *The Chiapas Rebellion*. Austin: Mexico Resource Center.
Said, E. 1979. *Orientalism*. New York: Vintage Books.
———. 1993. *Culture and Imperialism*. London: Vintage Books.
Schell, L.M., and A.M. Tarbell. 1998. "A Partnership Study of PCBs and the Health of Mohawk Youth: Lessons from our Past and Guidelines for our Future." *Environmental Health Perspectives* 106, 3. (A joint study of the Departments of Anthropology and Environment Research Projects/ Akwesasne Task Force on the Environment, Rooseveltown, New York). Abstract at http://ehpnet1.niehs.nih.gov/child1998/abs/Suppl-3/833-840schell/abstract.html
Schull, J. 1967. *The Nation Makers*. Toronto: Macmillan.
Scott, D.C. 1914. "Indian Affairs, 1867–1912." In A. Shortt and A. Doughty (eds.), *Canada and Its Provinces*. Toronto: University of Edinburgh Press.
———. 1926. *The Poems of Duncan Campbell Scott*. Toronto: McClelland and

Stewart.
———. 1947. *The Circle of Affection and Other Pieces in Prose and Verse*. Toronto: McClelland and Stewart.
Scott, D.C., and A.S. Bourinot. 1960. *More letters of Duncan Campbell Scott, C.M.G., LL. D., LITT. D., F.R.S.C., F.R.S.L.: 2nd series*. Ottawa: A.S. Bourinot.
Scott, D.C., E.K. Brown and R.L. McDougall. 1983. *The Poet and the Critic: A Literary Correspondence between D.C. Scott and E.K. Brown*. Ottawa: Carleton University Press.
Seton, K. 1999. "Fourth World Nations in the Era of Globalization: An introduction to contemporary theorizing posed by indigenous nations." Available at http://www.cwis.org/fwj/41/fworld.html.
Shkilnyk, A.M. 1985. *A Poison Stronger than Love: The Destruction of an Ojibwa Community*. New Haven, CT: Yale University Press.
Silverstein, Ken. 2000. "Gore's Oil Money." *The Nation*, May 22.
Smith, D. 1990. *Text, Facts and Femininity: Exploring the Relations of Ruling*. London: Routledge.
Solomons, D. 1991. "Accounting and Social Change: A Neutralist View." *Accounting, Organizations and Society* 16, 3.
Spiers, E. 1980. *The Army and Society: 1815–1914*. New York: Longman.
Stavenhagen, R. 2000. "Indigenous Movements and Politics in Mexico and Latin America." In C. Cook and J. Lindau (ed.) *Aboriginal Rights and Self-Government: The Canadian and Mexican Experience in North American Perspective*. Montreal: McGill-Queen's University.
Stephenson, J. 1995. *The 1994 Zapatista Rebellion in Southern Mexico: An Analysis and Assessment*. London: Strategies and Combat Institute.
Surtees, R. 1983. "Indian Land Cessions in Upper Canada, 1815–1830." In L. Getty and A. Lussier.
Suzuki, D. " The value of indigenous knowledge." Available at http://www.davidsuzuki.org/Dr_David_Suzuki/Article_Archives/weekly08119901.asp.
Sweetman, J. 1984. *War and Administration*. Edinburough: Scottish Academic Press.
Tello, C. 1995. *Chiapas La Rebelión de las Cañadas*. Madrid, España: Acento Editorial.
Tinker, T. 1980. "Towards a Political Economy of Accounting." *Accounting, Organizations and Society* 5, 1.
———. 1985. *Paper Prophets: A Social Critique of Accounting*. New York: Praeger.
———. 1991. "The Accountant as Partisan." *Accounting, Organizations and Society* 16, 3.
Titley, E.B. 1986. *A Narrow Vision: Duncan Campbell Scott and the Administration of Indian Affairs in Canada*. Vancouver: University of British Columbia Press.
Tobias, L. 1983. "Protection, Civilization, Assimilation." In L. Getty and A. Lussier.
Tollefson, C. 1996. "Strategic Lawsuits and Environmental Politics: Daishowa Inc v Friends of the Lubicon." *Journal of Canadian Studies* 31, 1.
Trend, J. B. 1967. *The Civilization of Spain*. New York: Oxford University Press.
Trigger, B.G. 1977. *The Indians and the Heroic Age of New France*. Ottawa:

Canadian Historical Association.

Venne, S. 1997. "Understanding Treaty Six." In M. Asch (ed.), *Aboriginal and Treaty Rights in Canada: Essays on Law, Equity, and Respect for Difference*. Vancouver: UBC Press.

Vescey, C. 1987. "Grassy Narrows Reserve: Mercury Pollution, Social Disruption, and Natural Resources: A Question of Autonomy." *American Indian Quarterly* 11, 4.

Villafuentes, D., S. Meza, G. Franco, M. Garcia, C. Rivera, M. Lisbona and J. Morales. 1999. *La Tierra en Chiapas, viejos problemas nuevos*. Chiapas: Universidad de Ciencias y Artes del Estado de Chiapas.

Weir, B. 2000. "Dignity, $1.4B what lawsuit is about." Available at http://www.ammsa.com/windspeaker/WINDNEWSJUNE2000.html#anchor2551709.

Weyler, R. 1992. *Blood of the Land: The Government and Corporate War Against First Nations*. Philadelphia: New Society.

Womack, J. 1999. *Rebellion in Chiapas: An Historical Reader*. New York: New Press.

Woodcock, G. 1974. *Colony and Confederation: Early Canadian Poets and Their Background*. Vancouver: University of British Columbia Press.

World Rain Forest Movement. 1998 (November). "Indigenous peoples fight for territorial rights in Guyana." Available at http://www.wrm.org.uy/bulletin/17/Guyana.html.

Wright, R. 1992. *Stolen Continents: The Americas through Indian Eyes Since 1492*. Boston: Houghton Mifflin.

York, G., and L. Pindera. 1992. *People of the Pines: The Warriors and the Legacy of Oka*. Toronto: Little Brown.

Young, B. J. 1986. *In its Corporate Capacity: The Seminary of Montreal as a Business Institution, 1816–1876*. Kingston: McGill-Queen's University Press.

Index

About the Authors
The poet and the professor

DEAN NEU is the Future Fund Professor of Accounting in the Haskayne School of Business at the University of Calgary. As an accounting activist committed to unveiling the presence of accounting where we might not otherwise expect to find it, he has in numerous articles and public appearances revealed how accounting plays a mediative role between governments and population segments. His research and writing demonstrate how accounting, working hand in hand with bureaucracies, shapes and constructs societal governance. In his work, the disguise of accounting as a boring, benign appendage to business and government is stripped away to reveal it as a key element in shaping public policy and the perceptions the public has of those policies.

RICHARD THERRIEN is a poet, researcher, cultural worker, editor, filmmaker, ghost-writer and landscape labourer. Mr. Therrien's film credits include NFB documentaries, educational films and dramas. His poems and articles have been published in a variety of journals, including: *Last Issue,* a cultural journal; *Blue Buffalo,* a literary quarterly; *Absinthe,* a literary quarterly; *Bush Mail,* a literary/alchemical/ecology journal; several book reviews have been published in the *Calgary Herald* and *Windspeaker,* a Native weekly in Edmonton. He makes his home in North Vancouver, B.C.